T0134351

Freiburger Studien zur Netzökonomie

Prof. Dr. Günter Knieps, Universität Freiburg

Volume 21

Günter Knieps | Volker Stocker [eds.]

The Future of the Internet

Innovation, Integration and Sustainability

 Nomos

The Deutsche Nationalbibliothek lists this publication in the
Deutsche Nationalbibliografie; detailed bibliographic data
are available on the Internet at http://dnb.d-nb.de

ISBN   978-3-8487-6080-0 (Print)
         978-3-7489-0209-6 (ePDF)

British Library Cataloguing-in-Publication Data
A catalogue record for this book is available from the British Library.

ISBN   978-3-8487-6080-0 (Print)
         978-3-7489-0209-6 (ePDF)

Library of Congress Cataloging-in-Publication Data
Knieps, Günter / Stocker, Volker
The Future of the Internet
Innovation, Integration and Sustainability
Günter Knieps / Volker Stocker (eds.)
245 pp.
Includes bibliographic references.

ISBN   978-3-8487-6080-0 (Print)
         978-3-7489-0209-6 (ePDF)

1st Edition 2019
© Nomos Verlagsgesellschaft, Baden-Baden, Germany 2019. Printed and bound in Germany.

Table of Contents

Table of Contents

Introduction: The Future of the Internet – Innovation, Integration and Sustainability

Günter Knieps and Volker Stocker

The evolution of the Internet may be characterized as a path-dependent process driven by strong dynamics and innovations interrelated with developments towards integration and sustainability. The transition from narrowband specialized telecommunication networks to a broadband Internet during the last decades fundamentally changes the industrial organization of the Internet, differentiating between All-IP broadband infrastructures, markets for Internet traffic and markets for application services. Due to the pervasive use of the Internet protocol (IP) of fragmented data packet transmission a variety of heterogeneous access network infrastructures are coexisting, all integrated via the IP layer. In addition, the dynamics of Internet traffic management has gained increasing importance.

The fundamental decision of the Internet Engineering Task Force (IETF) in favor of a multipurpose traffic network perspective implied the integrating of real-time application services and all other services (called best effort services). The avoidance of parallel specialized communication infrastructures thus became the starting point of a contentious debate about the pros and cons of active traffic management within the Internet and the related controversy on network neutrality. The traditional best effort data packet transmission of the Internet based on the equal treatment of all data packets has been challenged fundamentally; in particular considering the drawbacks of ad hoc rationing schemes (e.g., by the TCP), the limited capabilities of overlay networks, and increasing congestion problems within the Internet. It has been a substantial benefit of standardization organizations (in particular the IETF) to spend enormous efforts on developing the necessary ingredients for a variety of innovative traffic architectures. The latter enables the design of a wide range of QoS differentiation strategies through the introduction of a hierarchy of traffic classes implemented via packet prioritization or bandwidth capacity reservation. While this presents a precondition for the development of incentive compatible allocation schemes of network capacities, advanced congestion pricing approaches are required to enable price and investment models for stochastic as well as deterministic traffic qualities in All-IP broadband networks.

The Internet of Things (IoT) brings disruptive innovations. These are no longer limited to communication applications (e.g., voice over IP), but rather spur the transition of traditional network industries into intelligent (smart) networks. Relevant fields of applications comprise smart sustainable cities, smart electricity networks and microgrids, shared mobility, intelligent railroad systems, networked driverless vehicles, commercial drones, smart manufacturing, e-health, etc. The interaction between physical network infrastructures and physical network services with IP-based virtual networks is a crucial driver in transforming the traditional network industries into intelligent networks based on real-time, location-aware, and adaptive decision making. Critical inputs for a virtual network are QoS differentiated All-IP bandwidth capacities combined with sensor networks, geo-positioning services, and big data processing. The importance of guarantees for very low latencies within the tactile Internet is strongly increasing, requiring large investments into future 5G networks with a combination of very high throughput, very low latency, and big data processing capacities. Moreover, privacy and cybersecurity issues gain increasing importance in the future due to the relevance of the IoT in all areas of future life.

In celebration of the 50th Freiburg Seminar on Network Economics, the goal of our conference-workshop was to bring together leading international researchers to present their latest results on the dynamics of the future Internet. This volume offers a collection of the contributions made by the conference speakers and covers a variety of current and highly relevant topics. In his contribution *"Internet of Things (IoT), heterogeneous virtual networks and the future of the Internet"*, Günter Knieps examines the challenges that emerge in the context of the IoT from a network economic perspective. Beyond aspects related to privacy and security, the article discusses heterogeneous requirements for (i) end-to-end QoS levels, (ii) data processing and cloud computing, and (iii) geo-positioning. Bert Sadowski, Onder Nomaler and Jason Whalley explore the topic of *"Technological diversification into 'Blue Oceans'? A patent-based analysis of Internet of Things technologies"*. Examining a sample of 90 companies, the authors investigate technological diversification strategies of companies in the context of the IoT. In doing so, emphasis is placed on examining the relationship between technological diversification and technical performance. *"Net Neutrality in Europe after the Net Neutrality Regulation 2015/2120"* is examined by Thomas Fetzer. The article provides comprehensive discussions surrounding the application of the regulation and provides an insightful review and analysis of the regulatory assessment of zero rating and traffic shaping practices. Johannes Bauer examines *"Regulation and digital innovation."* The article provides comprehensive explanations of and detailed insights into the many dimensions of innovation processes which shape the evolution in the Internet ecosystem. Based on a (forward-looking) economic analysis, implications for future communication policy are derived. The topic of *"5G and the Future of Broadband"* is comprehensively examined by William Lehr. The article describes the role of softwarization and virtualization for meeting the diverse and complex demands that emerge in mobile next generation access networks. Changes in the economics of service provision and competition are discussed. Iris Henseler-Unger investigates *"Telecommunication 4.0 – Investment in Very High Capacity Broadband and the Internet of Things"*. This article provides a forward-looking discussion of the challenges telcos are facing to master the transition associated with the fourth industrial revolution. In doing so, a focus is placed on investments in very high-capacity networks. *"Ecosystem Evolution and End-to-End QoS on the Internet: The (Remaining) Role of Interconnections"* is examined by Volker Stocker. The author describes the state of evolution of the Internet ecosystem and explains the challenges associated with differentiated requirements for traffic delivery. In doing so, different mechanisms for increasing end-to-end QoS and their complementarities are explored, and the role of interconnections is discussed. Falk von Bornstaedt explores *"The evolution of interconnection in the Internet: New models of cooperation between Internet service providers and content"*. The article provides a state-of-the-art overview of the interconnection ecosystem and sheds light on the changes that have occurred and discusses potentials for cooperation between market players. Marlies Van der Wee, Frederic Vannieuwenborg and Sofie Verbrugge present *"Multi-objective technology selection for IoT solutions: A methodological approach"*. In this position paper, the authors investigate business case viability in the context of IoT services. In doing so, a conceptual framework of parameters that should guide the decision on a specific technology for deploying IoT services is presented. Christopher S. Yoo and Jesse Lambert examine *"5G and Net Neutrality"*. More specifically, this article investigates the impact of network neutrality on 5G and discusses the role and importance of exceptions from strict network neutrality rules to facilitate 5G-related innovations.

We would like to thank all participants for making our conference workshop held in Freiburg on 10-11 July 2017 a big success and for contributing to the many fruitful discussions we led. Of course, special thanks go to the speakers of the conference for their presentations and excellent contributions to this conference volume. We are extraordinarily grateful to the "Gesellschaft für Netzökonomie, Wettbewerbsökonomie und Verkehrswissenschaft" at the University of Freiburg for their financial support of the conference as well as the publication of this conference volume. Many thanks are also due to Ms. Monika Steinert for her highly competent and incomparable support in organizing the conference work-shop and her tireless work towards the publication of this volume.

Freiburg and Berlin, Spring 2019   Günter Knieps and Volker Stocker

Author Biographies

Johannes M. Bauer is the Quello Chair for Media and Information Policy in the Department of Media and Information at Michigan State University (MSU). He is trained as an engineer and social scientist with MA and PhD degrees from the Vienna University of Economics and Business, Austria. His research, published in leading journals in the field, covers a wide range of issues related to media and information policy, media economics and entrepreneurship, and the governance of information and communication technology to support the public interest. It has been funded by federal agencies such as the National Science Foundation and international organizations. Dr. Bauer has served as an advisor to public and private sector organizations in North and South America, Europe, and Asia. His most recent book, the Handbook on the Economics of the Internet (co-edited with Professor Michael Latzer at the University of Zurich), was published in 2016 by Edward Elgar. Dr. Bauer has held visiting professorships at the Delft University of Technology, the Netherlands (2000-2001), the University of Konstanz, Germany (Summer 2010), and most recently the University of Zurich, Switzerland (2012).

Falk von Bornstaedt is an Internet and telecommunications industry economist. He served as a product manager for Deutsche Telekom and pioneered the introduction of several IP products. Dr. von Bornstaedt holds a PhD in Economics from Cologne University. His most recent book published was "Internetwirtschaft" together with Rüdiger Zarnekow and Jochen Wulf in 2013. He has been teaching internet economics at the Universities of Freiburg, Cologne, Bonn, and currently the Technical University of Berlin, Germany. Since 2018 he has been working as a consultant and serving the RIPE NCC in Amsterdam as a member of the Executive Board.

Thomas Fetzer studied law at the University of Mannheim where he also received his doctoral degree in 2000 with a thesis on the taxation of Internet transactions. He graduated from the Vanderbilt University Law School with the degree of an LL.M. in 2003 and habilitated at the University of Mannheim in 2009 with a comparative treatise on the sector-specific regulation of the telecommunications sector in Europe and the U.S. He is an Adjunct Professor of Law at the University of Pennsylvania Law School Centre for Technology, Innovation and Competition since 2009. He held the Chair of Tax Law and Business Law at the TU Dresden Law School from 2010 to 2012. He has been holding the Chair of Public Law, Regulation Law and Tax Law at the School of Law and Economics at the University of Mannheim since 2012. He served as head of the Department of Law and Dean of the School of Law and Economics from 2014 to 2017. Moreover, he is an academic co-director of the Mannheim Centre for Competition and Innovation (MaCCI) as well as an academic co-director of the Leibniz ScienceCampus MannheimTaxation (MaTax). Thomas Fetzer specializes in Antitrust and Regulatory Law with a special focus on questions relating to digitalization. He has done several studies for the German Federal Ministry of Economic Affairs and Energy on the regulation of digital markets. Furthermore, he has testified several times as an expert for the German Parliament (Deutsche Bundestag).

Iris Henseler-Unger is the Managing Director of WIK and of WIK-Consult. Before joining WIK in November 2014 Dr Henseler-Unger served as Vice President of the Federal Network Agency for Electricity, Gas, Telecommunications, Post and Railway (BNetzA) in Bonn/Germany from 2004 to 2014, where she was in particular responsible for regulating telecommunications and railways, and represented Germany in European regulators' groups (BEREC, IRG).

Her experience in the telecommunications sector dates back to 1993 having served as an expert for the FDP parliamentary group in the field of liberalisation in the 1990s. Dr Henseler-Unger possesses in depth knowledge of telecommunications policy and regulation – both from a national and European perspective – and of the European regulatory framework and recommendations from the European regulators' perspective. In addition, she has extensive stakeholder contacts.

Dr Henseler-Unger studied economics at the Universities of Bonn and Zurich and holds a PhD from the University of Mannheim. After her research activities at the University of Mannheim, professional positions were in the Federal Ministry of Economics and at the FDP parliamentary group in the area of economic policy, posts, and telecommunications.

Dr Henseler-Unger is Member of the Board of the MÜNCHNER KREIS and Member of the "Wissenschaftlicher Arbeitskreis für Regulierungsfragen" of the Federal Network Agency.

Günter Knieps is Professor of Economics at the University of Freiburg, Germany, where he holds the Chair of Network Economics, Competition Economics and Transport Sciences.

He finished his studies at the University of Bonn, Germany with diplomas in mathematics as well as economics and obtained his PhD in Mathematical Economics from the University of Bonn. After that he held postdoc positions at Princeton and at the University of Pennsylvania and obtained his habilitation in Berne. Prior to joining the Faculty of Economics in Freiburg he held a Chair of Microeconomics at the University of Groningen in the Netherlands. He is a Member of the Scientific Council of the Federal Ministry for Economic Affairs and Energy as well as the Federal Ministry for Transport and Digital Infrastructure, a member of the Academic Advisory Board of the Walter Eucken Institute in Freiburg, and a founding member of *Ökonomenstimme*, an Internet platform for economists in Germany.

Professor Knieps' main research interests are the study of network economics, competition economics and the Industrial organization of the Internet, and sector studies on energy, telecommunications and transportation. In the last years the main focus of his research has been on the economics of smart networks, Internet of Things and big data virtual networks, with applications in smart sustainable cities, microgrids and shared mobility markets. He has published widely in academic and professional journals.

Jesse Lambert is a J.D. candidate at the University of Pennsylvania Law School (class of 2019).

Jesse's major research interests involve utilizing empirical techniques to gain better understanding of the intersections between law and technology and law and sport. Before joining the University of Pennsylvania, Jesse was an analyst at FanDuel, a fantasy sports company. Before that, Jesse studied business analytics while earning his Masters of Business Administration at Carnegie Mellon University's Tepper School of Business.

After graduating from the University of Pennsylvania, Jesse will join Dechert, LLP's Philadelphia office as a full-time Associate.

William Lehr is an Internet and telecommunications industry economist and research scientist in the Computer Science and Artificial Intelligence Laboratory (CSAIL) at the Massachusetts Institute of Technology (MIT) where he is part of the Advanced Network Architectures group. Dr. Lehr's research focuses on the economic implications of ICT technologies for public policy, industry structure, and the evolving Internet ecosystem. He is engaged in multiple multidisciplinary research projects focusing on issues such as broadband Internet access, cybersecurity, next generation network architectures, and spectrum management reform. In addition to his academic work, Dr. Lehr advises public and private sector clients in the US and abroad on ICT strategy and policy matters. Dr. Lehr holds a PhD in Economics from Stanford and an MBA in Finance from the Wharton School, and MSE, BA, and BS degrees from the University of Pennsylvania.

Onder Nomaler holds a BSc degree in Industrial Engineering and a MSc in Economics. He earned his PhD in Economics at Maastricht University in 2006. He worked at UNU-MERIT as a research fellow, and since 2002 he has been based in the Department of Innovation Sciences at the Eindhoven University of Technology, The Netherlands. His research interests include evolutionary economics, computational economics, complexity theory, network analysis, economics of innovation, measurement of innovation, input-output economics, and bibliometrics, especially in patent value assessment and (patent) citation network analysis.

Bert Sadowski is Associate Professor of the Economics of Innovation and Technological Change at the Eindhoven University of Technology, the Netherlands as well as Visiting Professor at Northumbria University, Newcastle, UK and the University of Trento, Italy. Over the past 15 years, his research interest has been in the areas of the economics of technological change and innovation, innovation management and technology analysis. He has carried out a number of projects for governmental and nongovernmental organizations as well as for a variety of private companies. He has been a special adviser to the European Commission, the Dutch Ministry of Economic Affairs as well as to different local and provincial governmental organizations in the Netherlands and abroad. He has served as a boardroom consultant to a number of private companies.

Volker Stocker is a Postdoctoral Researcher at TU Berlin and the Weizenbaum Institute for the Networked Society (German Internet Institute) in Berlin, Germany where leads the research group "Work and Cooperation in the Sharing Economy". Before joining TU Berlin and the Weizenbaum Institute, Volker was a doctoral researcher (research assistant) at the University of Freiburg and the MPI for Informatics in Saarbrücken. Volker studied at the Universities of Freiburg and Mannheim, Germany and the Hanken School of Economics in Helsinki, Finland and holds a Diplom degree in Economics. During his time as a doctoral researcher, he has been a Lecturer in Economics at the Baden-Württemberg Cooperative State University (DHBW) in Lörrach, Germany and spent time as a visiting research student at the TU Berlin, Germany, the University of Northumbria in Newcastle, UK, and the Massachusetts Institute of Technology (MIT) in Cambridge, US.

His major research interests are in the fields of network economics of the Internet, Internet evolution, and Internet policy. Volker is a regular speaker at international conferences and has published multiple papers on topics like network neutrality, content delivery networks, and broadband policy.

Marlies Van der Wee received an MSc degree in Engineering, option Industrial Engineering and Operations Research from Ghent University in July 2010. She joined the Techno-Economic research unit at IBCN in September 2010, at the same university. Funded by a personal research grant from the Agency for Innovation by Science and Technology (IWT, Flanders), she finished a PhD on social cost-benefit analysis of broadband networks in a multi-actor setting. Marlies is author or co-author of more than 35 publications, both in international journals and presented at conferences world-wide. Marlies is involved in several national and European research projects, where she performs techno-economic analysis and business modeling in different application domains (such as broadband networks, media, energy and eHealth).

Frederic Vannieuwenborg received a MSc degree in engineering, option Industrial Engineering and Operations Research from Ghent University (Belgium) in July 2011. Later that year, at the same university, he joined the Techno-Economics research group within the Internet and Data Lab (IDLab) which is affiliated to imec. A personal research grant of Flemish agency for innovation and entrepreneurship (Vlaio) allowed him to do a PhD on analyzing the impact of smart services via techno-economic modelling. His research focuses on techno-economic aspects such as value-network modelling, impact analyses, cost evaluation, technology choice, barrier detection and multi-actor analyses within the application domains of eCare/mHealth, smart energy, smart dairy farming, Industry 4.0 and IoT in general.

Sofie Verbrugge received an MSc degree in computer science engineering and a PhD degree from Ghent University (Ghent, Belgium) in 2001 and 2007 respectively. Since 2008, she has been working as a researcher affiliated to imec (previously iMinds), where she is the research coordinator for the techno-economic research group within the Internet and Data Lab (IDLab). Since October 2014, she is appointed as an associate professor at Ghent University. She teaches courses on Information Technology and Data Processing as well as on Engineering Economy. She also acts as the diversity coordinator for the Faculty of Engineering and Architecture. Sofie's main research interests include technology selection, infrastructure and operational cost modeling, real options and game theory as well as business modeling and value network analysis, applied to projects in a broad range of application domains based on fixed or wireless broadband networks as well as on the Internet-of-Things. Sofie has been involved in several European as well as national research projects in these domains. She is a member of the Editorial Board of Telecommunications Policy, the International Journal of ICT Economy, Governance and Society. She is also a member of the Young Academy of Flanders (Belgium).

Jason Whalley is Professor of Digital Economy, Northumbria University, Newcastle, UK and Affiliate Professor at Institut Mines-Télécom Business School, Evry, France. His research focuses on the telecommunications industry. One area of interest is the structure of both fixed and mobile tele-communication markets, while a second is the development of regulatory regimes. A third more recent area of interest relates to technological inno-vation, and how this interacts with and shapes the strategies of companies and regulatory regimes. He is the editor of Digital Policy, Regulation and Governance.

Christopher S. Yoo is the John H. Chestnut Professor of Law, Communi-cation, and Computer & Information Science at the University of Pennsyl-vania.

Repeatedly recognized as one of the most frequently cited scholars in administrative and regulatory law as well as intellectual property, he is the author of five books and over one hundred scholarly articles. His major research projects include investigating innovative ways to connect people to the Internet; analyzing the technical determinants of optimal interopera-bility; comparing antitrust enforcement practices in China, Europe, and the U.S.; promoting privacy and security for autonomous vehicles, medical devices, and the Internet's routing architecture; and studying the regulation of Internet platforms. He is also building innovative joint degree programs designed to produce a new generation of professionals with advanced training in both law and engineering.

Before entering the academy, Professor Yoo clerked for Justice Anthony M. Kennedy of the Supreme Court of the United States and Judge A. Raymond Randolph of the U.S. Court of Appeals for the D.C. Circuit. He also practiced law with the D.C. firm of Hogan & Hartson (now Hogan Lovells) under the supervision of now-Chief Justice John G. Roberts, Jr.

He is frequently called to testify before the U.S. Congress, Federal Communications Commission, Federal Trade Commission, foreign governments, and international organizations. He is currently serving as a member of the Federal Communication Commission's Broadband Deployment Advisory Committee, the Board of Advisers for the American Law Institute's Project on Principles of Law for Data Privacy and the Project on Principles for a Data Economy, and as co-convener of the United Nations Internet Governance Forum's initiative on Connecting and Enabling the Next Billions.

Internet of Things (IoT), heterogeneous virtual networks and the future of the Internet

Günter Knieps[1]

Abstract

The Internet of Things (IoT) makes it necessary to rethink the future role of the Internet. Different physical network services (e.g. shared mobility services, smart rail services, smart energy services) require different implementations of virtual networks, all based on QoS requirements for data packet transmission within mobile and fixed broadband networks. The focus of this chapter is on the heterogeneity of virtual networks for a large variety of physical network services. The heterogeneity of relevant dimensions of virtual networks is analyzed, specifically considering heterogeneous QoS requirements of all-IP bandwidth capacities, heterogeneous sensor network requirements, heterogeneous geopositioning services as well as heterogeneous data processing and cloud computing. A basic goal of network virtualization is to bundle the end-to-end responsibility for privacy and security concerns regarding the virtual side of IoT applications in the hands of the provider of the virtual networks.

Keywords: Internet of Things, Economics of virtual networks, Smart networks

---

1   University of Freiburg, Chair of Network Economics, Competition Economics and Transport Science; guenter.knieps@vwl.uni-freiburg.de

1. Introduction

Smart networks may be considered as an "envelope concept" focusing on the combination of Information and Communication Technologies (ICT) with traditional infrastructure networks providing physical network services. Smart bidirectional metering, sensors, actuators and remote control by interactive machine-to-machine communication, in combination making up the so-called Internet of Things (IoT),[2] are becoming increasingly important on the road towards smart networks (European Commission, 2015; OECD, 2012, 2013a, 2013b). The IoT makes it necessary to rethink the future role of the Internet. Real-time two-way communication between sensors and actuators as well as communication between physical and virtual networks is gaining importance, e.g. the remote tactile steering or control of an object via the Internet. For example, vehicles in a platoon need to be connected with 1-2 ms latency and thus have very low latency tolerance. Other examples requiring very low latency guarantees are remote driving and real-time control of microgrids. Hence ICT based steering and control of physical networks are becoming increasingly important in the future IoT.

The focus of this chapter is on IoT applications which are characterized as smart physical network services. The interaction between physical networks and ICT is challenging the industrial organization of network industries (Knieps, Bauer, 2016). On one hand, a fundamental change is taking place in traditional network industries and physical network services, with real-time, location aware and adaptive network capacity allocation becoming particularly relevant. On the other hand the traditional communication and entertainment oriented Internet is challenged to meet the ICT requirements of smart network industries and more general of the app economy.

The chapter is organized as follows: In the subsequent section 2 the design principle of IP based virtual networks required for various physical networks and for a large variety of physical network services is characterized. In section 3 the basic dimensions of virtual networks are considered. The intrinsic heterogeneity of virtual networks is analyzed, based on innovative entrepreneurial combinations of the heterogeneous dimensions of

---

2   The term Internet of Things (IoT) most probably dates back to Kevin Ashton, who pointed out the particular relevance of the physical world compared to the virtual ICT world: "Ideas and information are important, but things matter much more" (Ashton, 2009, p. 1).

virtual networks. In particular, heterogeneous Quality of Service (QoS) bandwidth capacities, heterogeneous sensor networks, heterogeneous geopositioning requirements, heterogeneous (big) data processing capacities and heterogeneous security requirements are identified. In section 4 a concluding outlook is provided.

2. IoT and the evolution of IP based virtual networks

2.1. The complementarity between physical networks and virtual networks

From a network economic point of view the conceptual differentiation between services of physical network infrastructures (e.g. roads, railways, electricity networks) and complementary virtual networks based on ICT services is important (Knieps, 2017c). Different physical network services (e.g. shared mobility services, smart rail services, smart energy services) require different implementations of virtual networks, all based on QoS requirements for data packet transmission within mobile and fixed broadband networks. Virtual networks may be interconnected with other virtual networks (e.g. ubiquitous sensor networks) or via the all-IP Internet with other actors. For example, within a microgrid the aggregator must bundle the prosumer consumption and generation decisions within the different home networks and communicate the real-time import/export decisions to the wholesale distribution network operator. Home networks may also use multipurpose broadband communication architecture, not only for electricity applications based sensors but also for other communication requirements, e.g. entertainment (Knieps, 2017a).

2.2 IP based virtual networks

The Archimedean point of virtual networks is the evolution of the IP towards the universal network protocol for internetworking: the IP as the common network layer protocol for interconnecting many different networks, for instance cable, fixed and mobile communication networks etc. (Tanenbaum, Wetherall, 2011, pp. 424 ff.). Alternative broadband access networks, such as mobile access networks, fixed telecom access networks, or cable access networks are characterized by convergence towards all-IP networks (Knieps, Zenhäusern, 2015, pp. 339 ff.; Knieps, Stocker, 2016).

Based on the well-established concept of Next Generation Networks (NGN)[3] the concepts of Future Networks (FNs) and network virtualization have been developed, emphasizing the need for advanced traffic management to realize a wide scope of application services and heterogeneous network architectures on a common multipurpose ICT infrastructure (ITU-T, 2012, p. iv). Traditional specialized communication networks are thus challenged by the concept of network virtualization: "Network virtualization is a method that allows multiple virtual networks, called logically isolated network partitions (LINPs), to coexist in a single physical network" (ITU-T, 2012, p. 2).

Virtual networks provide the necessities for increasingly important end user demand for a wide scope of heterogeneous application services requiring heterogeneous ICT support. Different virtual networks require different QoS bandwidth capacities offered by traffic service providers. Service continuity may also require multiple interconnected virtual networks. Property rights and decision competency for the traffic service providers are different from those for the virtual networks providers. Whereas traffic service providers are offering QoS guaranteed bandwidth capacities for QoS requirements driven by IoT applications, virtual network providers combine specific QoS bandwidth capacities with other ICT components (virtual resources), such as sensing, geopositioning, or data processing, to build a virtual network tailored for the requirements of complementary physical applications. Heterogeneous virtual networks have been analyzed for microgrids (Knieps, 2017a), smart sustainable cities (Knieps, 2017b), shared mobility services (Knieps, 2018a), and networked vehicles (Knieps, 2018b). Different (single purpose specialized) virtual networks may seamlessly cooperate without interoperability requirements between different traffic service providers. Cooperation between different virtual networks can serve as a substitute for interoperability agreements between different traffic services providers (Knieps, 2017c, pp. 243-246).

---

3   An NGN is defined as follows: "A packet-based network able to provide telecommunication services and able to make use of multiple broadband QoS-enabled transport technologies and in which service-related functions are independent from underlying transport-related technologies. It enables unfettered access for users to networks and to competing service providers and/or services of their choice. It supports generalized mobility which will allow consistent and ubiquitous provision of services to users." (ITU-T Y.2001, 2004, p. 2).

3.   *Heterogeneity of virtual networks*

Virtual networks for a large variety of physical network services are based on the following dimensions:

- All-IP based real-time and adaptive broadband communication networks
- IP based sensor networks
- Global navigation satellite systems and their overlay position correction networks
- (Big) Data processing, cloud computing and fog computing
- Privacy and security

The IoT application driven variety of virtual networks is based on entrepreneurial combinations of the different dimensions of virtual networks. In the following the heterogeneity requirements for the different dimensions of virtual networks are elaborated.

3.1   Heterogeneity of QoS requirements of all-IP bandwidth capacities

Due to the unified standardized Internet Protocol IP, different stationary and mobile broadband technologies can be used for data packet transmission in the future all-IP Internet. Utilization dependent user fees are also becoming indispensible for data packet transmission in the all-IP Internet. The prioritization of data packets within different QoS classes for providing deterministic or stochastic QoS guarantees necessitates access controls, and concomitant price and quality differentiation for different quality classes. Traffic services providers can use the resultant revenues, in addition to the fixed connection fees, for investment in broadband capacities. Heterogeneous traffic classes without deterministic QoS guarantees are characterized in Babiarz et al. (2006). A hierarchy of heterogeneous stochastic QoS classes can be established in such a way that the highest classes are Expedited Forwarding (EF), followed by Assured Forwarding (AF) and Default Forwarding (DF) providing the lowest "Low Priority Data service class" (for non-real time and elastic traffic). For deterministic QoS guarantees, see Ash et al. (2010).

The economic incentives for QoS differentiation traffic classes can only be analyzed if the entrepreneurial QoS potentials and related traffic architectures are taken into account. Prioritization of data packets can take place within the DiffServ architecture, enabling a hierarchy of traffic classes without deterministic QoS guarantees (Knieps, 2011). The Generalized DiffServ architecture provides the open set of flexible multipurpose traffic architectures supporting a variety of heterogeneous QoS classes required for different application services (Knieps, 2015, p. 739). Traffic QoS requirements cannot be considered from the perspective of IoT only, but have also to take into account all other application services provided within an all-IP network infrastructure. For deterministic QoS guarantees two complementary mechanisms are required: Firstly, admission control and associated priorities, secondly development of service restoration priority levels based on the criticality of services. As important network performance criteria delay, jitter and packet loss parameters are specified for stochastic and deterministic QoS guarantees. The hierarchy of traffic classes (implemented by admission control) is based on a monotone relation of more strictly defined QoS parameters with increasing opportunity costs of bandwidth capacity. The hierarchy of restoration priority is based on a monotone relation of opportunity costs of bandwidth capacity usage due to different restoration priority parameters.

The heterogeneous requirements of different deterministic and stochastic traffic qualities can be implemented by means of NGN, allowing the entrepreneurial search for QoS architectures and subsequent incentive compatible pricing schedules (Knieps, 2015; Knieps, Stocker, 2016). A well-defined hierarchy of traffic classes with different deterministic traffic quality guarantees is defined for NGN bandwidth allocations (Ash et al., 2010). It has been shown that QoS pricing for a hierarchy of deterministic traffic classes can be derived in an incentive compatible manner (Knieps, 2017c). The hierarchy of traffic classes is based on a monotone relation of opportunity costs of bandwidth capacity usage due to different QoS classes as well as restoration priority parameters. Network capacity (bandwidth) is allocated to each quality class (channel) separately, including the required reserve capacity due to the required restoration priority parameter to guarantee the deterministic parameters (delay, jitter, packet loss). Price and QoS differentiation pricing and investing rules for a hierarchy of deterministic QoS guarantees are derived, resulting in the following insights: The price for packet transmission increases with required traffic quality, because variable costs increase with traffic quality. For higher quality classes marginal cost functions are shifted upwards, resulting (ceteris paribus) in higher package charges.

3.2. Heterogeneous sensor network requirements

Heterogeneous sensor networks with strongly different characteristics can be differentiated, such as 6LoPan sensor networks (low costs, low speed) and camera based sensoring (high volume, very delay sensitive/tactile). During the last two decades there has been an evolution towards IP based sensor networks. Based on these standards for sensor networks, the innovation potentials of different virtual networks, which are complementary for the heterogeneous smart infrastructure services, can be realized. The important goal is to connect the metering and sensor networks to the all-IP Internet.

An important area for sensor networks is focused on low-cost, low-speed ubiquitous communication between devices based on low rate wireless networks with low transfer rates and very limited communication range. The IEEE 802.15.4. standard[4] specifies the physical layer as a required precondition for two major networking protocols, 6LoW PAN and ZigBee IP (Kushalnagar et al., 2007). Characteristics of Low-Power Wireless Personal Area Networks (LoWPANs)[5] are wireless sensors with small packet size, low bandwidth and Reduced Function Devices (RFDs). The benefits of IP v6 are the large address space, since a large number of devices are involved, as well as the seamless connectivity to other IP based networks without translation gateways (Kushalnagar et al., 2007). Interconnection can take place on the basis of existing IP network infrastructure. Even if different network carriers apply different QoS traffic architecture, only a mapping between the traffic classes of different carriers is required; emulation techniques like translation gateways are not necessary. Virtual networks can be designed by application providers based on the different QoS architectures of different traffic service providers.

The advantages of compatibility with the IPv6 network standard come at a cost. They require additional fragmentation due to the constraints regarding the size of the Maximum Transmission Unit (MTU) and lead to lower data rates. Since IPv6 requires the support of much larger packet

---

4   IEEE 802.15 WG (Working Group) develops Wireless Personal Area Network (WPAN) standards for short distance wireless networks, https://standards.ieee.org/develop/wg/WG802.15.html

5   "A LoWPAN is a simple low cost communication network that allows wireless connectivity in applications with limited power and relaxed throughput requirements. A LoWPAN typically includes devices that work together to connect the physical environment to real-world applications, e.g., wireless sensors." (Kushalnagar et al., 2007, p. 1).

sizes than the largest IEEE 802.15.4. frame size, a LoWPAN fragmenta-
tion and reassembly adaptation layer must be provided at the layer below
IP, because a full IPv6 packet does not fit in an IEEE 802.15.4 frame
(Montenegro et al., 2007).

ZigBee Alliance and IETF are cooperating on the design of an open
standard named ZigBee IP. The basic strategy is to use IPv6 whenever
possible and introduce required modifications. A protocol has been defined to compress IPv6 datagrams and send them over 802.15.4 radio link.
IPv6 Neighbor Discovery has been modified to find the IP addresses of
directly reachable neighbors; there was also a protocol developed for allowing neighbors to exchange data. ZigBee IP: IEEE 802. 15. based specifications are using 6LoWPAN header compressions as a high level communication protocol. ZigBee IP, the IPv6 based standard for wireless sensor networks, enables multipurpose applications, not only for virtual
microgrids but also for virtual networks supporting smart city IoT applications and smart water networks.

In contrast, tactile ad hoc radio networks require high data rates and
high mobility. For these applications the tactile Internet with high
throughput requirements and ultra-low latency guarantees combined with
big data processing is required. The ultra-low latency requirements of the
tactile Internet can be implemented within next generation 5 G networks,
enabling multipurpose-driven different IoT applications such as networked
vehicles, water sensors located within agricultural areas, or security cameras (Brake, 2016, pp. 2-6). Camera based sensing (which involves high
volumes of data) is implemented with compressor functions, combined
with big data processing for networked vehicles applications (Knieps,
2018b).

3.3   Heterogeneous geopositioning services

In Intelligent Transport Systems as well as in other application areas of the
IoT, in addition to real-time transmission, spatially differentiated data collection with an ever increasing positioning accuracy becomes increasingly
important. Thus satellite navigation systems gain increasing significance.
The geopositioning Overlay-System EGNOS (European Geostationary
Navigation Overlay Service) is fundamentally an enhanced infrastructure
system in the form of a satellite based differential GPS or Galileo.
EGNOS improves accuracy and reliability by correcting the measurements
in the GPS, respectively Galileo navigation systems. Galileo enhancement

is based on the accurate positioning of mobile vehicles. EGNOS combined with digital cellular technologies enables a large variety of real-time and locational tailored applications in the app economy. Various EGNOS based applications are evolving, such as airport approach control, networked driving, intermodal local traffic (e.g. bus on demand services), entering ports in conditions of reduced visibility, and location based services within the city. The EGNOS infrastructure consists of three geostationary satellites and a network of ground stations. EGNOS has been founded by an agreement between the European Space Agency (ESA), the European Commission (EC) and Eurocontrol (the European Organisation for the Safety of Air Navigation).

Three categories of EGNOS services are provided:[6]

(1) Safety of Life (SoL), enabling safety critical transport applications with particular focus on aviation applications
(2) Open Service (OS) enabling improving position accuracy for applications where safety is not critical
(3) EGNOS Data Access Service (EDAS) providing additional services such as the EGNOS information broadcast through the GEO Signal In Space (SIS). Access to EDAS servers enables additional performance, in particular regarding the QoS of data packet transmission in real time and within guaranteed delay boundaries not available via the use of best effort Internet.[7]

EGNOS provides its services, which can be received throughout Europe, free of charge. The full transmission of data provided by EDAS Servers is IP based, either via best effort Internet or by point to point direct link guaranteeing higher performance. The costs of direct communication access lines are borne by the users.[8]

EGNOS can be used in all areas where precise geopositioning is of particular importance, such as aviation, networked/autonomous driving, rail traffic control, navigation in smart cities, or agriculture. Geopositioning systems differ from those of broadband infrastructures insofar as there is no rivalry in the receiving of positioning data. Because of this perfect non-rivalry in consumption, the financing target cannot be met through utiliza-

---

6   https://gssc.esa.int/navipedia/index.php/Category:EGNOS_Services
7   https://www.gsa.europa.eu/egnos/edas/condition-use-edas
8   https://gssc.esa.int/navipedia/index.php/EGNOS_Data_Access_Service_ (EDAS)

tion dependent user fees. Government financing thus seems to be the obvious solution.

3.4   Heterogeneous data processing and cloud computing

The collection, processing and transmission of large volumes of real-time and location aware data may become an important ICT component in many IoT applications. In the context of smart cities and Intelligent Transportation Systems speed sensors and high-resolution cameras are collecting large volumes of real-time traffic data, enabling intelligent traffic management. Platforms for networked driverless vehicles depend on ultra-delay sensitive adaptation to road traffic conditions within the nearby local environment. The design of big data virtual networks enables the combination of big data analysis for sensor-compressing with ultra-low latencies in data transmission, taking into account strict positioning requirements (Knieps, 2018b, pp. 5 f.).

The question as to where to locate the data processing leads to the division of labor between cloud computing and fog computing. The result may depend on different criteria, including data processing, bandwidth consumption, latency requirements and security and safety. Fog computing within the edge cloud is focused on local, highly distributed computing concepts (e.g. Bonomi et al., 2012, pp. 13 f; Chang et al., 2014, p. 346). The ultra-low latency requirements of networked automated vehicles result in the necessity of combining the highest QoS traffic class for bandwidth capacity with fog computing (Knieps, 2018b). The literature on big data, cloud computing and fog computing leaves open the question of how to allocate the decision competence among the different actors involved. However, the concept of the big data virtual network requires that the end-to-end responsibility and the decision competence to combine the required ICT components rest with the virtual network provider.

3.5   Heterogeneous e-privacy and security requirements

A basic goal of network virtualization is to bundle the end-to-end responsibility for privacy and security concerns regarding the virtual side of IoT applications in the hands of the provider of the virtual network.[9] Virtual networks should not create security externalities and in particular not cause disruptions to other virtual networks or physical networks. Authentication, authorization, and accounting of virtual resources are required, preventing the abuse of virtual resources and malicious attacks (ITU-T, 2012, p. 12). Privacy protection and security measures are relevant within all dimensions of virtual networks. The advantage of IP based virtual networks is their ability to benefit from the efforts of the IETF to develop security measures for data packet transmission. The focus of Internet Protocol Security (IPsec) is on the security of the IP protocol located at the network layer, avoiding attacks on protocols.[10] In contrast, attacks on users are largely independent from protocol details. The disaggregated approach to security concepts differentiates between security measures on the network layer, the transport layer and the application layer. The basic principle of network layer security architecture is the split between time-consuming authentication and the key exchange protocol step; this also establishes a security architecture on one hand and the actual data traffic protection on the other hand (Baker, Meyer, 2011). Whereas security requirements regarding confidentiality (unauthorized disclosure), integrity (data integrity and data origin authentication) and availability (mitigating denial-of-service attacks) are typically required on all layers, heterogeneous implementations of security mechanisms combining network layer security with application layer security are up to the security requirements of different applications (Baker, Meyer, 2011, pp.10 ff.). There are many ways in which IPsec can be implemented with heterogeneous granularity as regards the security service provided (Kent, Seo, 2005, p. 10).

In addition to the requirements, which must be met by the network architecture of an all-IP Internet, there are important challenges from a data

---

9   "Since LINPs created by network virtualization are isolated and independently managed, conventional security considerations for non-virtualized networks should be independently applied to each LINP too. In addition to that, a security problem of an LINP should not be spread to other LINPs." (ITU-T, 2012, p. 6).

10   "IPsec is designed to provide interoperable, high quality, cryptographically-based security for IPv4 and IPv6. The set of security services offered includes access control, connectionless integrity, data origin authentication, detection and rejection of replays (a form of partial sequence integrity), confidentiality (via encryption), and limited traffic flow confidentiality. These services are provided at the IP layer, offering protection in a standard fashion for all protocols that may be carried over IP (including IP itself)." (Kent, Seo, 2005, p. 5).

privacy protection (e-privacy) and cyber security point of view, due to the increasing relevance of spatially differentiated real-time traffic data. In this context the principle of Geographic Location/Privacy (Geopriv) architecture has been developed: "A central feature of the Geopriv architecture is that location information is always bound to privacy rules to ensure that entities that receive location information are informed of how they may use it." (Barnes et al., 2011, p. 4).

Heterogeneous security requirements are also identified in the context of cloud computing, with a particular focus on data isolation, data protection and confidentially protection. Different cloud computing services require heterogeneous security mechanisms in order to avoid conflicts between different protection requirements (ITU-T, 2015, p. 12). Fog computing at the edges has particular protection requirements compared to cloud computing, because the fog devices are faced with a higher threat potential, which is typically not expected in the central cloud (Stojmenovic, Wen, 2014, p. 5). Security and privacy are also considered of particular importance for the 5 G networks of the future (Brake, 2016, p. 5). A disaggregated approach to security mechanisms within 5 G networks has been proposed, with a particular focus on the role of network slicing and heterogeneous application-specific security mechanisms (Ericsson, 2017, p. 8).

4.   Conclusions

The IoT poses new challenges for the Internet of the future. Real-time transmission as well as spatially differentiated data collection are growing in importance. The transition from a narrowband best effort Internet to a multi-purpose Internet with active traffic management based on all-IP broadband infrastructure with QoS differentiated bandwidth capacities gains increasing relevance. All-IP broadband infrastructures endowed with the Generalized DiffServ architecture function as General Purpose Technologies (GPTs) for applications and services driven by innovational complementarities between Internet applications (e.g. search engines, PC software) and traffic services (Knieps, Bauer, 2016, p. 45). The IoT strongly enlarges the scope of applications and services. The entrepreneurial development of heterogeneous virtual networks is driven by the requirements of new markets for IoT applications, such as microgrids, shared mobility services and smart city concepts, requiring traffic architectures in an all-IP broadband network that provide stochastic and deterministic QoS guarantees (Knieps, 2017c). The potentials of a GPT for ICT based complementary innovations between traffic services and IoT based applications should therefore not be hampered by network neutrality regulation (Bauer, Knieps, 2018).

References

Ash, G., Morton, A., Dolly, M., Tarapore, P., Dvorak, C., & El Mghazli, Y. (2010), Y.1541-QOSM: Model for Networks using Y.1541 Quality-of-Service Classes, RFC 5976.

Ashton, K. (2009), That ´Internet of Things´ Thing – In the real world, things matter more than ideas, RFID Journal, 22 June, https://www.rfidjournal.com/articles/view?4986

Babiarz, J., Chan, K., & Baker, F. (2006), Configuration Guidelines for DiffServ Service Classes, RFC 4594.

Baker, F. & Meyer, D. (2011), Internet Protocols for the Smart Grid, RFC 6272.

Barnes, R., Lepinski, M., Cooper, A., Morris, J., Tschofenig, H., & Schulzrinne, H. (2011), An Architecture for Location and Location Privacy in Internet Applications, RFC 6280.

Bauer, J.M., & Knieps, G. (2018), Innovational Complementarities and Network Neutrality, Telecommunications Policy, 42,172-183.

Bonomi, F., Milito, R., Zhu, J., & Addepalli, S. (2012), Fog Computing and Its Role in the Internet of Things, MCC, August 17, Helsinki.

Brake, D. (2016), 5 G and Next Generation Wireless: Implications for Policy and Competition, Information Technology & Innovation Foundation (ITIF), June, 1-22, www.ITIF.org.

Chang, H., Hari, A., Mukherjee, S., & Lakshman, T.V. (2014), Bringing the Cloud to the Edge, IEEE INFOCOM Workshop on Mobile Cloud Computing, 346-351.

Ericsson (2017), 5G Security: Scenarios and Solutions, Ericsson White Paper, Uen 284 23-3269, June.

European Commission (2015), A Digital Single Market Strategy for Europe, Brussels, 6.5. 2015, COM (2015)192 final.

ITU-T (2004), Next Generation Networks – Frameworks and functional architecture models: General overview of NGN, Recommendation ITU-T Y.2001.

ITU-T (2012), Framework of network virtualization for future networks, Recommendation ITU-T Y.3011.

ITU-T (2015), Security framework for cloud computing, Recommendation ITU-T X.1601.

Kent, S., & Seo, K. (2005), Security Architecture for the Internet Protocol, RFC 4301.

Knieps, G. (2011), Network neutrality and the Evolution of the Internet, International Journal of Management and Network Economics, 2(1), 24-38.

Knieps, G. (2015), Entrepreneurial traffic management and the Internet Engineering Task Force, Journal of Competition Law & Economics, 11(3), 727-745.

Knieps, G. (2017a), Internet of Things and the Economics of Microgrids, in: F. Sioshansi (Ed.), Innovation and Disruption at the Grid's Edge, Amsterdam et al.: Academic Press/Elsevier, 241-258.

Knieps, G. (2017b), Internet of Things and the economics of smart sustainable cities, Competition and Regulation in Network Industries, 18(1-2), 115-131.

Knieps, G. (2017c), Internet of Things, future networks and the economics of virtual networks, Competition and Regulation in Network Industries, 18 (3-4), 240-255.

Knieps, G. (2018a), Network Economics of Shared Mobility, Network Industries Quarterly, 20(3), September, 9-12.

Knieps, G. (2018b), Internet of Things, big data and the economics of networked vehicles, Telecommunications Policy, https://doi.org/10.1016/j.telpol.2018.09.002

Knieps, G., & Bauer, J.M. (2016), The Industrial organization of the Internet, in J.M. Bauer & M. Latzer (Eds.), Handbook on the Economics of the Internet, Cheltenham et al.: Edward Elgar, 23-54.

Knieps, G., & Stocker, V. (2016), Price and QoS differentiation in all-IP networks, International Journal of Management and Network Economics, 3(4), 317-335.

Knieps, G., & Zenhäusern, P. (2015), Broadband network evolution and path dependency, Competition and Regulation in Network Industries, 16(4), 335-353.

Kushalnagar, N, Montenegro, G. & Schumacher, C. (2007), IPv6 over Low-Power Wireless Personal Area Networks (6LoWPANs): Overview, Assumptions, Problem Statement, and Goals, RFC 4919.

Montenegro, G., Kushalnagar, N., Hui, J., & Culler, D. (2007), Transmission of IPv6 Packets over IEEE 802.15.4. Networks, RFC 4944.

OECD (2012), Machine-to-Machine Communications: Connecting Billions of Devices, OECD Digital Economy Papers, No. 230, OECD Publishing, http://dx.doi.org/10.1787/5k9gsh2gp043-en.

OECD (2013a), Building Blocks for Smart Networks, OECD Digital Economy Papers, No. 215, OECD Publishing, http://dx.doi.org/10.1787/5k4dkhvnzv35-en.

OECD (2013b), The App Economy, OECD Digital Economy Papers, No. 230, OECD Publishing, http://dx.doi.org/10.1787/5k3ttftlv95k-en

Stojmenovic, I., & Wen, S. (2014), The Fog Computing Paradigm: Scenarios and Security Issues, Proceedings of the 2014 Federated Conference on Computer Science and Information Systems, IEEE, ACSIS, Vol. 2, DOI: 10.15439/2014F503, 1-8.

Tanenbaum, A.S, & Wetherall, D.J. (2011), Computer Networks, 5th ed., Boston et al.: Prentice Hall.

Technological diversification into 'Blue Oceans'? A patent-based analysis of Internet of Things technologies

Bert Sadowski,[1] Onder Nomaler[2] and Jason Whalley[3]

Abstract

The Internet of Things (IOT) promises to be the 'next big thing' in the development of information and communication technologies (ICT). The widespread application of technology to devices will facilitate the large-scale collection and analysis of data that, in turn, promises to have a far-reaching impact wherever it occurs. The rapid technological change associated with IOT creates both challenges and opportunities for companies. In this chapter, we explore how companies react to the uncertainties that they face by implementing 'Blue Ocean' strategies that entail entering markets that are uncontested. Drawing on a sample of 90 companies, all from sectors that will be significantly affected by the IOT, and using patent data, the technological diversification of companies in our sample from one market to another is investigated. Our analysis finds that unrelated technological diversification is negatively associated with market and technological performance, while in contrast related technological diversification has a positive effect on technological performance. We also show how the relationship between the market capitalisation of companies and the number of IOT patents that they own differs between both sectors and companies. These differences may be due to a variety of factors, which are used to suggest a series of areas where further research is required.

Keywords: Technological diversification, Blue Ocean strategy, Internet of Things, Patenting Profiles

---

1   TU Eindhoven, Eindhoven, The Netherlands and Northumbria University, Newcastle, UK

2   TU Eindhoven, Eindhoven, The Netherlands

3   Northumbria University, Newcastle, UK and Telecom Ecole de Management, Evry, France; corresponding author: jason.whalley@northumbria.ac.uk

1. Introduction

Over the course of the last 30 or so years, information and communication technologies (ICT) have changed beyond all recognition. The mobile telecommunications industry has emerged as a significant global industry, enabling individuals and businesses to be connected through an ever more versatile series of mobile technologies that support a wide array of services (Curwen and Whalley, 2010; Goggin and Hjorth, 2014). The growth of the Internet, from the mid-1990s onwards, has revolutionised many industries, changing among other things how we communicate, access news and shop (Broadband Commission for Sustainable Development, 2017; Comino and Manenti, 2014; Wheen, 2011). Integral to the widespread attractiveness of mobile telecommunications and the Internet are improvements in devices, which have not only dramatically declined in size and weight but are increasingly powerful.

Arguably the most recent development in ICT is the Internet of Things (IOT). At its most basic, the IOT involves the application of technology to devices. While the estimates of the number of IOT connections varies, from just a few billion to more 50 billion (Nordrum, 2016), through their collection and then the sharing and analysis of large volumes of data the IOT promises to profoundly change wherever it occurs (Barkai, 2016; Miller, 2015; Schwab, 2016). Within the home, for example, the IOT will enable households to manage their energy consumption as well as to monitor the elderly or infirm, while applying IOT to transportation gives rise to the possibility of managing traffic flows more efficiently than at present (Greengard, 2015; Kranz, 2017; Miller, 2015).

Periods of rapid technological change, which characterises ICT, creates both uncertainty and opportunities for companies. These uncertainties challenge business models, while enabling new ones to emerge. Companies can react to these uncertainties through creating markets by following a 'Blue Ocean Strategy' (Kim and Mauborgne, 2005, 2017), which involves entering uncontested market space instead of battling their competitors that are found to be in traditional 'Red Oceans'. By entering a 'Blue Ocean' market, companies are able to unlock demand as competition is irrelevant in these new markets (Kim and Mauborgne, 2014). As companies seek to combine new breakthrough innovations and thus create new markets, companies need to take into account their existing portfolio of incremental innovations (Kim and Mauborgne, 2017).

In this chapter, we explore the extent to which a sample of established and highly successful companies, as measured by their market capitalisation, have diversified from one market into another. We do this through identifying the patent portfolios for these companies in two related areas, namely, ICT in general and IOT in particular. By identifying the patent portfolio of companies, we can examine the extent to which they have diversified from ICT into IOT and thus shed some light on the degree to which they are engaging in a 'Blue Ocean' strategy – such diversification, where companies enter a new market, has been conceptualised as such a strategy (Kim and Mauborgne, 2005, 2014), whose aim is to discover and then benefit from pioneering innovations in these markets (van de Vrande, Vanhaverbeke and Duysters, 2011).

With this in mind, the remainder of this chapter is divided into five main sections. In the following section, relevant literature is briefly recounted before in Section 3 our attention turns to the methodology adopted and the data that we use in our analysis. The findings of our analysis are presented in Section 4, and discussed in Section 5. Conclusions are drawn in the final section of this chapter.

2.   Literature

Although the knowledge base of a firm provides it with a series of strategic options to exploit and explore technological opportunities (Krafft, Quatraro and Saviotti, 2014), these options are shaped by the strategies that the company has previously adopted as well as the experiences and resources that it has gained during earlier phases of its growth and development (Mendonça, 2006; Fransman, 2010). In other words, while the knowledge base of a company is a necessary component of any strategy it may adopt, it alone is insufficient as it needs to be combined with the other resources that it possesses. With this in mind, our focus here is on the degree to which the patent portfolios of a number of companies affect via technological diversification their technological performance in IOT technologies.

Technological diversification has been defined as the extent to which companies use their knowledge base to diversify into new markets (Kodama, 1986; Lin, Chin and Wu, 2006). It has been argued that through such a strategy, companies strengthen their competitive advantage (Garcia-Vega, 2006). As most companies are operating in different markets using a variety of technologies, their technological profiles will differ as these reflect company histories, initial positions in a market, the extent to which a company is specialised in one area or has diversified into (numerous) others etc. (Granstrand, Patel and Pavitt, 1997; Pavitt and Patel, 1997; Breschi, Lissoni and Malerba, 2003). Having said this, it has been shown that companies continue to develop their technological competences in areas where they initially gained some form of technological advantage in the past (Cantwell, 2004; Fai, 2003). This may result in the technological diversification of companies being uneven, favouring some technological areas over others.

However, technological diversification in the area of IOT might have a different effect on the technological performance of firms in the short and in the long term. In the long term, companies consider whether they should enter new markets, regardless of whether they are related or not, where patents can provide them with a competitive advantage (Mihm, Sting and Wang, 2015). The scope of a company's patent portfolio may reflect the underlying technological complexity of the products and services that it provides (Rycroft and Kash, 1999), as well as the need to familiarise itself with new technologies to ascertain their potential (Lynn, Morone and Paulson, 1996). As technologies develop at different rates, there is a degree of unpredictability in how technological opportunities emerge. This uncertainty is partially mitigated by the company's technological diversification, but if this is too broad the company may lack the ability to initially identify and then exploit the emerging opportunities. As companies address the technological complexity that they face and assess the potential of technologies, they are required to allocate their often scarce resources. Thus, companies may focus their limited resources, either on areas that they are already familiar with or where they possess valuable resources. Therefore, the following hypotheses will be tested:

- H1a: The higher the degree of related technological diversification of a company, the greater the positive impact on its technological performance in IOT.
- H1b: The higher the degree of unrelated technological diversification of a company, the greater the negative impact on technological performance in IOT.

In the short term, these effects can be visible in the market capitalization of the company. Technological unrelated diversification can have negative effects on the short-term market performance of the firm, but related technological diversification can have positive effects. Hence:

- H2a: The higher the degree of unrelated technological diversification, the greater the negative impact on the short-term market performance of the company.

- H2b: The higher the degree of related technological diversification, the greater the positive impact on short-term market performance of the company.

3. *Methodology and data*

3.1. Defining IOT technologies

As IOT is rooted in the notion of machine-to-machine (M2M) systems (OECD, 2012, 2015), it can be defined as a set of complex technologies that use sensors to monitor and control users/machines, generate large amounts of data that is transmitted via a management platform so that it can be analysed to predict future developments. IOT systems contain the following elements:

- A user / machine monitored by devices and controlled by a M2M end user where data are generated.
- A M2M management platform where data are transmitted
- Back-office where data is collected (OECD, 2012).

To facilitate the collection and analysis of large amounts of data and predict how the system may develop in future, IOT systems include cloud computing and 'big data' analytics. To this machine learning and artificial intelligence are being added, thereby giving rise to, for example, remote controlled machines combined with machine learning that enable autonomous machines and intelligent systems (OECD, 2015). For an illustration of how these technologies can be combined together see, among others, Sheng, Yang, Yu, Vasilakos, McCann and Leung (2013).

A series of differences exist between 'traditional' ICT and IOT. IOT is characterised by its use of new Internet protocols (IPv6) as well as the application of new software protocols called 'Constrained Application Protocol' (COAP) that enable basic electronic devices with the option to interactively communicate over the Internet. Even so, there is some overlap between 'traditional' ICT and IOT technologies – for example, WiFi standards are defined with respect to IEEE 802.x and are also used for IOT as well. Having said this, some WiFi standards like 802.15.4, which define the physical and media access control for low-powered wireless sensors, are specific to IOT.

The above combine to define a IOT value chain that is composed of three key stages, namely: sensors, transport infrastructure and big data analytics and applications. The application areas where IOT is deployed is diverse, stretching from assisted living to e-health, domotics (smart home) and smart transportation (Atzori, Iera and Morabito, 2010). Moreover, the IOT will change traditional, that is, established, sectors like logistics, industrial automation and security (Botta, de Donato, Persico and Pescape, 2016). The scope of IOT, with examples, is illustrated by Table 1.

Table 1:   Illustrative IOT application sectors

Application area	Definition	Examples	Sectors affected
Smart wearables	Designed for a variety of purposes as well as for wear on a variety of parts of the body, or embedded into different elements of attire	Wearables - Fitbit	Health
Smart home	Solutions make the experience of living at home more convenient and pleasant	Sprinkler installations	Construction
Smart city	Finding sustainable solutions to the growing problems of a city	Smart grids, smart traffic	Energy, traffic management
Smart environment	Finding sustainable solutions to growing environmental problems	Air and water quality monitoring, smart farming	Agriculture
Smart industry	To support infrastructure and more general purpose functionalities in industrial locations	Real time shipping tracking	Logistics

3.2.   Patenting activities

Patent analysis is commonly undertaken to ascertain the knowledge positions of firms and countries (Krafft, 2010; OECD, 2015). The usefulness of patents as an indicator of innovation has been discussed – see, for example, Kleinknecht, van Montfort and Brouwer (2002) or van Zeebroeck (2011) – with the strengths of such an approach being highlighted. Such an approach, in essence, assumes that the greater the number of patents provides for a stronger knowledge position for a company (OECD, 2013). The OECD has developed an approach that classifies ICT technological fields using IPC codes in a number of areas including telecommunications, consumer electronics, computers and office machinery. Such a classification has been utilized to examine ICT firms, and to compare OECD member states with respect to their competitive position (OECD, 2010).

Patent analysis facilitates understanding the knowledge positions of firms (Krafft, 2010; Krafft, Quatraro and Saviotti, 2014, OECD, 2015). In order to examine the impact of technological diversification and the current knowledge position of firms on their technological performance in the emerging area of the IOT, a panel data set was created. In order to examine the patenting activities in the ICT area, we use the classification developed by the OECD (OECD, 2009, 2013, 2015) to identify all ICT patents according to IPC in the USPTO database. The OECD developed a classification of technological fields for ICT using IPC codes in areas such as telecommunications, consumer electronics, computers and office machinery and so forth. This classification has been utilised to examine ICT firms and compare OECD member states with respect to their competitive position (OECD, 2010).

In a second step, we identified patents in the IOT area based on patents in the following IPC classes:

- Transmission technology (H04L, transmission of digital information)
- Wireless technologies (H04W, wireless communication networks)
- Digital computing (G06C, computing, calculating counting)

Through this approach we created a dataset of potential IOT patents that included all of the different components of IOT networks such as sensor technologies, big data applications as well as wired transmission technologies. To check the veracity of the resulting dataset, we compared the results in terms of the IPC classes identified with previous studies, finding that a significant overlap existed (Intellectual Property Office, 2014; Lex-Innova, 2015). By following this classificatory approach, we were able to identify all relevant patent applications in the USPTO database at the global level between 1920 and 2015. This provided the overall sample for our analysis.

3.3.   Sectoral focus

In contrast to previous research (Sadowski, Nomaler and Whalley, 2016), which looked at ICT firms, our focus is on a range of manufacturing and service sectors that are associated with the IOT. For more than a decade, the Financial Times published an annual list of the world's largest companies as defined by market capitalisation. Those companies listed among the world's most valuable are (sometimes) categorised by sector, with the list including all those companies with a free float of at least 15% of the available shares (Dullforce, 2015). Companies are allocated to a sector, enabling a comparison to be drawn between the value of, say, 'oil and gas providers' and 'banks'.

The sectoral classification facilitates the identification of companies in areas where the IOT is expected to make a significant impact. Drawing on Greengard (2015) and Miller (2015) it is possible to identify ten different sectors where IOT is likely to make a significant impact. These are:

- Aerospace and defence
- Automobiles and parts
- Electronic and electrical equipment
- General industrials
- General retailers
- Healthcare equipment and services
- Industrial engineering
- Industrial transportation
- Software and computer services
- Technology hardware and equipment

Using these ten sectors it is possible to identify 134 companies in the last FT500 that is publicly available (Financial Times, 2015). To these companies, which are, of course, significant in value by virtue of their inclusion in the FT500 list, can be added another 26 that are telecommunication companies. 11 of these are 'fixed line telecommunications', while another 15 are classified as 'mobile telecommunications' companies. Through this approach we were able to identify 160 companies. However, not all of these 160 companies can be found in the USPTO database, that is, some of these companies do not hold ICT or IOT patents. When these are removed from our sample, it is possible to identify 90 companies that our analysis will focus on in the remainder of the chapter. It is worth noting that the companies in our sample with most IOT patents are located in the same sector, namely, 'technology hardware and equipment', with this sector also providing almost half of all IOT patents in our sample – see Table 2 for more details. Compared to the distribution of IOT patents provided by all of the different sectors identified in Table 2, companies from the 'technology hardware and equipment' sector are arguably overrepresented.

Table 2:   IOT companies according to sector

Sector	Number of companies	Number of IOT patents	Sector IOT patents as per cent of all IOT patents
Aerospace & defense	7	7,575	2.37%
Automobiles & parts	12	15,437	4.83%
Electronic & electrical equipment	6	4,370	1.4%
Fixed line telecommunications	8	19,651	6.14%
General industrials	7	29,946	9.37%
General retailers	5	2,399	0.75%
Health care equipment & services	3	588	0.18%
Industrial engineering	8	6,907	2.16%
Industrial transportation	1	187	0.06%
Mobile telecommunications	4	4,511	1.41%
Software & computer services	11	73,522	23.00%
Technology hardware & equipment	18	154,494	48.34%
Total	90	319,587	100%

3.4.   Dependent variables

We use two dependent variables to measure the effects of technological diversification on the technological and market performance of a company. The first measure of long term technological performance is total patent applications by a company in the IOT area between 1920 and 2015 (*PATIOT*). Patent applications as an indicator of a company's technological performance have been widely discussed (see, for example, Brouwer and Kleinknecht, 1999; Hagedoorn and Cloodt, 2003) and extensively been used to examine technological diversification of companies (Leten,

Belderbos and van Looy, 2007). The use of patent applications enables long periods of technological development to be included in the analysis, as well as provides detailed information at the company level regarding these developments. Having said this, the disadvantages of using patent applications in the analysis are related to, for example the different motivations of companies to patent technologies and the variations that exist across different industries regarding the propensity of companies to patent (Blind, Elder, Frietsch and Schmoch, 2006; Brouwer and Kleinknecht, 1999). The second measure on short term market performance is the market valuation of the company (*MarkValue*) defined as the total market value of the company as reported in the FT500 in 2015.

As the dependent variables take only nonnegative integer values, a negative binominal regression model was considered as appropriate (Greene, 2003; Hilbe, 2011) to estimate the effects of technological diversification on the technological and market performance of companies in the IOT area. By using this estimation method, we are able to control for the impact of unobserved firm-specific characteristics related to the market and technological performance, which might bias the results of the analysis (Greene, 2003; Hilbe, 2011). The empirical model tested in the analysis is the following:

$$(1)\ Perf = \alpha + \beta_1 logPATICT + \beta_2 DIV + \beta_3 REL$$

in which the dependent variable on technological and market performance (*Perf*) uses two variables *PATIOT*, that is, the total number of IOT patents and *MarktValue*, i.e. market valuation of the company. In addition, the variable *DIV* denotes the degree of unrelated technological diversification of the company, defined as unrelated diversity and the variable *REL* denotes the degree of related technological diversification. As a control variable for knowledge base of the firm we used the variable *PATICT* indicating the total number of ICT patents of the firm. As Table 3 shows there are large variations in the total number of IOT patents (*PATIOT*) and ICT patents (*PATICT*) as well as in the market value of the companies in the sample (*MarkValue*) as indicated by large standard deviations – see Table 3.

Table 3:   Descriptive statistics

Variable	Description	Number	Mean	Standard Deviation
PATIOT	Number of patent application in IoT	90	3549	6701
PATICT	Number of patent application in ICT	90	9586	17298
MarkValue	Market value of company	90	84434	96283
DIV	Technological unrelated diversification	90	0.02	0.04
REL	Technological related diversification	90	3.77	0.94

Figure 1 shows that market performance - measured in market capitalization in US$ billions - and technological performance - measured in total number of IOT patents - are related to one another.

Figure 1:   Market and technological performance of major IOT firms

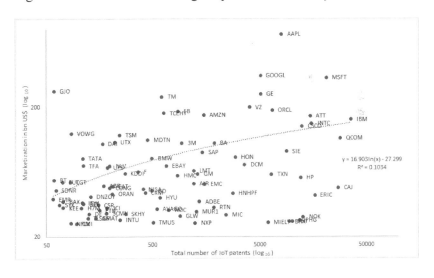

All companies in the sample are identified by their ticker symbol. The fit of the statistical model is significant ($R^2 = 0.1034$). Most IOT companies

are located in the lower left-hand corner of the graph. A few companies are located close to the fitted line of the statistical model, for example, AT&T (ATT), Cisco (CSCO) and Intel (INTC). However, there is also a group of companies – for instance, Cannon (CAJ), IBM (IBM) and Qualcomm (QCOM) – that have a very high number of IOT patents that are not reflected in the higher valuation of the company. In contrast, another group of companies – for instance, Apple (AAPL), Google (GOOGL) and Microsoft (MSFT) – combine a higher market capitalisation with lower numbers of IOT patents.

In Table 4, we specify the coefficients of correlation between the variables of interest. As expected, market valuation (MarkValue) and technological performance in IOT (PATIOT) are positively correlated (coefficient 0.249). Furthermore, technological performance in IOT (PATIOT) is highly correlated with the total patent stock in ICT (PATICT) (0.896), negatively with the level of unrelated technological diversification (DIV) (-0.237), but positively with the level of related technological diversification (REL) (0.482). The market valuation of companies is positively related to the total patent stock in ICT (PATICT) (0.225), negatively to the extent to unrelated technological diversification (DIV) (-0.248) and to related technological diversification (REL) (-0.381).

Table 4:   Correlation matrix

	PATIOT	PATICT	MarketValue	DIV	REL
PATIOT	1				
PATICT	0.896*	1			
MarketValue	0.249*	0.225*	1		
DIV	-0.237*	-0.245*	-0.248*	1	
REL	0.482*	0.531*	- 0.381*	-0.498*	1

Note: * Correlation is significant at the 0.05 level (2-tailed).

Technological diversification (*DIV*) is defined as the extent to which the patent portfolio of a company is spread across different technology classes. In contrast to HHI index, the traditional measure used for technological diversification (Hall and Trajtenberg, 2004), an entropy measure is utilised to decompose the measure at a sectoral level. In order to account for the extend of (un-)relatedness of technological diversification, we use the notion of related and unrelated variety (Franken, van Oort and Verburg, 2007) to examine the distinction between patents that are related to one another within the same IPC class and those that are not. Related technological diversification addresses the variety that occurs in IPC codes within the same patent class. In terms of the entropy measure, we define technological diversification as:

$$(2) \qquad H_0 = \sum_{g=1}^{G} P_g \, log_2 \left(\frac{1}{p_g} \right)$$

In equation (2), $H0$ is the variable for unrelated technological diversification between IPC codes and pi is the variable for the share of each IPC code (*DIV*). According to hypothesis H1a, we expect a negative sign for *DIV*.

Technological related diversification (*REL*) is defined as the degree to which technologies share the same underlying knowledge base, that is, technologically related areas. In order to calculate the technological related variety of a company's patent portfolio it is necessary to have for each pair of technology classes – for example, H04L digital transmission technology and H04M telephonic communication H04M – in a patent portfolio a measure of their level of technological relatedness. The expected sign for the variable REL is positive (hypothesis H1b).

4. Findings

Table 5 displays the results of the negative binomial estimation of the relationship between technological and market performance, technological unrelated diversification and technological related diversification. In order to control for endogeneity, a Hausman test was performed to examine whether there is a correlation between the predictor variable and the error term in the model (Greene, 2003; Hausman and Doreian, 1984; Hilbe, 2011). The results of test rejected the appropriateness of using random effects for the estimation.

As shown in Table 5, both models are significant. In the first model, we use as a dependent variable for technological performance the total number of patent applications *(PATIOT)*. As expected, the linear term of unrelated technological diversification *(DIV)* shows a negative sign. These results strongly confirm hypothesis 1a (H1a), namely, that the marginal effect of unrelated technological diversification is negative for all companies in relation to their technological performance in IOT. Furthermore, the sign for related technological diversification *(REL)* is positive and significant. The control variable for the knowledge base of the company in the area of ICT *(PATICT)* is significant.

Table 5:   Results of Negative Binominal Regression Analysis of Firm's Market and Technological Performance

	PATIOT	**MarkValue**
PATICT	0.0001*** (0.0001)	0.0001** (0.0000)
DIV	-9.5445*** (2.4035)	-3.998** (1.949)
REL	0.5088** (0.1998)	- 0.147 (0.135)
_cons	4.1745 (0.8857)	11.888 (0.612)
N	90	90
Ll	-731.1379	-1098.6444
Chi-Square	121.52	13.09

Note: * Indicates significance at .1; ** Indicates significance at .05; *** Indicates significance at .01

In model 2, the dependent variable for market performance is the market value of IOT patents *(MarkValue)*. Similar to Model 1, the sign for unrelated technological diversification (*DIV*) is negative for the linear term. Therefore, the hypothesis (H2a) is confirmed. The sign for related technological diversification *(REL)* is not significant. Therefore, hypothesis H2b cannot be confirmed. The control variable for the knowledge base of the company in the area of ICT (*PATICT*) is significant.

5. Discussion

The 90 companies in our sample, which are drawn from 11 different sectors, have all acquired, albeit to lesser or greater extent, ICT patents and they have all diversified into the new and emerging technological area of the IOT. Given the far-reaching impact that many commentators believe the IOT will have across the whole economy (Greengard, 2015; Miller, 2015), this diversification is arguably unsurprising, but it is only slowly becoming visible. Through examining the technological diversification of the companies in our sample, we are able to gain a better understanding of the breakthrough potential of IOT innovations.

Recent research on the diversification of companies, based on a combination of radical innovation and market creation, has been described as a 'Blue Ocean' strategy (Kim and Mauborgne, 2014, 2017). Such a strategy assumes that the company enters an uncontested market instead of competing against their rivals in traditional 'Red Ocean' markets. In this context, the IOT is considered to be a 'Blue Ocean' where competition has yet to emerge. Based on previous research on technological diversification (Krafft, Quatraro and Saviotti, 2014), this chapter has examined the extent to which technological diversification into IOT has had a positive effect on the long-term technological and short-term market performance of companies.

Our analysis demonstrates that unrelated technological diversification, that is, diversification that explores a new technological area, has a negative effect on market and technological performance. In contrast, related technological diversification, namely, the exploration of technological areas that are more similar, has a positive effect on the (long term) technological performance. However, these effects cannot be found with respect to the (short-term) market performance of companies in our sample. These results suggest that the 'Blue Ocean' strategies adopted by companies are based on exploiting more closely related technologies.

It is axiomatic that the extent to which companies in our sample have diversified into IOT differs. For example, if we examine the market and technological performance of telecommunication companies, of which there are 12 in our sample, then clear differences emerge. As can be observed from Figure 2, the majority of the companies are clustered close together – companies like BCE (formerly Bell Canada Enterprises), BT, KKDI and Orange (formerly France Télécom) are all characterised by their relatively low market valuation and minimal number of IOT patents. In contrast, however, are three – NTT DoCoMo (DCM), Verizon Communications (VZ) and AT&T (ATT) – companies. The former is character-ised by its relatively low value but considerably larger number of IOT pa-tents, while the latter two companies have a market value that is considera-bly higher than the other telecommunication companies in our sample.

Figure 2:   Market and technological performance of telecommunication
            firms

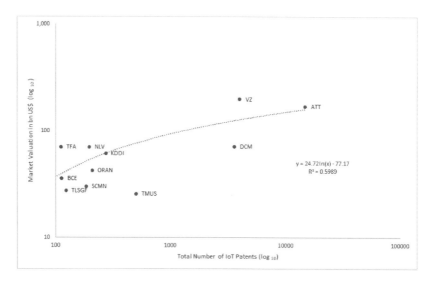

One possible explanation for the differences between telecommunication companies highlighted by Figure 2 relates to how they undertake research and development (R&D). The difference between, for example, BT and NTT DoCoMo may be due not only to how they undertake R&D but also the areas that they focus on - see, among others, Fransman (1994b) for a discussion of the different ways that BT and NTT undertake R&D. Fransman (1994b) also includes AT&T in his analysis. The large number of IOT patents held by AT&T could arguably reflect its longstanding ownership, throughout numerous restructurings (Curwen and Whalley, 2004; Fransman, 1994a; Whalley and Curwen, 2007), of Bell Labs. But, given the more or less similar number of IOT patents, why is Verizon Communications valued so much more highly than NTT DoCoMo? This may be due to their difference in size – AT&T has, for example, almost twice as many mobile subscribers as NTT DoCoMo (AT&T, 2017; NTT DoCoMo, 2017), and also provides other services as well. In other words, market value is shaped by the interaction between technology and the attractiveness of products and services to consumers.

Figure 3 charts the relationship between the market capitalisation of companies against the number of IOT patents that they own for two sectors: 'general industries' and 'industrial engineering'. As can be observed from Figure 3, the companies in these sectors are grouped into two: most are characterised by a small number of IOT patents and low market capitalisation. This is perhaps surprising, especially when it is noted that companies like ABB (ABB) and Deere (DE) are in this group, though it may be the case that they have only recently become aware of the potential of IOT in those markets in which they operate. In other words, they are on the cusp of moving away from 'Red Oceans' to 'Blue Oceans' where competition is not yet present.

Figure 3:   Market and technological performance of companies in the 'general industries' and 'industrial engineering' sectors

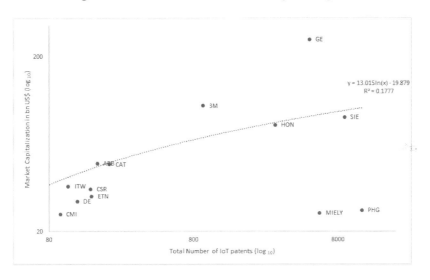

There are just six companies in the second group, united by little except their sectoral classification by the Financial Times. Two European manufacturing companies – Siemens (SIE) and Philips Electronics (PHG) – are among these six, with Philips owning more IOT patents than Siemens but being valued considerably lower. Such a stark difference may reflect their different histories. Both were wide-ranging conglomerates, and while they have over time narrowed their operational scope this has been more extensive for Philips than it has for Siemens. The broader operational scope of Siemens may be reflected in its higher market capitalisation, while Philips' longstanding key role in the Dutch R&D landscape may explain its relatively large number of IOT patents.

General Electric is also conglomerate, though one that is worth considerably more than either Siemens or Philips. The broad based nature of General Electric, which generates revenues from lines of business as diverse as power generation, healthcare, aviation, and renewable energy, arguably well positions the company to exploit the emerging opportunities associated with the IOT. However, General Electric is struggling – the value of its shares has declined while the rest of the market has risen, large recent acquisitions are underperforming, and the company is forecast to be reliant for revenue growth and profits on just a handful of its businesses (The Economist, 2017a, 2017b). As the newly installed boss of General Electric seeks to transform the fortunes of the company, the management is likely to be more concerned with the "Red Oceans' that it is currently present in than identifying and then expanding into 'Blue Oceans'. In other words, while General Electric may be well positioned in terms of the number of patents that it owns and has a long pedigree in manufacturing, it is unlikely that it will pioneer the development of IOT shaped markets. Instead, a more plausible scenario is that the company will enter these markets after another company has pioneered their development.

The 'Blue Ocean' approach outlined by Kim and Mauborgne (2005, 2014, 2017) has been used within the academic community, either to understand the strategies that have been adopted or to suggest how strategies may develop in the future. As can be observed from Table 6, the approach has been applied to a broad array of issues at a variety of analytical levels.

Some commentators, however, have noted that making the competition irrelevant is "easier said than done" (Wee, 2017), while others have suggested that the approach outlined by Kim and Mauborgne (2005, 2014) is difficult to operationalise. Not only do Parvinen, Aspara, Hietanen and Kajalo (2011) suggest that in its early incarnations 'Blue Ocean' strategy is outlined in largely descriptive terms, but also that it is unclear as what the appropriate level of analysis actually is. To this Kampa, Cziulik and Amodio (2012) add that procedures need to be developed to operationalise 'Blue Ocean' strategy, suggesting that this can be achieved through adopting a strategic planning process approach. Similarly, Gandellini and Venanzi (2011) suggest combining 'Blue Ocean' strategy with a dashboard approach to operationalise it.

Table 6:   Examples of where 'Blue Ocean' strategy has been used in the academic literature

Reference	Focus
Barros, Moreira, Filho, Albuquerque, Carvalho and Ramalho (2013)	Computer games
Bourletidis (2014)	Regional development in Greece
Chang (2010)	Mobile handsets in emerging markets
Hollensen (2013)	Game consoles
Kamal and Dionne-Odom (2016)	Palliative care
Kampa, Cziulik and Amodio (2012)	Product development
Kim, Yang and Kim (2008)	Development and adoption of logistics technology
Lindic, Bavdaz and Kovacic (2012)	Factors underpinning development of high-growth companies in Slovenia
Rebón, Ocariz, Gerrikagoitia and Aluua-Sorzabala (2015)	Behaviour of visitors to a tourism related website
Straub (2009)	Academic citations
Serio, Tedeschi and Ursino (2016)	Low cost airlines
Wubben, Düsseldorf and Batterink (2012)	Identification of new markets within the fruit and vegetable industry

Our analysis operationalises 'Blue Ocean' through adopting a company level approach. Patent data is used to shed light on both company and sectoral developments. Through facilitating the identification of differences both between companies as well as between and within sectors, this approach has arguably been fruitful. This approach could be extended to include other companies listed on successive FT500 lists, though, of course, it is likely that not all of these companies will engage in patenting activities with respect to either ICT or IOT.

Most, if not all, of the companies listed on successive FT500 lists are multi-divisional companies where the various parts make an uneven contribution to the technological performance and market valuation of the parent company. While it may be analytically attractive to analyse the relationship between technological diversification and market valuation, it does not necessarily follow that the data will be available to make this possible. Patents may be owned by a division or centrally by a company, and for almost every company listed in the FT500 it is the parent company and not one or more of its subsidiaries that are listed on the stock exchange.

Probably a more productive approach would be to extend the current analytical approach longitudinally, thereby enabling technological diversification over several years to be investigated. One advantage of such an approach would be that it would facilitate identifying the shift in the technological profile of companies over time, while another is that the data requirements are relatively straightforward to address. Furthermore, as some companies, such as Philips, have divested significant operations to become a narrower focused company, while others, like General Electric, have acquired companies, the analysis could be extended by identifying how the patent portfolio of the company changes as structural changes occur. This would, among other things, shed light on whether companies are using mergers and acquisitions to quicken the pace at which they develop and commercialise new technologies.

6. Conclusion

This chapter has focused on the technological diversification of companies into IOT. Using a sample of 90 companies, all in sectors where the IOT is likely to have a major impact, and drawing on patent and financial data, our analysis investigated whether companies are engaged in related or unrelated technological diversification. Our analysis found that there are positive effects of related technological diversification on the technological performance of companies in IOT, and that greater the related technological diversification by companies the stronger the impact is on their short-term market performance.

The chapter has also sought to operationalise 'Blue Oceans' within the context of IOT. While a substantial literature has emerged surrounding the notion of 'Blue Ocean Strategy' since it was first outlined by Kim and Mauborgne (2005, 2014, 2017), and the notion of expanding into 'uncontested markets' is intuitively attractive, it is not easy to operationalise. Having said this, the approach adopted in this chapter has been analytically fruitful – we have been able to identify the patent portfolios of companies, and have begun to understand how the knowledge bases of companies in one area have been leveraged by them to enter new markets. Furthermore, by combining the number of patents with the market capitalisation of companies, the relationship between technological and financial performance has been explored.

Notwithstanding the insights gained from our analytical approach, it can be further developed. A longer period of market related data could be included in the analysis, thereby enabling not only a more detailed analysis of the relationship between technological and market performance to occur but also one that is longitudinal in nature as well. Secondly, the impact that merger and acquisition activity has on both the number of patents and the market performance of the company needs to be taken into account. Acquisitions offer a company a quick, if sometimes expensive, way for them to enhance their knowledge base and enter new markets. Conversely, the sale or divestment of a division narrows the operational scope of a company, which, in turn, will impact on its knowledge base and thus its ability to enter new markets. Thirdly, a more nuanced approach to the value of each patent could be adopted. The value of patents between sectors is not the same (Abrams, Akcigit and Popadak, 2013), and may be shaped by the different approaches to patenting – such as productive and strategic – that companies adopt. Incorporating such a distinction into the analysis would enable the relationship between technological and market performance to be enhanced.

References

Abrams, D.S., Akcigit, U. and J. Popadak (2013) *Patent Value and Citations: Creative Destruction or Strategic Disruption?* Penn Institute for Economic Research, Working Paper 13-065, available at: ssrn.com

AT&T (2017) A Global Leader in Telecommunications, Media and Technology – 2016 Annual Report, AT&T: Dallas, Texas, USA

Atzori, L., A. Iera and G. Morabito (2010) "The Internet of Things: A survey", *Computer Networks*, Vol.54 (15), pp. 2787-2805.

Barkai, J. (2016) The Outcome Economy – How the industrial Internet of Things is changing every business, Create Space Independent Publishing Platform.

Barros, G.A.B., Moreira, A.V.M., Filho, V.V., Albuquerque, M.T.C.F., Carvalho, L.V. and G.L. Ramalho (2013) "Applying Blue Ocean strategy to game design: A path to innovation", *Proceedings of SB Games 2013*, available at: www.sbgames.org

Blind, K., Elder, J., Frietsch, R. and V. Schmoch (2006) "Motives to patent: Empirical evidence from Germany", *Research Policy*, Vol.35 (5), pp. 655-672.

Botta, A., de Donato, W., Persico, V. and A. Pescape (2016) "Integration of cloud computing and Internet of Things; A survey", *Future Generation Computer Systems*, Vol. 56, pp. 684-700.

Bourletidis, D. (2014) "The strategic model of innovation clusters: Implementation of blue strategy in a typical Green region", *Procedia Social and Behavioural Sciences,* Vol.148, pp.645-652.

Broadband Commission for Sustainable Development (2017) *The State of Broadband: Broadband catalysing sustainable development,* September, available at: www.itu.int.

Breschi, S., F. Lissoni and F. Malerba (2003) "Knowledge-relatedness in firm technological diversification", *Research Policy*, Vol.32 (1), pp. 69-87.

Brouwer, E. and A. Kleinknecht (1999) "Innovation output and a firm's propensity to patent. An exploration of CIS micro data", *Research Policy*, Vol.28, pp. 615-624.

Cantwell, J. (2004) An Historical Change in the Nature of Corporate Technological Diversification. The Economics and Management of Technological Diversification, Routledge: England, UK.

Chang, S-C. (2010) "Bandit cellphones: A blue ocean strategy", *Technology in Society*, Vol.32, pp. 219-223.

Comino, S. and F.M. Manenti (2014) Industrial Organisation of High-Technology Markets: The Internet and information technologies, Edward Elgar: Cheltenham, England, UK.

Curwen, P. and J. Whalley (2004) *Telecommunications Strategy – Cases theory and applications*, Routledge: Abington, Oxford, UK.

Curwen, P. and J. Whalley (2010) Mobile Telecommunications in a High-Speed World: Industry structure, strategic behaviour and socio-economic impact, Gower: Farnham, UK.

Dullforce, A-B. (2015) "FT500 2015 Introduction and methodology", *Financial Times*, 19 April, available at: www.ft.com

The Economist (2017a) "Flannery unveils his strategy to revive GE", *The Economist*, 16 November, available at: www.economist.com

The Economist (2017b) "Why General Electric is struggling", *The Economist*, 30 November, available at: www.economist.com

Fai, F. M. (2003) Corporate technological competence and the evolution of technological diversification, PhD dissertation, University of Reading, Reading, UK.

Financial Times (2015) "Global 500", *Financial Times*, 19 April, available at: www.ft.com

Franken, K., van Oort, F. and T. Verburg (2007) "Related variety, unrelated variety and regional economic growth", *Regional Studies*, Vol.41 (5), pp. 685-697.

Fransman, M. (1994a) "AT&T, BT and NTT – A comparison of vision, strategy and competence", *Telecommunications Policy,* Vol.18 (2), pp. 137-153.

Fransman, M. (1994b) "AT&T, BT and NTT – The role of R&D", *Telecommunications Policy*, Vol.18 (4), pp. 295-305.

Fransman, M. (2010) *The New ICT Ecosystem: Implications for Policy and Regulation*, Cambridge University Press: Cambridge, UK

Gandellini, G. and D. Venanzi (2011) "Purple ocean strategy: How to support SMEs' recovery", *Procedia Social and Behavioural Sciences*, Vol.24, pp. 1-15.

Garcia-Vega, M. (2006) "Does technological diversification promote innovation? An empirical analysis of European firms", *Research Policy*, Vol.35 (2), pp. 230-246.

Goggin, G. and L. Hjorth (2014) *The Routledge Companion to Mobile Media,* Routledge: New York, New York, USA.

Granstrand, O., P. Patel and K. Pavitt (1997) "Multi-technology corporations: why they have" distributed" rather than" distinctive core" competencies", *California Management Review,* Vol.39 (4), pp. 8-25.

Greene, W. (2003) *Economic analysis,* Prentice Hall: Upper Saddle River, New Jersey, USA.

Greengard, S. (2015) *The Internet of Things,* MIT Press: Cambridge, Massachusetts, USA.

Hagedoorn, J. and M. Cloodt (2003) "Measuring innovative performance: Is there an advantage in using multiple indicators?", *Research Policy*, Vol.32 (8), pp. 1365-1379.

Hall, B.H. and M. Trajtenberg (2004) *Uncovering GPTs with patent data,* National Bureau of Economic Research, Cambridge, Massachusetts.

Hilbe, J.M. (2011) *Negative binomial regression*, Cambridge University Press: Cambridge, UK.

Hollensen, S. (2013) "The blue ocean that disappeared – the case of Ninendo Wii", *Journal of Business Strategy*, Vol. 34 (5), pp. 25-35.

Intellectual Property Office (2014) *The Internet of Things: A patent overview*, Intellectual Patent Office: Newport, UK.

Kamal, A.H. and J.N. Dionne-Odom (2016) "A blue ocean strategy for palliative care: Focus on family caregivers", *Journal of Pain and Symptom Management*, Vol.51 (3), March.

Kampa, J.R., Cziulik, C. and C.C.E. Amodia (2012) "A critical analysis on the blue ocean strategy and an approach for its integration into the product development process", *Product: Management & Development*, Vol.10 (2), pp. 79-86.

Kim, W. C. and R. Mauborgne (2005) *Blue Ocean Strategy: How to create uncontested market space and make the competition irrelevant*, Harvard Business School Press: Boston, Massachusetts, USA.

Kim, W. C. and R. Mauborgne (2014) Blue Ocean Strategy, expanded edition: How to create uncontested market space and make the competition irrelevant, Harvard Business Review Press: Boston, Massachusetts, USA.

Kim, W.C. and R. Mauborgne (2017) *Blue Ocean Shift – Beyond competing*, Macmillan: London, UK.

Kim, C., Yang, K.H. and J. Kim (2008) "A strategy for third-party logistics systems: A case analysis using blue ocean strategy", *Omega*, Vol. 36, pp. 522-534.

Kleinknecht, A., van Montfort, K. and E. Brouwer (2002) "The non-trivial choice between innovation indicators", *Economics of Innovation and New Technology,* Vol.11 (2), pp. 109-121.

Kodama, F. (1986) "Technological diversification of Japanese industry", *Science*, Vol.233, pp. 291-297.

Krafft, J. (2010) "Profiting in the info-coms industry in the age of broadband: Lessons and new considerations", *Technological Forecasting & Social Change,* Vol.77, pp. 265-278.

Krafft, J., Quatraro, F. and P.P. Saviotti (2014) "The dynamics of knowledge-intensive sectors knowledge base: Evidence from biotechnology and telecommunications", *Industry and Innovation*, Vol.21 (3), pp. 215-242.

Kranz, M. (2017) *Building the Internet of Things*, Wiley: Hoboken, New Jersey, USA

Leten, B., Belderbos, R. and B. van Looy (2007) "Technological diversification, coherence and performance of firms", *Journal of Product Innovation Management*, Vol.24 (6), pp. 567-579.

LexInnova (2015) *Internet of Tings. Patent landscape analysis,* LexInnova: San Francisco, USA.

Lin, B-W., Chin, C-J. and H-L. Wu (2006) "Patent portfolio diversity, technology strategy and firm value", *IEEE Transactions on Engineering Management,* Vol.51 (1), pp.17-26.

Lindic, J., Bavdaz, M. and H. Kovacic (2012) "Higher growth through the blue ocean strategy: Implications for economic policy", *Research Policy*, Vol.41, pp. 928-938.

Lynn, G.S., Morone, J.G. and A.S. Paulson (1996) "Marketing and discontinuous innovations: The probe and learn process", *California Management Review*, Vol.38 (3), pp. 8-37.

Mendonça, S. (2006) "The revolution within: ICT and the shifting knowledge base of the world's largest companies", *Economics of Innovation and New Technology*, Vol.15 (8), pp. 777-799.

Mihm, J., Sting, F.J and T. Wang (2015) "On the effectiveness of patenting strategies in innovation races", *Management Science,* Vol.61 (11), pp. 2662-2684.

Miller, M. (2015) The Internet of Things – How smart TVs, smart cars, smart homes and smart cities are changing the world, Que Publishing: Indianapolis, Indiana, USA.

Nordrum, A. (2016) "Popular Internet of Things forecast for 50 billion devices by 2020 is outdated", *IEEE Spectrum*, 18 August, available at: //spectrum.ieee.org

NTT DoCoMo (2017) Beyond – Annual Report 2017, Year ended 31 March 2017, NTT DoCoMo: Tokyo, Japan.

OECD (2009) Guide to Measuring the Information Society 2009, OECD: Paris, France.

OECD (2010) Information Technology Outlook 2010, OECD: Paris, France.

OECD (2012a) *Machine-to-machine Communications: Connecting billions of devices.* OECD Digital Journal 192, available at: www.oecd.org

OECD (2013) *Communications Outlook 2013*, OECD: Paris, France.

OECD (2015) *Digital Economy Outlook 2015*, OECD: Paris, France.

Parvinen, P., Aspara, J., Hietnanen and S. Kajalo (2011) "Awareness, action and context-specificity for blue ocean practices in sales management", *Management Decision*, Vol.49 (8), pp. 1218-1234.

Pavitt, K. and P. Patel (1997) "The Technological Competencies of the World's Largest Firms: Complex and Path-Dependent, But Not Much Variety", *Research Policy*, Vol.26 (2), pp. 141-156.

Rebon, F., Ocariz, G., Gerrikagoitia, J.K. and A. Aluza-Sorzabal (2015) "Discovering insights within a blue ocean based on business intelligence", *Procedia Social and Behavioural Sciences*, Vol. 175, pp. 66-74.

Rycroft, R.W. and D.E. Kash (1999) *The Complexity Challenge: Technological Innovation for the 21st century*, Cengage Learning: Andover, England, UK.

Sadowski, B., Nomaler, O. and J. Whalley (2016) "Technological pervasiveness and speciation in the Internet of Things (IOT): A patent-based analysis", *27th European Regional Conference of the International Telecommunications Society*, 7th – 9th September, Cambridge, UK

Schwab, K. (2016) *The Fourth Industrial Revolution*, World Economic Forum: Geneva, Switzerland.

Serio, L., Tedeschi, P. and G. Ursino (2016) "Making sense of (ultra) low-cost flights: Vertical differentiation in two-sided markets", *Management Science*, forthcoming

Sheng, Z., Yang, S., Yu, Y., Vasilakos, A., McCann, J. and K. Leung (2013) "A survey of the IETF protocol suite for the Internet of Things: Standards, challenges, and opportunities", *Wireless Communications*, Vol.20 (6), pp. 91-98.

Straub, D.W. (2009) "Editor's comments – creating blue oceans of thought via highly citable articles", *MIS Quarterly*, Vol.33 (4), pp. iii-vii.

van de Vrande, V., Vanhaverbeke, W. and G. Duysters (2011) "Technology insourcing and the creation of pioneering technology", *Journal of Production Management Innovation,* Vol.28 (6), pp. 974-987.

Wee, C.H. (2017) "Think tank – Beyond the five forces model and blue ocean strategy: An integrative perspective from Sun Zi Bingfa", *Global Business and Organizational Excellence*, January/February, pp. 34-45.

Whalley, J. and P. Curwen (2007) "Whatever happened to the Baby Bells?", *Minnesota Journal of Law, Society and Technology*, Vol.8 (1), pp. 149-173.

Wheen, A. (2011) Dot-dash to dot.com: How modern telecommunications evolved from the telegraph to the Internet, Springer: Heidelberg, Germany.

Wubben, E.F.M., Dusseldorf, S. and M.H. Batterink (2012) "Finding uncontested markets for European fruit and vegetables through applying blue ocean strategy", *British Food Journal,* Vol.14 (2), pp. 248-271.

van Zeebroeck, N. (2011) "The puzzle of patent value indicators", *Economics of Innovation and New Technology,* Vol.20 (1), 33-62.

Net Neutrality in Europe after the Net Neutrality Regulation 2015/2120

Thomas Fetzer[1]

Abstract

The need for net neutrality regulations has been discussed in Europe as well as in the U.S. for many years. In Europe the EU has enacted a Regulation on Net Neutrality, which aims to strike a balance between net neutrality on the one hand and allowing for innovative services, that require a guaranteed quality of service. However, the Regulation has not brought the net neutrality debate to an end in Europe. Rather this discussion now goes on at the level of the application of the Regulation. This article will assess the permissibility of two common practices by Internet Service Providers based on the new Regulation: zero rating and traffic shaping. It will also deal with a first decision by the German Regulatory Agency on the application of the European Net Neutrality Regulation.[2]

Keywords: network neutrality, zero rating, BEREC, regulation

1.   Introduction

The net neutrality debate has taken many twists in Europe. The debate has been heavily influenced by parallel discussions in the United States even though the regulatory environment as well as the level and kind of competition for broadband Internet access is very different in the U.S. and in Europe.[3] Nevertheless, there was pressure on the European Parliament to enact some kind of net neutrality regulation in Europe after it seemed that the at that time rather strict net neutrality regulation would be eased in the

---

1   University of Mannheim School of Law and Economics and Mannheim Centre for Competition and Innovation (MaCCI); fetzer@jura.uni-mannheim.de

2   The article is based on legal opinion that the author has written for a telecommunications provider. A less comprehensive German version of the article is available at MMR 2017, 579.

3   Fetzer et al., Wirtschaftsdienst 2013, 695; Peitz et al., Wirtschaftsdienst 2012, 777; see for the U.S. Yoo, 2008 U. Chi. Leg F. 179.

U.S. in 2014.[4] After controversial discussions, the European Parliament enacted the "Regulation laying down measures concerning open internet access and amending Directive 2002/22/EC on universal service and users' rights relating to electronic communications networks and services and Regulation (EU) No 531/2012 on roaming on public mobile communications networks within the Union"[5] (Regulation 2015/2120) on November 25th 2015 which went into force on April 30th 2016 as far as the net neutrality provisions are concerned.

With the enactment of Regulation 2015/2120 the net neutrality debate has reached a new stage in Europe. The Regulation has brought the discussion whether there is a need for legislative net neutrality measures to a tentative end. However, that discussion has been followed by an equally intense and controversial discussion about the application and the interpretation of Regulation 2015/2120. This does not come as a surprise since the Regulation ultimately is a compromise, which tries to ensure the openness of the Internet by prohibiting certain practices by Internet Service Providers (ISPs) that harm the open Internet on the one hand. On the other hand, the Regulation aims at allowing innovative new services that require a specific (guaranteed) quality of service. Moreover, the Regulation acknowledges that certain traffic management practices are useful and, therefore, should also be permissible. Since the Regulation offers some ambiguity regarding what should be permissible, the Body of Regulators for Electronic Communications (BEREC) received a mandate to issue guidelines in order to ensure the uniform application of the Regulation in Europe.[6] Troublesome ambiguity exists especially regarding the permissibility of zero rating practices under which the use of specific services or categories of services do not count against the in an Internet access contract included data allowance. Accordingly, BEREC published such guidelines that inter alia deal with zero rating and other potential practices by

---

4   Wyatt, New York Times, April 23, 2014, "F.C.C., in a Shift, Backs Fast Lanes for Web Traffic", https://www.nytimes.com/2014/04/24/technology/fcc-new-net-neutrality-rules.html (accessed June 4, 2018).

5   Regulation (EU) 2015/2120 of the European Parliament and of the Council of 25 November 2015 laying down measures concerning open internet access and amending Directive 2002/22/EC on universal service and users' rights relating to electronic communications networks and services and Regulation (EU) No 531/2012 on roaming on public mobile communications networks within the Union, OJ L 310, 26.11.2015, p. 1-18.

6   Art. 5 par. 3 Regulation 2015/2120.

ISPs in August 2016.[7] Even though from a legal point of view these guidelines are not binding but just a mere interpretation aid to the Regulation their practical importance cannot be overstated.[8]

Regulation 2015/2120 takes a two-tier approach: It distinguishes between Internet Access Services (IAS) and other services. According to Art. 2 par. 1 No. 2 Regulation 2015/2120 IAS are such services, that enable users to access all content and/or services that are generally available on the Internet. For IAS Art. 3 par. 3 Regulation 2015/2120 states a general obligation to treat all traffic the same. However, the Regulation provides for exceptions to this strict net neutrality approach. According to Art. 3 par. 3 and par. 4 Regulation 2015/2120 ISPs can under further specified conditions apply certain traffic management techniques to the IAS. Art. 3 par. 2 Regulation 2015/2120 gives ISPs and end-users the right to enter agreements that eventually include certain deviations from strict net neutrality. "Other services" are addressed by Art. 3 par. 5 Regulation 2015/2120. Accordingly, ISPs are allowed to offer other electronic communication services which do offer a certain quality of service by prioritizing selected content. Traditionally, such services are called "managed services" or "specialized services". However, according to Art. 3 par. 5 subpar. 2 Regulation 2015/2120 ISPs must offer such "other services" only if a minimum quality of the IAS is actually required for specific uses, if the "other service" does not use the capacity of an ISP but additional network capacity, and if such "other services" do not harm the IAS, e.g. by degrading the IAS so much that all customers will want to switch to an "other service" (at an extra fee). Moreover, ISPs need to be transparent on the conditions of an "other service" and must not market it as "Internet Access".

It did not take long before the first cases mainly concerning zero rating came up, that required national regulatory agencies to assess, which practices should be permissible under the new Regulation. The two most prominent examples in Germany concern an offer by Vodafone ("Vodafone Pass") and Deutsche Telekom ("StreamOn"). Vodafone Pass offers different tariff arrangements, which customers can choose from and which

---

7   BEREC, Guidelines on the implementation by National Regulators of European Net Neutrality Rules, BoR 2016 (16) 127.

8   For a critical assessment whether this kind of delegating interpretative authority to BEREC see Klement, EuR 2017, 532.

give customers effectively unlimited data for specific uses.[9] For example, the Social-Pass enables customers to use selected social network sites without the usage being counted against an included data volume of their tariff. StreamOn on the other hand allows customers to use certain stream-ing-services of streaming providers that have an arrangement with Deutsche Telekom.[10] Moreover, under certain conditions Deutsche Tele-kom will shape video streams in a way that the bandwidth, that is availa-ble for video streaming, will be limited so that customers can only watch SD-video quality. StreamOn is free of charge for customers as well as for streaming providers. The first Vodafone Pass is free of charge; for addi-tional passes customers have to pay between 5 and 10 Euros per pass.

The German Regulatory Agency "Bundesnetzagentur" (BNetzA) launched an investigation against Vodafone as well as against Deutsche Telekom. The investigation against Deutsche Telekom ended with an or-der by BNetzA generally allowing the zero rating of streaming services and banning the traffic shaping of video streams.[11] The agency considered the zero rating aspect of StreamOn to be in accordance with the Net Neu-trality Regulation. However, the traffic shaping aspect was considered a violation of the regulation's rules on traffic management. Moreover, BNetzA ordered Deutsche Telekom to enable StreamOn customers to benefit from the zero rating not only in Germany but also while being abroad based on the European Roaming Regulation.[12] This article will fo-cus on the two questions related to the European Net Neutrality Regula-tion but not deal with the roaming issues. Hence, this article will ask which limits Regulation 2015/2120 puts on zero rating and traffic shaping. It will argue that BNetzA was correct in finding that the zero rating com-ponent as offered by Deutsche Telekom is legal but that the Regulation

9   https://www.vodafone.de/privat/service/vodafone-pass.html (accessed June 4, 2018).

10 https://www.telekom.de/unterwegs/tarife-und-optionen/streamon   (accessed June 4, 2018).

11 Bundesnetzagentur, December 15, 2017, Bundesnetzagentur sichert Netzneut-ralität – Teilaspekte von "StreamOn" werden untersagt [Press release], https://www.bundesnetzagentur.de/SharedDocs/Downloads/DE/Allgemeines/P resse/Pressemitteilungen/2017/15122017_StreamOn.pdf?__blob=publicationFi le&v=2 (accessed June 4, 2018).

12 Regulation (EU) No 531/2012 of the European Parliament and of the Council of 13 June 2012 on roaming on public mobile communications networks within the Union (recast), OJ L 172, 30.06.2012, p. 10-35.

would also allow for traffic shaping measures as implemented by Deutsche Telekom but banned by BNetzA.

2. Zero rating and the European Net Neutrality Regulation

Zero rating usually requires two contractual arrangements: One arrangement between an ISP and its customers, which determines that the consumption of certain Internet (content) services does not count against a data allowance included in the Internet access contract between the ISP and its customers. This is mainly relevant for contracts, which do not offer truly unlimited data. Mostly this concerns contracts for mobile data usage whereas fixed IAS usually offer unlimited data anyway. Usually a second contractual arrangement exists between the ISP and content providers (CP), whose services should benefit from the zero rating. Both contracts can be free of charge but also can include a payment that the customer and/or a CP must make to the ISP in order to benefit from the zero rating.

The European Net Neutrality Regulation contains no provision dealing explicitly with zero rating. Since the above-mentioned zero rating schemes are offered through an IAS, the question whether such zero rating offers are permissible must be answered based on the general rule for contracts with ISPs as laid down in Art. 3 par. 2 Regulation 2015/2120.[13] According to Art. 3 par. 2 Regulation 2015/2120:

> "2. Agreements between providers of internet access services and end-users on commercial and technical conditions and the characteristics of internet access services such as price, data volumes or speed, and any commercial practices conducted by providers of internet access services, shall not limit the exercise of the rights of end-users laid down in paragraph 1."

This provision confirms the – also constitutionally protected – freedom to contract of ISPs and their customers.[14] Accordingly, ISPs and their customers do have the right to conclude a contract tailor-made to the demand of the customer. In order to decide whether zero rating is permissible based on a contractual basis, the first question is whether a zero rating ar-

---

13   Since the available zero rating schemes are offered as part of the IAS their legality is not determined on the basis of Art. 3 par. 5 Regulation 2015/2120.

14   Jarass, in: Jarass, Charta der Grundrechte der Europäischen Union 2016, Art. 16 Recital 2 with further references; Bernsdorff, in: Meyer, Charta der Grundrechte der Europäischen Union 2014, Art. 16 Recital 10 ff. on the freedom to contract in EU law.

rangement is an "agreement" within the meaning of Art. 3 par. 2 Regulation 2015/2010. Clearly the contract on an IAS is an "agreement" in that sense. However, is this a contract on "commercial and technical conditions of internet access services"? The Regulation does not explicitly mention zero rating as being covered by Art. 3 par. 2 Regulation 2015/2120 but refers only generally to "commercial and technical conditions and the characteristics of internet access services". It also gives examples for such conditions and characteristics by listing "price, data volumes or speed". Zero rating effectively is a kind of a pricing mechanism: ISP and customer agree that the ISP will not charge the customer for certain uses of her IAS. Hence, zero rating agreements fall under the scope of Art. 3 par. 2 Regulation 2015/2120. This view is confirmed by the guidelines that BEREC has issued on the implementation of the Regulation 2015/2120. According to Art. 5 par. 3 Regulation 2015/2120 BEREC had to issue such guidelines on the implementation of the Regulation in order to ensure a uniform application of the Regulation in the Member States.[15] According to recital 40 of those guidelines zero rating shall not be prohibited per se but needs to be assessed based on a case-by-case approach by the national regulatory agencies.

Neither the constitutionally protected nor the by the Regulation 2015/2120 defined freedom to contract of ISPs and their customers is guaranteed without limitations. Rather, the Regulation determines that contracts between ISPs and customers are only permissible if they do not limit the exercise of the rights of end-users laid down in Art. 3 par. 1 Regulation 2015/2120. According to this provision:

> „1. End-users shall have the right to access and distribute information and content, use and provide applications and services, and use terminal equipment of their choice, irrespective of the end-user's or provider's location or the location, origin or destination of the information, content, application or service, via their internet access service."

Neither Art. 3 par. 2 nor par. 1 Regulation 2015/2120 explicitly address the question whether zero rating is limiting any end-user's rights and therefore should be prohibited. Hence, one must apply the tools of statutory interpretation in order to assess whether the Regulation bans zero rating. Those tools are the legislative text, legislative history, the context of the relevant provisions and the purpose of a provision.

---

15   BEREC, Guidelines on the implementation by National Regulators of European Net Neutrality Rules, BoR (16) 127.

The text of Art. 3 Regulation 2015/2120 does not give any guidance for the assessment of zero rating practices since it does not mention zero rating explicitly. However, a first argument in favor of the permissibility of zero rating can be derived from the legislative history of the regulation. Even though the European legislator was aware of the existence of zero rating practices[16] – and the fact that some commentators considered such practices to be a serious threat to net neutrality during the legislative procedure – it did not explicitly ban those practices. If the legislator is aware of the possibility that a certain conduct occurs in the future but does not ban or even regulate this conduct, this is a clear indicator that the respective conduct should not be generally banned.

The context of Art. 3 Regulation 2015/2120 does not really give any clear indication whether zero rating should be permissible or banned. This means that the purpose of the provision is going to be important for the assessment whether zero rating is legal or not: The regulation aims at protecting the end-user's right as laid down in Art. 3 par. 1 Regulation 2015/2120. If zero rating should endanger those rights, contracts on zero rating would not be permissible under Art. 3 par. 2 Regulation 2015/2120. It is important to note that not any limitation of end-users' rights laid down in Art. 3 par. 1 Regulation 2015/2120 is relevant in this context. According to recital 7 of the Regulation only materially reductions are relevant. Such a material reduction requires an "undermining of the essence of the end-users' rights." The question whether such a significant reduction of end-users' rights is caused by a zero rating offer requires a differentiated answer: It is necessary to distinguish between different end-user groups: customers of an ISP using zero rating offers, all end-users and CPs.

Generally speaking, customers using zero rating offers are not harmed by such offers but benefit from them since they can use more services than they actually could based on their general data allowance: First, the zero rated content does not count towards the included data allowance and, therefore, the customer can consume this content unlimitedly. Second, as a consequence of the zero rating of some content more included data is also available for the consumption of content, which is not zero rated. Of course, it is possible that specific zero rating offers are not beneficial to customers, e.g. if ISPs block all content except for the zero rated and

---

16   European Parliament, October 22, 2015, Was bedeutet Netzneutralität?, http://www.europarl.europa.eu/news/de/news-room/20151022STO98701/was-bedeutet-netzneutralit%C3%A4t (accessed June 4, 2018).

thereby create walled-gardens. Also, zero rating that enables the customer to use zero rated content even after an included data allowance has been used might have a negative impact.[17] However, if this is not the case, the individual customer's rights laid down in Art. 3 par. 1 Regulation 2015/2120 are generally not harmed by zero rating offers.

The European Regulation does not only aim at protecting individual customers but also at the protection of all customers as a group and their ability to access a wide variety of content on the Internet. Net neutrality proponents generally have voiced three potential dangers resulting from zero rating offers for the variety and plurality of content that is available on the Internet: (1) Zero rating practices give those services benefiting from zero rating a competitive advantage over such services, which are not zero rated. This potentially leads to a reduction of the overall number of available services if customers prefer zero rated content over non-zero rated content, which then eventually will disappear. (2) If ISPs charge CPs for the participation in a zero rating offer, this favors established and financially strong CPs over non-commercial and new start-up CPs. CPs with deep pockets have a competitive advantage over financially weaker CPs and can drive them out of business. (3) Vertically integrated ISPs have an incentive to favor affiliated CPs over unaffiliated CPs, which potentially results in an overall reduction of CPs.

However, it has been demonstrated that all three threats are only plausible under certain market conditions:[18] First of all, much depends on the level of competition on the Internet access market. The more competition on this market exists the less likely is it that the described threats actually materialize. If end-customers and CPs can choose from different ISPs, this makes it much harder for a single ISP to charge either the end-customer or the CP a fee for the participation in the zero rating scheme. Secondly, regarding the effects of zero rating on the variety of available content much depends on the specific conditions of zero rating offers. The assessment whether zero rating offers endanger the variety and plurality of content mainly depends on two factors: (1) Do CPs get non-discriminatory access to the zero rating offer? If any CP can benefit from such offers on equal terms, such offers do not distort competition between different ISPs, including the competition between independent CPs and CPs affiliated with

---

17   BEREC, Guidelines on the implementation by National Regulators of European Net Neutrality Rules, BoR (16) 127, Guideline No. 40.

18   Fetzer et al., Wirtschaftsdienst 2013, 695; Peitz et al., Wirtschaftsdienst 2012, 777.

an ISP. (2) Does an ISP charge an extra fee from CPs? If the participation in a zero rating scheme is free of charge for CPs, it is not plausible that popular (mainstream) content of financially strong CPs gets a competitive advantage over non-commercial content or start-up CPs, which lack the ability to pay for the participation in a zero rating scheme. In sum, zero rating schemes, which are open to any CP and are free of charge, are not threatening the variety and plurality of content and, hence, do not limit the rights of all end-users as laid down in Art. 3 par. 1 Regulation 2015/2120. Hence, a zero rating arrangement between an ISP and its customers does not violate Art. 3 par. 2 Regulation 2015/2120 due to a violation of the rights of all end-users laid down in Art. 3 par. 1 Regulation 2015/2120.

Lastly, the European Regulation does also protect the right of CPs to distribute their content to any end-user. As just mentioned zero rating can potentially distort competition between different CPs if it is not offered on a non-discriminatory basis at no charge. If any ISP can benefit from a zero rating scheme without having to pay for it an extra fee, it is not plausible that zero rating causes distortions of competition between different CPs.

Overall, it can be stated that the European Regulation does not generally ban zero rating. The permissibility must be evaluated based on a case-by-case approach. The legal basis for this evaluation is Art. 3 par. 2 Regulation 2015/2120, which protects the freedom to contract of ISPs as well as end-consumers. Only zero rating offers that materially limit the rights of end-users laid down in Art. 3 par. 1 Regulation 2015/2120 are prohibited. Zero rating schemes, which are open to all CPs on a non-discriminatory basis and which are free of charge are clearly permissible. To all other offers strict scrutiny applies. Consistent with these findings BNetzA found the zero rating component of StreamOn to be generally permissible under Regulation 2015/2120.[19]

---

19   Bundesnetzagentur, December 15, 2017, Bundesnetzagentur sichert Netzneutralität – Teilaspekte von "StreamOn" werden untersagt [Press release], https://www.bundesnetzagentur.de/SharedDocs/Downloads/DE/Allgemeines/P resse/Pressemitteilungen/2017/15122017_StreamOn.pdf?__blob=publicationFi le&v=2 (accessed June 4, 2018).

3. *Traffic shaping and the European Net Neutrality Regulation*

Traffic shaping refers to traffic management techniques, which reduce the amount of data used for a service. Such techniques can be based on data compression technologies or on a reduction of the available bandwidth for a specific service. Traffic shaping oftentimes is combined with zero rating schemes by ISPs. The reason for that combination is that customers with a zero rating tariff tend to consume more data and thereby to use more network capacity. In order to avoid congestion on the network caused by this effect ISPs might want to shape the zero rated content in order to reduce the overall amount of data flowing through the network. From an economic point of view ISPs want to reduce the cost of providing zero rating. One of the first cases raising the question whether traffic shaping violates net neutrality involved the U.S. based mobile network operator MetroPCS.[20] MetroPCS only had limited spectrum resources that would have made it hard to offer streaming services to its customers. Hence, MetroPCS reduced the quality of videos by shaping the traffic. That way MetroPCS was able to offer a service to its customers that it otherwise could not have offered to them. The current StreamOn case also involves a traffic shaping component. The ISP shapes video streams of StreamOn customers in a way that customers will experience only SD-quality instead of HD-quality. From a technical point of view this is achieved by limiting the bandwidth that is available for video streams. However, from a customer experience point of view normally customers with a smartphone or tablet will not be able to tell a difference between SD and HD due to the relatively small screen of mobile devices. The traffic shaping will be applied to all video streams once a customer has opted for StreamOn no matter whether it concerns CPs that are StreamOn partners or not. According to the ISP it would be hard to distinguish video streams coming from different sources without engaging in too intrusive deep packet inspection (DPI).

---

20 Singel, Wired, January 7, 2011, MetroPCS 4G Data-Blocking Plans May Violate Net Neutrality, https://www.wired.com/2011/01/metropcs-net-neutrality (accessed June 4, 2018).

BNetzA ruled that the traffic shaping component of StreamOn violates Art. 3 par. 3 Regulation 2015/2120 due to the application of an impermissible traffic management technique.[21] It is questionable, however, whether the agency was correct in applying Art. 3 par. 3 Regulation 2015/2120 in addition to Art. 3 par. 2 Regulation 2015/2120 in that case. Arguably Art. 3 par. 3 (and 4) Regulation 2015/2120 only applies to unilateral traffic management measures by ISPs whereas Art. 3 par. 2 Regulation 2015/2120 governs traffic management measures which are based on a contractual agreement between an ISP and its customers.

Since the European Net Neutrality Regulation does not explicitly state whether traffic shaping should be allowed, Art. 3 Regulation 2015/2120 needs to be interpreted based on the above-mentioned tools of interpretation. The text of the provision is silent regarding traffic shaping. One could make the argument that traffic shaping should be generally permissible since the legislator did not explicitly ban it. However, the argument is weaker in this context than in the context of zero rating since the discussion on traffic shaping during the legislative process was much less prominent than the discussion on zero rating. Since the context of Art. 3 Regulation 2015/2120 does also not provide for any conclusive arguments in favor or against the legality of traffic shaping measures, eventually the purpose of the Net Neutrality Regulation will play an important role in the assessment of the legality of traffic shaping measures.

According to the internal norm hierarchy of Art. 3 Regulation 2015/2120 the first step is to examine whether traffic shaping can be summarized under Art. 3 par. 2 Regulation 2015/2120 before moving on to the par. 3 of that provision.

Art. 3 par. 2 Regulation 2015/2120 requires an agreement between an ISP and its customers. In the case of StreamOn the traffic shaping component has been based on such an agreement. Customers can only benefit from the zero rating of video streams if they also accept the traffic shaping of these streams. Art. 3 par. 2 Regulation 2015/2120 does not explicitly mention traffic shaping as a permissible content for an agreement between ISP and its customers. However, the provision explicitly states that agreements on technical conditions of an IAS are allowed. Traffic shaping

---

21   Bundesnetzagentur, December 15, 2017, Bundesnetzagentur sichert Netzneutralität – Teilaspekte von "StreamOn" werden untersagt [Press release], https://www.bundesnetzagentur.de/SharedDocs/Downloads/DE/Allgemeines/P resse/Pressemitteilungen/2017/15122017_StreamOn.pdf?__blob=publicationFi le&v=2 (accessed June 4, 2018).

can be interpreted as a specific kind of technical condition of the IAS. Specific traffic will be treated on a technical level in a specific way so that the data packages, that are required to consume video streams, are reduced. This is achieved by limiting the available bandwidth for these services. Since Art. 3 par. 2 Regulation 2015/2120 explicitly mentions speed as one permissible condition that ISPs and their customers can agree on, it seems convincing to subsume agreements on traffic shaping measures under Art. 3 par. 2 Regulation 2015/2120.

As mentioned in the context of zero rating such agreements are only permissible under Art. 3 par. 2 Regulation 2015/2120 if they do not limit the end-users' rights as laid down in Art. 3 par. 1 Regulation 2015/2120. In order to assess whether traffic shaping measures cause such an interference with those rights one has to distinguish again between different groups of end-users: The customer of the ISP, all end-users and the CPs. As mentioned earlier not any interference with the rights of these groups will lead to a violation of the Regulation but only material ones.[22]

Regarding the customers of an ISP much depends on the concrete design of a traffic shaping measure. If the traffic shaping does not degrade the customer experience by reducing the (sensible) quality of the IAS but instead effectively gives the customer more data allowance since less of her allowance is used for the zero rated content, the customer benefits from such a measure. For a conclusive assessment it is also important whether the customer can deactivate the traffic shaping (and the zero rating) easily provided she desires to get the best available quality for any content. If this is ensured and the customer gets full autonomy whether she wants the traffic shaping to be applied, such traffic shaping measures should not be considered to be diminishing the rights of the ISP's customers.

Regarding all end-consumers a threat to their rights laid down in Art. 3 par. 1 Regulation 2015/2120 is not clearly identifiable. The only thinkable negative impact on all end-users would be that CPs do no longer offer any HD content since they know that their content will be treated in a way that consumers will not be able to receive it in HD but only in SD anyway. However, as long as there is sufficient competition on the ISP as well as on the CP market such a danger seems to be rather hypothetical.

Remains the group of the CPs that might be negatively affected by traffic shaping measures. Here a further distinction is necessary: Such CPs

---

22   Regulation 2015/2120, OJ L 310, 26.11.2015, p. 1-18, Recital 7.

which have a contract with an ISP on zero rating and traffic shaping are not negatively affected by the traffic shaping of their content since they at the same time benefit from the zero rating of their offers. However, the current offers, namely StreamOn, do not only shape the traffic of partners of the ISP applying zero rating and traffic shaping but of any video stream provider. At first glance, this clearly seems to violate rights of such CPs which do not participate in StreamOn: They are affected by the shaping of their traffic but do not benefit from the zero rating of their content. In the case of StreamOn one could argue that the potential harm to CPs is limited since every streaming provider could become a partner of Deutsche Telekom free of charge and, hence, there is no reason to complain. However, such a view effectively would lead to an obligation to become a StreamOn partner which would be problematic from a freedom to contract point of view. However, the decisive question is whether Art. 3 par. 1 Regulation 2015/2120 actually includes a right for CPs to be received by any end-user with the best possible quality rather than just a right for the CP towards its ISP to get any content distributed over the network of that specific ISP. The first understanding would be a too extensive interpretation of the Regulation 2015/2120. Art. 3 par. 2 Regulation 2015/2120 gives end-users the right to agree with their ISP on commercial and technical conditions of "their" IAS. In other words: End-users have a contract with their ISP and CPs have a similar contract with their ISP. Accordingly, end-users have a right towards their ISP to get access to any available content on the Internet. CPs have a comparable right towards their ISP that it makes the content of the CP available to everybody. However, if an end-user refuses to access the content by a CP or to receive this content only with a specific quality, this does not infringe the right of that CP. Art. 3 par. 1 Regulation 2015/2120 does not give CPs a right towards any ISP to get their content delivered with maximum quality to any end-user if the end-user does not want that. This view is supported by the fact that Art. 3 par. 2 Regulation 2015/2120 explicitly allows contracts on the speed of an IAS. However, any contract on the speed (meaning bandwidth) of the IAS will have a positive or negative impact on the ability of CPs to distribute their content to consumers. If an end-user decides to book a 1 Mbit/s IAS, that will inevitably make it impossible for video streaming providers to provide their service to this customer. However, Regulation 2015/2120 gives end-users the right to reduce the quality of their IAS for any CP this should include the end-user's right to reduce the quality only for selected services. If the end-user decided autonomously that she only wants a certain quality for her IAS, this decision must be respected by CPs. Eventually that expresses ideally the concept of the entire Regulation 2015/2120: End-users should have full control over their IAS rather than ISPs or CPs.

Arguably traffic shaping that is based on an agreement between an ISP and its customers only needs to be complying with Art. 3 par. 2 Regulation 2015/2120 in order to be legal. However, BNetzA argued that traffic shaping also needs to comply with Art. 3 par. 3 Regulation 2015/2120 since traffic shaping is a specific kind of traffic management, which is governed by Art. 3 par. 3 and par. 4 Regulation 2015/2120.[23] BNetzA relied heavily on the BEREC guidelines when pursuing this road. According to those guidelines National Regulatory Agencies (NRA) need to consider always Art. 3 par. 3 Regulation 2015/2120 when deciding on the legality of traffic management measures that are based on a contract between ISP and its customers.[24]

However, the structure of Art. 3 Regulation 2015/2120 makes it also possible to argue that traffic management measures, that are based on an agreement between an ISP and a customer, only must be assessed based on Art. 3 par. 2 Regulation 2015/2120 whereas Art. 3 par. 3 and 4 Regulation 2015/2120 only apply to such traffic management measures, which an ISP wants to apply unilaterally: Firstly, Art. 3 par. 2 Regulation 2015/2120 only refers to par. 1 of that provision and not to par. 3 and 4 when limiting the rights of ISPs and end-users to enter agreements on the conditions of an IAS. If the legislator would have wanted that right to be limited also by the limitations laid down in Art. 3 par. 3 and 4 Regulation 2015/2120, it would have been easy to mention that in Art. 3 par. 2 Regulation 2015/2120 explicitly. Besides this textual argument a contextual consideration also speaks for an interpretation according to which contractually-based traffic management measures only have to satisfy the requirements of Art. 3 par. 2 Regulation 2015/2120 but not the requirements of par. 3 of that provision: Art. 3 par. 2 Regulation 2015/2120 explicitly permits agreements on commercial conditions of an IAS. Art. 3 par. 3 subpar. 2 Regulation 2015/2120, however, prohibits any traffic management measure to be based on commercial considerations. If one interprets

---

23   Bundesnetzagentur, December 15, 2017, Bundesnetzagentur sichert Netzneutralität – Teilaspekte von "StreamOn" werden untersagt [Press release], https://www.bundesnetzagentur.de/SharedDocs/Downloads/DE/Allgemeines/P resse/Pressemitteilungen/2017/15122017_StreamOn.pdf?__blob=publicationFi le&v=2 (accessed June 4, 2018).

24   BEREC, Guidelines on the implementation by National Regulators of European Net Neutrality Rules, BoR (16) 127, Guideline No. 17.

Art. 3 par. 3 Regulation 2015/2120 to be an implicit part of Art. 3 par. 2 Regulation 2015/2120, it is hard to explain how one provision allows for commercial agreements whereas the second provision prohibits traffic management measures that would be required to execute the (permissible) commercial agreement. To exemplify that argument: Art. 3 par. 2 Regulation 2015/2120 allows clearly for agreements on data caps for the IAS. Such data caps require traffic management measures: If the included data allowance has been exhausted by the customer, the traffic needs to be throttled or blocked. However, such throttling or blocking would not be permissible under Art. 3 par. 3 Regulation 2015/2120 – provided it was actually applicable to this case. Since such a result would be contradictory this is a further argument that Art. 3 par. 3 and par. 4 Regulation 2015/2120 are not applicable to cases that fall within the scope of Art. 3 par. 2 Regulation 2015/2120 at all. Such an interpretation of Art. 3 Regulation 2015/2120 is also most consistent with the general idea of the European Net Neutrality Regulation to give the end-user full discretion to decide on the performance of her IAS as long as the rights of others are not negatively affected. As shown above such a relevant negative effect is not caused by traffic shaping measures. Hence, they should be permissible under Regulation 2015/2120.

4. Summary

The European Net Neutrality Regulation only has put a tentative end to the net neutrality debate in Europe. The discussion on the need for legislative actions regarding net neutrality has been succeeded by an intense debate on the interpretation of Regulation 2015/2120. This is no surprise, since the Regulation tries to strike a balance between strict net neutrality and the ability of ISPs to offer innovative new services. This is no easy balance to strike in general. This is even more true for specific deviations from strict net neutrality like zero rating and traffic shaping. Since the Regulation does not mention zero rating or traffic shaping explicitly, the question whether those two business models are permissible must be assessed based on Art. 3 Regulation 2015/2120. Much depends here on the concrete design of zero rating and traffic shaping offers. However, if they are offered in a way that end-users and CPs can fully decide whether they want to be included in a zero rating scheme or not, at least zero rating should be permissible. This is especially true if zero rating is offered free of charge to end-users as well as to CPs.

Regarding traffic shaping the relevant question is whether an end-user can decide autonomously whether to participate or not. If this is the case, also traffic shaping – depending on the concrete design – is not generally prohibited by the Regulation 2015/2120.

First cases show, however, that there is a high level of legal uncertainty existing. Eventually, this will have to be resolved by the courts. Based on past experiences with court procedures a final decision might not be issued within years. Based on past experience with the net neutrality debate in the U.S. even a final court decision might not be able to settle the net neutrality anytime soon.

References

BEREC. (2016, August 30). BEREC Guidelines on the Implementation by National Regulators of European Net Neutrality Rules. *BoR* (16) 127.

Bundesnetzagentur. (2017, December 15). Bundesnetzagentur sichert Netzneutralität – Teilaspekte von "StreamOn" werden untersagt [Press release]. Retrieved from https://www.bundesnetzagentur.de/SharedDocs/Downloads/DE/Allgemeines/Presse /Pressemitteilungen/2017/15122017_StreamOn.pdf?__blob=publicationFile&v=2 [Accessed June 4, 2018].

European Parliament. (2015, October 22). Was bedeutet Netzneutralität?. Retrieved from http://www.europarl.europa.eu/news/de/headlines/society/20151022STO9870 1/was-bedeutet-netzneutralitat [Accessed June 4, 2018].

Fetzer, T., Peitz, M., & Schweitzer, H. (2013). Flexible Geschäftsmodelle in der Tele-kommunikation und die Netzneutralitätsdebatte. *Wirtschaftsdienst*, 93(10), 695-701.

Jarass, H. D. (2016). *Charta der Grundrechte der Europäischen Union.* Munich: C.H.Beck.

Klement, J. H. (2017). Netzneutralität: der Europäische Verwaltungsbund als Legisla-tive. *Europarecht*, 2017(4), 532-561.

Meyer, J. (2014). *Charta der Grundrechte der Europäischen Union.* Baden-Baden: Nomos.

Peitz, M., Fetzer, T., & Schweitzer, H. (2012). Die Netzneutralitätsdebatte aus ökono-mischer Sicht. *Wirtschaftsdienst*, 92(11), 777-783.

Regulation (EU) 2015/2120 of the European Parliament and of the Council of 25 No-vember 2015 laying down measures concerning open internet access and amending Directive 2002/22/EC on universal service and users' rights relating to electronic communications networks and services and Regulation (EU) No 531/2012 on roam-ing on public mobile communications networks within the Union. (2015). *Official Journal of the European Union*, L 310, 1-18.

Regulation (EU) No 531/2012 of the European Parliament and of the Council of 13 June 2012 on roaming on public mobile communications networks within the Un-ion. (2012). *Official Journal of the European Union*, L 172, 10-35.

Singel, R. (2011, January 7). MetroPCS 4G Data-Blocking Plans May Violate Net Neutrality. Wired. Retrieved from https://www.wired.com/2011/01/metropcs-net-neutrality [Accessed June 4, 2018].

Wyatt, E. (2014, April 23). F.C.C., in a Shift, Backs Fast Lanes for Web Traffic. *The New York Times*. Retrieved from https://www.nytimes.com/2014/04/24/technology/fcc-new-net-neutrality-rules.html [Accessed June 4, 2018].

Yoo, C. S. (2008). Network Neutrality, Consumers, and Innovation. *University of Chicago Legal Forum*, Volume 2008(1), 179-262.

Regulation and digital innovation

Johannes M. Bauer[1]

Abstract

Telecommunication liberalization, regulatory reform, and privatization were premised on the notion that more intense competition would improve the static and dynamic efficiency of the sector. Many observations support these expectations, but there is also evidence of regulatory interventions that had unanticipated and unwanted effects on investment and innovation. New potential challenges for policy have arisen with the accelerating convergence of traditional telecommunications and the historically much less regulated Internet with its strong record of vibrant innovation. Received regulatory theory and practice typically use optimization models that are rooted in static equilibrium theory and pay only limited attention to innovation. This has changed recently with the desire to harness the power of the emerging digital economy. Countries worldwide are seeking to design regulation that also promotes innovation. This chapter extends the emerging literature in several directions. First, it enriches the prevailing view of digital innovation with a detailed discussion of the diversity of innovation processes and the prevalence of innovational complementarities in advanced communication systems. Second, it develops a general framework of the factors that influence innovation in which the effects of regulatory design can be positioned and examined. Finally, it derives implications for the design of future communication policy.

Keywords: Internet, Regulation, Innovation, Modularity, Complementarity

1   Department of Media and Information, Michigan State University, bauerj@msu.edu

1. Introduction

The Internet has become an indispensable infrastructure for innovation in the digital economy. It was designed in the 1960s as an alternative network based on very different principles than traditional telecommunications. For example, it envisioned services to be configured from computers connected to the network, rather than based on functionality engineered into the network, as had been the earlier practice. In contrast to telecommunication, which had been state-owned or highly regulated for most of the twentieth century, the Internet was widely admired as an alternative electronic space, a new frontier to be exploited and explored in new ways. Key technical design features, such as end-to-end connectivity, layering, and modularity, combined with the enormous cost reductions generated by digital technology and the plasticity of software, greatly expanded the space of innovation opportunities. The open architecture of the Internet allowed innovation experiments to be launched without permission from network operators. Pioneers and policy makers alike believed that the innovative potential of the Internet could best be explored by keeping traditional forms of regulation and state ownership minimal. The expansion of the number of Internet users and services, the resulting diversity and heterogeneity of services, and the exponentially increasing traffic loads are now challenging some of these initial architectural principles.

All-IP networks, made possible by the deployment of Internet protocols in fixed and wireless networks, are replacing older generations of infrastructure. With the diversification of historical voice and video service providers into the provision of broadband access and Internet services, traditional approaches to network regulation and the different principles governing the Internet need to be reconciled. As in past technological transitions, this begs the question of whether one of the existing approaches should be applied to new and emerging issues, whether a hybrid that combines existing approaches should be used, or whether an entirely new set of principles and practices should be developed. Because most regulatory choices create real or perceived winners and losers, stakeholders bring widely differing proposals to these policy matters and how best to pursue them.

The network neutrality discussion is one recent example in which such boundary and domain conflicts have surfaced and prompted varying policy responses across countries, ranging from more to less stringent regulatory interventions. Another example is the unfolding debate about a framework to govern emerging 5G wireless services. Operating in upper layers of the Internet, service and application providers favor an approach with strong, open, access provisions to the functions at lower layers (e.g., regulatory mandates on network operators to provide Mobile Virtual Network Operator (MVNO) access and regulated, unbundled backhaul from antenna towers). In contrast, network operators, providing lower level functionalities, which require costly network upgrades, are concerned about the potentially negative effects of such regulatory interventions on their ability to carry out necessary infrastructure investment (Bauer & Bohlin, 2018).

In these discussions, the repercussions of regulatory choices on innovation are crucial. Alas, the consequences of alternative models for the level and patterns of innovation activity are not well understood. Historically, telecommunication regulation focused on creating conditions that mimicked static efficiency. It considered impacts on innovation only in a roundabout way, realizing that achieving lasting efficiency gains required both efficient operations and a reasonable rate of innovation. For example, interest in optimizing regulatory lag or the later reliance on price cap regulation to increase productivity were partially motivated by using regulation to facilitate innovation processes. These considerations placed more emphasis on process innovation than on product and service innovation. Many of the deregulatory policies adopted since the 1970s assumed that competition and less regulation would improve static efficiency (e.g., lower prices and increase productivity within the existing technology) while, at the same time, accelerating innovation and hence dynamic efficiency (e.g., investment in superior networks or new services). Many observations corroborate that this model has often succeeded, but there is also evidence of regulatory interventions, which have had unanticipated and unwanted effects on investment and innovation, often with high associated welfare losses. With many countries seeking to position themselves strategically in the rising digital economy, dynamic efficiency and innovation have become core concerns of information and communication policy (Vogelsang, 2017a, 2017b). A nascent literature has started to examine the diversity of Internet-based, innovation processes and the importance of innovational complementarities among network, service, and application layers (Bauer & Knieps, 2018; Fransman, 2010). These developments are slowly generating more nuanced insights into the conditions under which regulation and governance facilitate or hinder innovation.

This chapter builds on the existing research to develop a general model of innovation in advanced, highly connected, and interrelated communication systems. To provide structure and organization to the chapter, section two briefly outlines the diversity of innovation processes in the Internet. Building on the innovation economics literature, sections three, four, and five develop the elements of a framework to position and conceptualize the influence of regulation on innovation in the information and communication technology (ICT) system. Section three discusses traditional and evolutionary models of innovation. Section four examines the role of contestability, appropriability, and opportunities, and section five focuses on innovational complementarities and coordination costs. Section six expands the basic model by looking at alternative modes of innovation that have been important in the Internet and in the ICT sector more generally. Section seven examines how different types of regulatory instruments affect players in the ICT ecosystem. This reveals several trade-offs and the need to apply a differentiated lens to policy design. The conclusion reiterates the main aspects of the chapter.

2. The diversity of Internet-based innovation

Combining digital technology with an ingenious network architecture, the Internet constitutes a rich space for innovation experiments. The Internet was designed to allow innovation to unfold from the logical edges of the network. Many new services can be launched by changing software on a server, typically at low cost. In response to more heterogeneous services and the need for some quality of service differentiation, new network con-figurations and players entered the Internet. These include content delivery networks (CDNs), internet exchange points, and novel ways to access the Internet via apps. Consequently, that early technical architecture has evolved into a network infrastructure in which open and proprietary net-working coexist, but not always in a harmonious relationship (claffy & Clark, 2016). The emergence of new computing architectures, such as cloud and fog computing, increasing heterogeneity of traffic in the Internet of Things (IoT), and the development of advanced cyber-physical systems will further change the Internet. Despite these developments, certain types and patterns of innovation persist, even though their relative importance may vary over time. Like in other areas examined by innovation economics, several types of innovation processes, each characterized by specific constellations of technical and economic features, co-exist in the Internet. Important attributes include the scope, magnitude, and degree of comple-mentarity of the innovation. As will be discussed in more detail, these different types of innovation flourish under alternative economic and policy conditions.

Innovations can range in scope from modular to architectural. Modular innovations affect one or several elements that contribute to the working of a larger technical artefact. Because they affect only functions within one module but not the broader architecture of the system, technical and economic interfaces between modules are typically effective to ensure the coordination and interoperability with other modules and functions. Changes in individual modules often stimulate innovations in related modules and contribute to a cascading process of innovation. Innovations can unfold dynamically, one module at a time. The open and transparent nature of the Internet greatly facilitates such modular innovations, and they have been a main driver of the innovative prowess of the Internet economy. Often changes at the edge are sufficient for such innovations, but they also affect lower layers of the infrastructure and may trigger complementary infrastructure innovations. To some degree, CDNs, internet exchange points, and increased bandwidth are all such responses. Although modular innovations are powerful engines of digital innovation, they also have limitations. They cannot solve problems that require redesigning the inter-relationships in the broader, technical system (Yoo, 2016) between modules. Such architectural innovations require different types of economic and governance arrangements among the players who are providing these modules (Henderson & Clark, 1990). Finding the right balance between modular and architectural innovations is critical for the overall innovation dynamics of the Internet.

A second important dimension is the magnitude of an innovation. Incremental innovations change a limited number of attributes of a process, product, or service, whereas discontinuous innovations (sometimes referred to as "radical" or "drastic" innovations) change many attributes simultaneously. Radical innovations may be the cumulative outcome of a series of incremental innovations. However, if implemented in one sweep, discontinuous innovations typically require considerable sunk investment and the building of a large user base to utilize economies of scale and scope efficiently in efforts to recover upfront expenses. Consequently, dis-continuous innovations are typically riskier and less frequent than incre-mental innovations. They will be contingent on different types of coordination than modular innovations and will thrive under different economic and policy conditions (Bauer & Bohlin, 2008).

Figure 1: A typology of Internet-based innovation

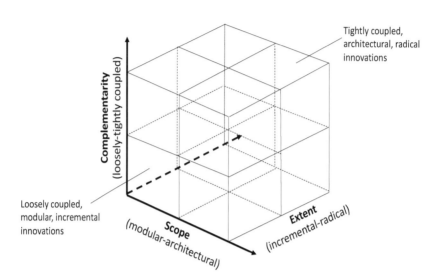

The degree of complementarity is a third important feature of innovation in the ICT system. Such interdependencies may be weak, or they may be very strong. This dimension is sometimes referred to as "coupling," ranging from independence (no coupling), to weak forms of dependence ("loose coupling"), to strong interdependence ("tight coupling") (Perrow, 1984). Technologies may be very flexible to configure these interdependencies ("plasticity"), or they may offer no flexibility (and thus resemble a fixed input Leontief technology). If technology is plastic, it is possible that innovations that begin as tightly coupled efforts (such as the introduction of smartphones, which required the coordination of multiple players) can eventually be organized in a modular fashion, once the major coordination tasks have been specified. The full realization of these complementarities is often contingent on supportive economic and governance arrangements.

These dimensions are not completely independent of each other. Certain constellations are more likely than others. For example, modular innovations are often incremental and loosely coupled, whereas architectural innovations are discontinuous (radical) and more tightly coupled. Historically, the main emphasis of the discussion about Internet-based innovation strongly emphasized modular, edge-driven innovations. The vision continues to be widely held that the Internet enables "permission-free" innovation, and that the ease with which new services can be configured from servers on the edges of the Internet accelerates digital innovation (Lee & Wu, 2009). However, new challenges arise with the proliferation of heterogeneous services and networking needs. This implies that other innovation types have gained in importance and that the forms of complementarities are changing. If complementary services and coordination mechanisms required by tightly coupled innovations (e.g., microgrids, telehealth) are not available or working poorly, innovation experiments involving such types of innovation may not happen or only happen at an undesirably low level.

3. Traditional and evolutionary views of digital innovation

The essence of innovation is the creation of novelty that contributes to sustainable efficiency increases (Antonelli, 2011). Research in economics, management, and policy typically conceptualizes innovation as a new production process, a product or service, an organization, marketing method, or design ("soft innovation") that is introduced to the marketplace (OECD, 2005; Stoneman, 2010, 1995). Digital technology greatly expands the role of software in the design of new products and services. Not only is digital technology more plastic than mechanical technology, it also accelerates the speed of change in many areas by reducing the costs of innovation. To capture this dynamic more fully, it is useful to complement traditional notions of innovation with an evolutionary perspective that highlights the trial-and-error process, which propels innovation. This view is a more accurate representation of the dynamics of the creation of novelty. It describes the process of innovation as a sequence, which is made up of the combination and recombination of knowledge, the selection of projects in the marketplace or by some form of collective action, and the replication and scaling-up of successful projects (Antonelli & Patrucco, 2016; Fransman, 2010, 2011; Nelson & Winter, 1982).

For the purposes of this chapter, Internet-based innovation is therefore conceptualized as a *directed* evolutionary process of combining and recombining knowledge to create new products and services that generate value. It is a directed search in that variations in this trial-and-error process are not random but the outcome of deliberate decisions by players who are influenced by economic and non-economic incentives (i.e., it is a process of cultural evolution) (Hodgson & Knudsen, 2010; Laland, 2017). Successful innovations will be selected in market and/or non-market environments and replicated to reach larger numbers of users. Competition will result in imitation by other players and further increase adoption of successful innovations. Not all innovations that generate private and social value are realized. Successful innovations need to be attractive to a sufficient number of customers to support their provision from market transactions or other funding mechanisms (e.g., crowdsourcing, advertising, public funding). Innovations regularly displace and disrupt existing firms, production technologies, and products. Although it would be desirable to have the welfare benefits of innovation outweigh its costs, an evolutionary perspective does not necessarily imply that this process of "creative destruction" (Schumpeter, 1942) is constrained to the subset of welfare-increasing changes (Nelson & Winter, 1982).

Figure 2: Factors influencing innovation

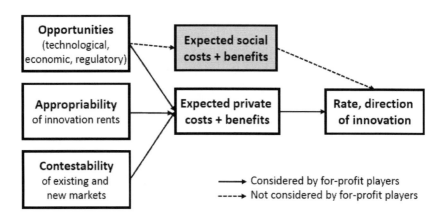

Advanced information and communication technologies (ICTs) constitute a highly diverse and dynamic socio-technical system. Innovation can be examined at the level of individual agents (e.g., a network operator, a service provider, a device manufacturer), segments of agents (e.g., the component industry, application developers), and the ICT system overall. Creativity is an out-of-equilibrium process, which is difficult to model with the tools of traditional economics, such as marginal analysis. Recent contributions have raised fundamental doubts about whether one can even identify a stable generative process that drives creativity (Koppl, Kauffman, Felin, & Longo, 2015). Although, in principle, it is sympathet-

ic to these concerns, this chapter proceeds on the assumption that the factors that influence the rate and direction of innovation can be identified
and examined, even though it may not be possible to model them mathe-
matically. At higher levels of aggregation, innovation becomes an emer-
gent phenomenon, resulting from the interactions of players at lower levels of the socio-technical system, each within the opportunities and constraints of their local environment.

Internet-based innovation is pursued in several distinct modes, including innovation efforts by profit-oriented commercial firms, peer production, government supported innovation, and venture capital-financed innovation. (We will discuss these modes and their specific advantages and
shortcomings in more detail in section 6.) Several common forces propel
these modes, even though the relevance of specific factors varies between
modes (see Figure 2). When deciding whether to innovate and the level of
resources to devote to it, players form expectations about the benefits and
costs of innovation to assess its expected contribution to individual and
organizational goals. Profit-oriented players primarily consider private
benefits and costs, which can be monetized, but players who operate in
other innovation modes may also consider social benefits, which may be
difficult to convert into revenue streams. There is a duality between investment and innovation in that many investments in ICTs also entail innovation. In turn, most innovations require resource commitment and investment. Thus, the standard, discounted cash-flow (DCF) approach used
to evaluate investment opportunities can also shed light on relevant aspects of an innovation decision, even though it does not capture the uncertainty with which many, non-marginal, innovation decisions are confronted.

4. Competition, appropriability, and innovation opportunities

Market and technology conditions will, in turn, influence considerations of
expected benefits and costs. The relative importance of these factors will
vary between the various modes of innovation. In the case of for-profit
firms, research on the economics of innovation suggests that the intensity
of competition, the appropriability of innovation rents, and the opportunities to innovate play a role. In the fast-paced and interdependent ICT system, complementarities with other players also have an influence. Regulation primarily affects innovation decisions by interacting with these factors.

Innovation decisions at the firm level are embedded into a broader innovation system as documented in a rich, scientific literature (Nelson, 1993; Nelson & Rosenberg, 1993; Nelson & Sampat, 2001). The working of financial markets and institutions, organizations governing standardization, patent laws, government and subsidy programs, and interactions with universities all may have an influence. In a similar way, firm capabilities will shape innovation activity (Nelson & Rosenberg, 1993; Teece, 2010). This chapter will largely abstract from these dimensions, although regulation can affect aspects of firm capabilities and the national, innovation system. For example, during the era of regulated monopoly, the Bell Laboratories was a major powerhouse of research and development (R&D) (Gertner, 2013). Other telecommunication carriers had much higher R&D budgets as well. With liberalization, much of that activity has migrated to equipment manufacturers and other players in the digital economy (Fransman, 1994, 2010).

A voluminous discussion in industrial economics explores the effects of market structure and competition on innovation, often seeking to settle the seemingly contradictory analyses offered by Joseph A. Schumpeter (1942) and Kenneth J. Arrow (1962) (see, for example, Cohen, 2010; Kamien & Schwartz, 1982). Schumpeter emphasized that temporary market power was conducive to the advance of large-scale innovation, whereas Arrow recognized that uncontested, monopoly power was detrimental to innovation. The two views can be reconciled by considering in more detail the intensity of competition, appropriability conditions, innovation opportunities, and different types of innovation. Although he discusses these issues in the context of antitrust policy, Shapiro (2012) provided an original take by showing how contestability, appropriability, and synergies interact. Contestability influences innovation activity if it enhances the "prospect of a firm to gain or protect profitable sales" (Shapiro, 2012). Contestability increases the innovation incentives of firms seeking to defend their market against emerging competitors as well as firms seeking to capture existing or develop new markets. Innovation incentives in uncontested markets are weak, although not entirely absent. Incentives for cost-reducing, process innovations and market-expanding, product innovations that increase profits still remain. In a similar way, innovation incentives in ultra-contested markets are weak, because any innovation can easily be imitated by competitors. Even so, there remain incentives for firms to continuously improve their performance relative to their competitors. Most likely, such improvements will be incremental and low risk, given the high contestability of the market. However, in rare cases, firms may seek to pursue more radical innovations even in fiercely competitive markets, if they allow an escape from an intense rivalry (Aghion, Bloom, Blundell, Griffith, and Howitt, 2005).

These insights are deepened if one also considers the appropriability conditions. Because innovations are risky, profit-oriented firms operating in market environments require an opportunity to earn temporary, supernormal profits to accept the innovation risk. Other things being equal, more risky innovation will require an opportunity to earn a higher markup and possibly over a longer period. Contestability and appropriability are related but not identical, because they capture different features of markets and the competitive process. Innovation incentives will be lower if contestability or appropriability are weak and will be highest if both are present. How different combinations affect the incentive to innovate will be contingent on innovation opportunities and the type of innovation. It is plausible and likely, but only superficially explored empirically, that the relationship between these explanatory factors and the rate and direction of innovation vary between different types of innovation. Incremental, modular innovations will likely be more responsive to contestability, whereas radical architectural innovations will be more contingent on achieving appropriability.

The potential costs and benefits of innovation are also shaped by the available technological and economic opportunities. They include technological, organizational, and business model improvements. A broader range of technical opportunities and the perception of wider unexplored spaces—conditions created by digital technology—offer more opportunities for innovation experiments. Such experiments constitute opportunities to explore the "adjacent possible" (Kauffman, 1993) and to find new combinations and re-combinations of knowledge that might result in sustainable innovations. Because of its strong reliance on software to build infrastructure, applications, and services, digital technology is highly plastic and flexible. This is amplified by the general-purpose technology of the Internet. Many services can be offered in multiple configurations. For example, video can be delivered to multiple devices (smartphones, tablets, TVs), via multiple channels (wireless, wireline) and alternative networking technologies (copper wires, coaxial cable, fiber, LTE, WiFi, and others). In a similar way, reliance on software greatly expands the range of business models that are potentially available and the ability to employ novel forms of pricing. For instance, digital technology enables strategies, such as versioning, bundling, and behaviorally targeted advertising, which help improve the ability to generate revenue streams (Anderson, 2009;

Bakos & Brynjolfsson, 2000; Shapiro & Varian, 1999). All this suggests that the innate characteristics of ICTs offer a vast space of innovation opportunities.

Transitions from one generation of technology, products, and services to the next entail costs associated with upgrades of equipment and practices and potential costs associated with the retirement of the existing technology. The latter constitute opportunity costs, which rational investors will consider as part of the cost of innovating. Designing new technologies and services as "backwards" compatible may mitigate these costs, but it may also limit the potential functionality gains of emerging solutions. Other things being equal, such transition costs will slow the speed of innovation and the adoption of new technologies as they reduce the expected net benefits of innovation. The new Internet protocol, IPv6, is a case of a networking technology that was deliberately designed in a way that was not backwards compatible. The new protocol has sizeable public benefits that are not considered in a private for-profit innovation decision. Although other factors were in play, this has likely delayed its adoption by private ISPs and the benefits it was supposed to provide.

5. *Innovational complementarities and coordination costs*

Many Internet-based services depend on complementary technologies. For example, mobile broadband services require appropriate network support, devices, and applications. Similarly, networks require applications and services to generate value. Given such interdependencies, the efforts of specific players (e.g., application developers) will be affected by innovation conditions in their own market segment and by the innovation activities of related players (e.g., network service providers). Bresnahan and Trajtenberg (1995) demonstrate the positive effects of the quality of a general-purpose technology (GPT) on the innovation opportunities of applications sectors and vice versa. Bauer and Knieps (2018) discuss the overarching relevance of such complementary innovations for the advanced Internet. Such complementarities exist between the network infrastructure and applications and services configured at higher levels of the Internet stack. They exist between devices and the network, between devices and applications, and between services. Advances in one area typically enable further advances in related technologies and services. In addition, constraints in a key technology may slow down advances in related areas.

Figure 3: Complementary innovation

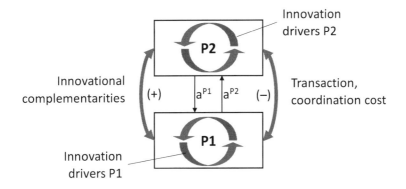

P1, P2 ... interrelated players (e.g. network operators, application developers;
a^{P1}, a^{P2} ... access charges between players (may be positive, negative or zero)

Fransman (2010, 2011) discusses another widespread complementarity — the symbiotic nature of much of the new knowledge needed to successfully innovate. Innovators often benefit from feedback provided by suppliers and users, as also evidenced in the work by von Hippel (2005). This process is often organized in a highly agile way. Brynjolfsson (2011) explains it as a cycle in which continuous experimentation with changes in product and service design allows the generation of real-time feedback, selection of successful changes, and their replication at scale. This has accelerated the race to market in the form of "minimally viable products," launched as early as possible after a beta-version, which are subsequently improved based on feedback from users.

A third example of complementarities is the need to integrate multiple technologies as in the case of smartphones, which combine computing, communications, entertainment, and other functions. Mazzucato (2013) demonstrates for the iPhone that many of the component technologies were developed with sustained government assistance. This is an example of a broad, cumulative, complementarity in which activities funded by the public sector expand the subsequent innovation opportunities of the private sector.

Two different types of coordination costs—transaction costs and adaptation costs—affect these complementary innovation processes. Transaction costs are related to the negotiation and enforcement of agreements among interdependent players. They might include direct and indirect costs of negotiating access to a network or technology. As the number of network operators and technology platform increases, these costs could be high. They are mitigated by standardization, technical design conventions, and supportive business arrangements. Adaptation costs arise if products and services need to be adapted to multiple, heterogeneous, complementary technologies. For instance, an application may need to be adapted to multiple operating systems or network environments. Such costs affect vertical coordination among firms on different layers of the Internet (e.g., application developers and network operators), and they may exist in horizontal relations among players on the same layers (e.g., between Internet Service Providers, ISPs).

Figure 4: Effects of transaction and adaptation costs on innovation

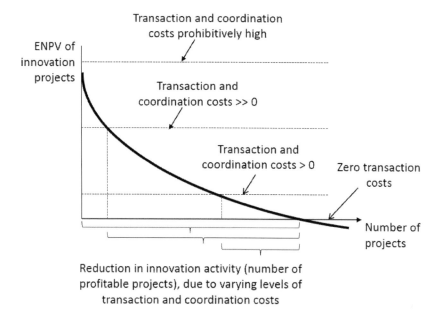

Reduction in innovation activity (number of profitable projects), due to varying levels of transaction and coordination costs

Other things being equal, transaction and adaptation costs will negatively influence innovation activity, because they will reduce the number of potentially profitable projects. Figure 4 illustrates several scenarios. If coordination costs are prohibitively high, no innovation project will be realized. If coordination costs are positive but lower than the anticipated net benefits of some projects, the number of profitable projects will be positive but lower than the number of projects pursued if coordination costs were zero.

Because all of these different types of innovation are important, the Internet must support an increasingly heterogeneous range of innovation processes. Regulation influences the mechanisms needed to coordinate interrelated innovation processes. How and whether such coordination is achieved will shape the types of innovation that are explored. Coordination costs will reduce, other things being equal, innovation incentives. If market coordination, or coordination via standards and protocols, are not effective, firms will seek to integrate activities into their operations (e.g., via vertical and horizontal integration or the takeover of startups). Some regulatory interventions, such as network neutrality provisions, non-discrimination provisions, or open access obligations can mitigate coordination costs for players in higher layers of the Internet. Although lower coordination costs are generally beneficial, well-intended regulatory interventions may inadvertently also reduce appropriability. These potential trade-offs must be navigated carefully.

6. *Alternative innovation modes*

Internet-based innovation unfolds in multiple other modes in addition to profit-seeking players. Important innovation modes other than activities of profit-driven players are peer production, government programs, and speculative capital. Profit-oriented firms innovate to grow their profitability (or firm value) and protect it against the intrusion of competitors offering substitute products and services. Unless mechanisms exist to monetize them, private firms will not take into consideration the social benefits of innovation. Many innovation processes in advanced technologies are cumulative and may require years of investment in projects whose ultimate payoffs are unknown. Pressures of shareholders and financial markets will also limit the incentives of private firms to consider benefits that accrue in the distant future. Consequently, private firms will not pursue innovation projects that create strong externalities, spillover effects, and network effects that cannot be monetized within a reasonably short period of time.

To some extent, private businesses have responded to this challenge with organizational innovations. Platform businesses help internalize such externalities and network effects by facilitating the creation of revenue streams from transactions for the service and third-party revenue streams such as advertising. For example, the improved searches enabled by training Google's algorithms with many users can be monetized via an associated stream of advertising revenues (Parker, Van Alstyne, & Choudary, 2016). New digital intermediaries, such as Airbnb and Uber, capture same- and cross-sided, network effects among the participants. These organizational and market innovations expand the realm of profit-driven innovation in the digital economy. They move the efficiency of decentralized private transactions closer to socially desirable outcomes (even though they also coincide with massive wealth distribution effects to the platform owners). However, they cannot overcome the challenges of innovations for which the generation of third-party revenue streams is difficult, for which uncertainty is high, and which require a long time-horizon. Other institutional modes are needed to pursue such projects.

One novel form that is closely associated with digital innovation is peer production, also referred to as social production (Benkler, 2016). Facilitated by the capabilities of the Internet to coordinate decentralized individuals, peer production allows aggregating and channeling distributed knowledge in innovative ways. Software platforms, such as the Linux operating system, Apache web servers, and many of the protocols developed by the Internet Engineering Task Force (IETF), are examples. Key attributes of peer production are its decentralized organization and execution, the coexistence and diversity of non-monetary and monetary incentives and motivations to participate, and novel forms of governance. Frequently, governance is separated from ownership and is based on a combination of charisma, meritocracy, and participation, which is quite different from property-based or contractual forms of governance (Benkler, 2006, 2011, 2016). The broader and more diverse, often non-monetary but not necessarily non-economic, motivations of participants allow them to pursue innovations that have strong social benefits (Lerner & Tirole, 2005). In a similar way, the network governance of technical and business coordination in the Internet in organizations, such as the Internet Engineering Task Force (IETF), the Internet Society (ISOC), the Internet Corporation for Names and Numbers (ICANN), and the Internet Governance Forum (IGF), in principle, allows consideration of social objectives and benefits better than profit-driven organizations (Mueller 2010; DeNardis, 2009). The open and transparent architecture of the public Internet is a result of this constellation of public interest motivations and visions (Abbate, 1999; Garcia, 2016; Hafner & Lyon, 1996).

The collective funding of innovation projects is another option to take social benefits into account and address the problem of long-time horizons and uncertainty. Government programs in support of basic research and of applied R&D have long recognized this and recently achieved it on a much lower scale with forms of crowdfunding. Often, the public sector uses its procurement activities to advance the boundaries of knowledge and technology. Massive government spending, often by defense departments, has helped develop technologies that greatly benefited the ICT sector. In the United States with heavy public funding, technologies, such as solid-state storage capability, Lithium-ion batteries, touchscreens, language recognition, and global positioning technology (GPS) were developed years and decades before their commercial use. Technology companies such as Apple and Microsoft later integrated these components into successful products, such as the iPhone (Mazzucato, 2013, chapter 5). The role of the public sector as a supporter of high risk but potentially high pay-off research has declined in many Western countries because of a more skeptical attitude toward the problem-solving capacity of government.

This approach risks underestimating the role of the public sector and of the importance of basic research pursued with a longtime horizon in mind. Mazzucato (2013) argues that the failure of ambitious, state-sponsored projects, such as the Concorde (super-sonic air transport) or Solyndra (photo-voltaic panels), does not generally question the ability of the state to advance large-scale projects. Rather, it is to be expected that some projects fail, as they do in the private sector. By the same token, state-sponsored programs brought us the highly successful Internet and numerous other useful technologies. This illustrates the importance of mission-driven, longer-term research initiatives to fund critical research and innovations. Rational policy makers could indeed support innovations that have strong externalities and public good effects or require very long time periods. Such policies are more likely to be adopted in nations with a highly skilled public administration and clear policy visions and priorities. It seems less likely that such enlightened policies will be pursued in nations, which have recently been shaped by populist movements, often driven by a fundamental distrust in the ability of government to act in the public interest.

Possibly as an institutional response to these shortcomings of the public sector, long-term, radical, and risky innovation efforts clouded by high levels of uncertainty will increasingly be supported by speculation-like motives in the private sector (Janeway, 2018). Capital available to invest in speculative, high-tech projects comes in two major forms. It can be cash reserves accumulated by successful companies. Apple, Google, Amazon, Facebook, Alibaba, and Tencent are leading examples of players with considerable internal cash reserves. These resources can either be directed to pursue ambitious research and innovation projects or they can be used to acquire promising technology developed by startups. For example, the purchase of Deep Mind by Google greatly accelerated its capabilities in artificial intelligence. Alternatively, capital for risky innovation projects may come from venture capital funds. A recent example is Softbank's $100 billion Vision Fund. Although speculative capital is ultimately motivated by profitability, the unique funding model allows pursuit of very risky, and longer-term, innovation types.

Even though a systematic empirical analysis has not been conducted, there is evidence that the coexistence of these different modes of innovation positively influences the diversity of innovation. As the discussion in this section illustrates, the various modes are complementary in that they support different types of innovation. In that sense, they increase the diversity of search processes and innovation experiments. In an evolutionary perspective, simultaneous searches in different directions are desirable and, other things being equal, create a higher likelihood of success than a narrow search strategy. Commercial, profit-driven innovation is strongly influenced by the contestability of the market segment, appropriability conditions, and technological opportunities. In its speculative forms, innovation will also explore uncertain directions with potentially long-term paybacks. Other modes, such as peer production or publicly funded innovation projects allow the pursuit of an innovation space that promises substantial social benefits.

This brief analysis generates several insights. First and foremost, there is a correspondence between the economic conditions of innovation and the type of innovation that will most likely be pursued. Incremental innovation will flourish under conditions of high contestability, whereas radical innovations will be less likely under intense competition. Thus, if voluntary arrangements, regulation, or other forms of policy create such conditions, firms will engage predominantly in incremental innovation, possibly biasing sectoral innovation in that direction. Innovations that require higher appropriability will only be forthcoming if institutional arrangements allow it. This could be achieved by higher forms of market concentration or other arrangements, such as innovation leadership by a firm organizing a market (e.g., Intel in WiFi), or exclusive contractual arrangements (e.g., during the introduction of the iPhone in the United States, Apple initially contracted exclusively with AT&T). If markets can evolve freely, one would expect that they would develop the institutional diversity appropriate to enable the pursuit of different innovation types. This is visible in the digital innovation system, where modular, incremental innovations dominate in the open Internet, but where higher levels of market concentration accompany more radical innovations (cloud computing, smartphones). If regulation or competition policy prohibit such arrangements, these types of innovations will not occur or will happen at a lower rate than might be desirable.

The introduction of the first smartphones in Asia and the United States, where one strong player organized the value chain and hence improved appropriability, offers one case, which clearly exhibits several of these trade-offs (Ehrlich, Eisenach, & Leighton, 2010; Hazlett, 2017). That innovation modes and innovation activity need to be aligned is an insight, which also emerges from work in innovation economics. Research by Breschi, Malerba, and Orsenigo (2000) and by Malerba and Orsenigo (1996) reveals different innovation types and processes that are advanced by different sector conditions. This is also reflected in the recent empirical literature on non-linear relations between the intensity of competition and innovation incentives. Early work by Aghion, Bloom, Blundell, Griffith, and Howitt (2005) reveals inverted U-shaped relations that vary for different sectors. More recent work, critical of these earlier studies, shows a wider variety of positive, negative, and inverted U-shaped relations (Hashmi, 2013). It does not principally challenge the insights from our analysis of contestability and appropriability, which suggests that different innovation types will flourish under alternative conditions. From this perspective, regulation shapes innovation through its effects on innovation drivers. In turn, this influences the composition of the portfolio of innovation types and modes and the rate and direction of innovative activity.

7. *Regulation and Internet-based innovation*

In most countries, for the past decades, regulatory intervention was specifically designed to alleviate bottlenecks and prevent the abuse of monopoly power. In addition, regulation pursued social objectives such as universal service or a narrowing of digital divides. This resulted in measures to unbundle local access facilities, govern vertical arrangements between players, interconnection and interoperability obligations, and complementary programs to overcome digital divides. Within these broad categories, there is some national variation. For example, unbundling was aggressively pursued in the United States in the wake of the Telecommunications Act of 1996. It was greatlycurtailed after evidence emerged that it did not stimulate facilities-based competition as anticipated (Bauer, 2005). It continued to play a much stronger role outside of the United States. Several countries have introduced network neutrality obligations that limit the ability of network operators to differentiate services and prices for players at higher layers of the Internet stack (Bauer & Knieps, 2018; Krämer, Wiewiorra, & Weinhardt, 2013). Countries with a tradition of very detailed regulation, such as France, have introduced geographically differentiated regulation (Bourreau, Cambini & Hoernig, 2012).

Although these regulations are targeted at players with significant market power, they influence the innovation system more broadly, given the strong complementarity between regulated and unregulated players. Indirect repercussions on complementary players may strengthen or weaken the effect of regulation on innovation. The aggregate effects on Internet-supported innovation are often more difficult to predict ex ante than effects on specific players, because they are contingent on the relative magnitude and direction of the direct and indirect effects (see also Bauer, 2010, 2014). General predictions are further complicated by the non-linear nature of the relationships. Table 1 summarizes important, first-round effects on different players in the ICT innovation system.

In many cases, there are additional indirect feedback effects that will further influence the overall direction of innovative activity. For example, although strict network neutrality will have a negative, direct effect on the innovation incentives of network operators, it stimulates modular types of innovations among application and service providers. This may create additional demand for bandwidth, which mitigates the negative direct effect on network operators. If that indirect effect trumps the direct effects, net neutrality may stimulate innovation, although possibly less strongly than an alternative approach that avoids the initial negative influence. The last column of Table 1 provides a qualitative assessment of the contingencies that will affect the overall outcomes on the rate and direction of innovation. It illustrates that the effects of regulation on innovation incentives of individual players are often ambiguous. Positive and negative effects co-exist, and the net effect will often depend on the specific details of regulation.

Table 1: Effects regulation on innovation in the ICT system

	Network operators (facilities-based)	Service providers (non-facilities-based)	Application developers	Component manufacturers	Device manufacturers	Overall effect on innovation incentives
Regulation of end-user service prices	Reduces appropriability (–)	Reduces appropriability (–)	N/A	N/A	N/A	Reduces innovation (–)
Unbundling of essential facilities at regulated prices	Reduces appropriability (–); increases contestability (+)	Increases appropriability (+); increases contestability (+)	Increases appropriability (+); increases contestability (+)	Reduces appropriability via procurement (–)	Likely increases incentives for complementary innovation (+)	Contingent on stringency of regulation and component effects (+/–)
Regulation of interconnection prices	Reduces appropriability (–); increases contestability (+)	Reduces transaction costs (+)	Reduces transaction costs (+)	Reduces transaction costs (+)	Reduces transaction costs (+)	Net effect depends on details of regulation (+/–)
Obligation to provide MVNO access	Reduces appropriability (–); increases contestability (+)	Increases appropriability (+); increases contestability (+); reduced transaction costs (+)	Increases appropriability (+)	Affects appropriability via procurement (+/–)	Increases appropriability (+); increases contestability (+)	Reduces innovation incentives of network operators if regulation undermines appropriability (–)
Network neutrality	Reduces appropriability (–); potentially reduces synergies (–);	N/A	Affects appropriability (+/–); affects transaction costs (+/–); affects coordination costs (+/–);	Reduces appropriability via procurement (–)	Increases appropriability (+);	Strict neutrality will bias innovation in favor of modular incremental innovations (+); strict neutrality will disadvantage innovations requiring QoS differentiation (–) and network innovation (–)
Structural separation of networks and services	Reduces synergies (–); Reduces appropriability (–)	Increases contestability (+)	May increase transaction costs (–)	N/A	May increase contestability (+), may increase appropriability (+)	Net effects will depend on details of regulation (+/–)

Because of space constraints, we will limit the discussion to the innovation effects of three forms of intervention: retail price regulation, wholesale price regulation, and network neutrality provisions. With few exceptions, such as essential basic services in some countries, retail price regulation has been largely phased out. It is briefly included because its effects on innovation are better understood than other forms of intervention, and a relatively clear picture emerges. Because such regulation reduces appropriability of innovation rents, it will generally reduce innovation incentives. This suggests that the gradual elimination of end-user price controls has had beneficial consequences on innovation in the ICT sector; the empirical evidence is largely consistent with that expectation (Prieger, 2001, 2002). (It does not imply that there could not be other legitimate reasons, for example, distributional issues or the provision of universal services, which may suggest some form of price control.) If price reviews take place only periodically, the regulatory lag may temporarily strengthen incentives to pursue cost-reducing, process innovation (Bailey, 1974). Since the 1980s, price regulation has shifted to wholesale markets and from rate-of-return regulation to price-cap regulation. Both are forms of cost-based price control, although the latter more strongly links profitability with performance.

Many countries introduced unbundling of local loops to open the access to bottleneck facilities (Bauer, 2005). In the European Union, two forms coexist: local loop unbundling (LLU), providing access at the users-side of local switches and bitstream access, a wholesale process, which provides access points in other parts of local network. Other things being equal, unbundling reduces the ability of the regulated firm to appropriate innovation rents from the network infrastructure (thus weakening innovation incentives), but it increases the contestability of (local) service markets, which increases innovation incentives. At the same time, unbundling increases appropriability of innovation rents for service-based competitors who are leasing wholesale access as well as the contestability of the market segments, both of which strengthen incentives to invest in complementary assets. However, incentives to invest in competing network infrastructure were not as strong as anticipated in early versions of the ladder-of-investment model, which assumed a staged transition from service-based to facilities-based competition (Cave, 2010, 2014; Cave, Fournier, & Shutova, 2012). If unbundling of local access stimulates demand for services, it will likely also have positive effects on innovation in applications and devices. It may increase or dampen innovation incentives in components, depending on the net effect on infrastructure investment. The strengths of these effects and the overall net effect on innovation activity depend to some degree on the specific implementation of wholesale price regulation. It can be hypothesized that all effects will decrease with the size of the markup over incremental costs embedded in unbundled prices.

Subsequent work clarified the trade-offs associated with the pricing of unbundled access on network investment with an emphasis on the repercussions on network upgrade investment and migration to next-generation networks. Three effects influence the consequences for investment and innovation of the interaction of incumbent network operators, new entrants, and users: a replacement effect, a wholesale effect, and a migration effect. Facilities-based incumbents will compare the potential profitability of investment and innovation in a next generation of technology with the profitability of the existing network. The lost profitability of the existing assets is an opportunity cost, which is often referred to as the "replacement effect" (of existing profits by profits from new investment). If existing network costs are sunk, this may be a significant hurdle. Likewise, a service-based entrant will consider the lost ("replaced") profits from offering services based on unbundled access as an opportunity cost that reduces the potential profitability of investing in a facilities-based operation. The price of unbundled access affects these two replacement effects in opposite directions: higher prices increase the replacement effect for incumbents (and hence reduce the incentive to innovate) but decrease the replacement effect for competitors who purchase unbundled network access (and hence increase their incentive to innovate).

Whether the overall effect is positive or negative depends on the strength of the contestability effect between competitors and incumbents. If that effect is strong, both incumbents and competitors will have a stronger incentive to innovate, which might help turn the ambiguous replacement effect into a positive overall innovation effect. The interaction is further modified by the wholesale revenue effect, which refers to the incentive of an incumbent to phase in a next-generation network in addition to the existing network. This requires a sufficiently high difference in the wholesale access price that can be charged for the existing (e.g., copper) and the new network (e.g., fiber) (Bourreau, Cambini, & Doğan, 2012). Finally, it is affected by the migration effect, which refers to the incentives of users to migrate to new technology. Migration will be faster if the cost difference between the existing and the new technology is smaller. This dynamic interaction has many potential outcomes, which greatly complicate finding the most efficient, regulatory approach. It might be a superior approach to keep ex ante interventions to an absolute minimum and rely more strongly on ex post methods, such as ex post regulation and antitrust supervision.

Network neutrality has recently emerged as a major policy debate. Many political and economic concerns influence stakeholder positions and policy solutions. At the heart of the controversy are the rules and obligations that should govern vertical relations in the Internet innovation system. The open and transparent design of the Internet reduced transaction and coordination costs of edge innovators and greatly stimulated creativity in the digital economy. Public ownership was compatible with this open and transparent, best-effort, network architecture. Network neutrality provisions are a response to the weakening of regulations that initially imposed similar obligations on private providers. It is also a response to the increasing importance of the Internet for human rights. But the tensions among these alternative policy rationales complicate policy design (Bauer & Obar, 2014). No clear and widely shared definition of "neutrality" is available. Stringent network neutrality implies that network operators should treat every datagram alike. Weak network neutrality allows reasonable quality of service differentiation if it is not used in a discriminatory way. Although widely endorsed by advocates, stringent network neutrality raises many more innovation concerns than weak forms. It reduces the appropriability of premiums for network innovation and reduces the ability to realize synergies between networks and higher layers. This will likely reduce innovations that require quality of service (QoS) differentiation. At the same time, it might boost modular innovations on the logical edges of the Internet and hence bias the overall direction of innovation in favor of modular edge innovations. (It might also increase the incentives or major players on either layer to integrate vertically.)

In other words, innovation opportunities that require differentiated network support may not be pursued with sufficient vigilance or they may not be pursued at all. Thus, strict network neutrality obligations will narrow the search space for innovations in a specific direction. Innovations that might require searching outside of that space are prevented at a potential cost to society that is unknown. It is likely that such innovations will be pursued in other organizational forms, such as private closed networks, that are not subject to network neutrality obligations (Bauer & Knieps, 2018). This is already visible in some countries with massive investments in clouds, apps that replace open Internet searches, and CDNs. It would be a pity if regulations intended to preserve innovation in the public Internet starve it of opportunities. This is not to say that concerns about vertical and horizontal discrimination are unwarranted. Safeguards to assure differentiation without unreasonable discrimination are desirable to protect the overall dynamics of the system of complementary innovations. As in the case of unbundling, ex post regulation or strengthened forms of competition policy might serve that purpose.

Regulation and other forms of public policy may affect Internet-based innovation in more roundabout ways. As discussed, innovation requires experimentation, the search in novel directions for new processes, products, and services that lead to new combinations and re-combinations of knowledge. It is possible that the accumulation of regulations, all individually well-intended and designed, may together constrain the space for available innovation experiments and narrow the direction in which searches go. Such a "regulatory thicket-effect" may be very difficult to show empirically, but it may be one of the reasons why less or less stringent regulation often coincides with more innovation activity. There is a potential counterargument in research on creativity: obstacles can motivate the development of innovative workarounds. This would imply that more stringent regulation stimulates innovation. One could look at the development of the Internet as a major instance of this effect, because one goal was to overcome the constraints of the historical, hierarchical, and specialized telecommunication networks. However, such instances must be deemed rare exceptions and do not support the conclusion that more stringent regulation supports innovation in general.

8.   Conclusion

This chapter examined the direct and indirect effects of regulation on the rate and direction of innovation. Given the many interdependencies and complementarities in the advanced ICT system and the observation that novelty often springs from obstacles, these effects are difficult to determine analytically and ex ante. The general hunch that less regulation would probably allow more and more diverse innovation experiments is weakly supported by theory and anecdotal evidence. However, as was discussed, it would be premature to conclude that exclusive reliance on unfettered market forces is superior in governing innovation. What then, are lessons and insights for public policy and Internet governance?

A first insight is that institutional diversity is beneficial for innovation. Each of the four modes discussed (and there are others) offers a setting to explore innovation opportunities in different and complementary ways. Commercial, profit-seeking innovation relentlessly generates novelty in dimensions that promise to be directly or indirectly monetized. Large cash reserves and operating cash flows in firms and capital amassed by the venture capital industry allow the exploration of radical, highly risky opportunities beyond the activities of many commercial firms. Public sector funding and support for visionary technology and innovation can help pursue projects whose benefits accrue to society at large and may be difficult to monetize by commercial players. Projects may range from local investment in advanced connectivity (e.g., to support wireless Internet of Things applications) to large ventures on the frontiers of science. Finally, peer production is yet another mode to process decentralized, distributed knowledge in projects that may have private appropriability but also have significant public good characteristics. Public policy therefore would benefit from allowing and possibly actively supporting such institutional diversity. This shifts the focus of policy on the institutional environment in which innovation processes are embedded. Policies that prohibit or underfund public sector involvement or other modes of innovation will complicate the exploration of some available innovation opportunities.

A second takeaway is that the consequences for innovation of ex ante forms of regulation should be analyzed explicitly when designing regulation. They should also be periodically evaluated. Both require assessing likely and possible unexpected effects of regulatory choices. Because regulation has repercussions beyond the immediately regulated firms, it will be important to examine whether indirect effects are likely to be weak (and thus able to be safely ignored) or whether they are potentially substantial and might support or undermine the goals of the intervention. Regulatory intervention may influence the level of resources that will be dedicated to research and development and innovation. Most likely, the regulatory model may have implications for the direction of innovation. If it is biased to one of the modes, innovation efforts will reflect the strengths and weaknesses of that specific mode. For example, strict network neutrality regulation will likely bias generativity toward modular edge innovations. This does not exclude the generation of other innovation types, but it reduces their likelihood compared to a scenario that also allows network differentiation. The absence of any non-discrimination safeguards, on the other hand, also raises concerns and may lead to underinvestment in edge innovations. Finding the right balance may not be easy ex ante, and forms of adaptive regulation may yield superior outcomes.

A third insight is that regulation affects innovation processes in the context of a broader innovation system. Because there are considerable differences across nations and regions, the role of regulation, contrary to current dominant thinking, may vary, depending on these conditions. For example, its role may have to be construed differently in an innovation system with a strong culture of venture capital funding and limited government support of ICT innovation than in one that has a strong, mission-driven government, public resources for R&D, and limited venture capital. The role of regulation will also be influenced by the historical path of reforms, with systems emerging from state ownership rather than from a history of private infrastructure provision. Many of the issues addressed in this paper require coordination and collaboration among multiple stakeholders. Innovation systems with a strong tradition and capacity to find solutions to such multi-faceted problems (e.g., the Nordic countries and several Asian countries) will allow a different role for regulation than adversarial systems in which such collaboration is difficult to orchestrate (e.g., the United States).

Finally, additional research is needed to better understand the drivers of innovation in the highly interconnected ICT system. Multiple complementarities among players exist and affect the dynamics of innovation. There will be many instances in which traditional models of innovation will capture the unfolding processes well. However, there will also be other situations with strong interdependencies and interactions in which indirect effects cannot be ignored analytically and practically. Such situations may be better modeled with dynamic and possibly computational methods. As part of these efforts it would be desirable to create better metrics of innovation. Widely used indicators such as R&D expenses, patents, ICT performance metrics such as download speeds, or the number of employees in certain occupations, are useful but do not fully document the nature of Internet-based innovation.

References

Abbate, J. (1999). *Inventing the Internet*. Cambridge, MA: MIT Press.

Aghion, P., Bloom, N., Blundell, R., Griffith, R., & Howitt, P. (2005). Competition and Innovation: An Inverted-U Relationship. *Quarterly Journal of Economics, 120*(2), 701-728.

Anderson, C. (2009). *Free: The Future of a Radical Prices*. New York: Hyperion.

Antonelli, C. (Ed.) (2011). *Handbook on the Economic Complexity of Technological Change*. Cheltenham, UK; Northampton, MA: Edward Elgar.

Antonelli, C., & Patrucco, P. P. (2016). Organizational Innovations, ICTs and Knowledge Governance: The Case of Platforms. In J. M. Bauer & M. Latzer (Eds.), *Handbook on the Economics of the Internet* (pp. 323-343). Cheltenham, UK; Northampton, MA: Edward Elgar.

Arrow, K. J. (1962). Economic Welfare and the Allocation of Resources for Invention. In Universities-National Bureau Committee for Economic Research Committee on Economic Growth of the Social Science Research Council (Ed.), *The Rate and Direction of Inventive Activity: Economic and Social Factors* (pp. 609 - 626). Princeton, NJ: Princeton University Press.

Bailey, E. E. (1974). Innovation and Regulation. *Journal of Public Economics, 3*(3), 285-295.

Bakos, Y., & Brynjolfsson, E. (2000). Bundling and Competition on the Internet. *Marketing Science, 19*(1), 63-82.

Bauer, J. M. (2005). Unbundling Policy in the United States: Players, Outcomes and Effects. *Communications & Strategies*(57), 59-82.

Bauer, J. M. (2010). Regulation, Public Policy, and Investment in Communications Infrastructure. *Telecommunications Policy, 34*(1-2), 65-79.

Bauer, J. M. (2014). Platforms, Systems Competition, and Innovation: Reassessing the Foundations of Communications Policy. *Telecommunications Policy, 38*(8-9), 662-673.

Bauer, J. M., & Bohlin, E. (2008). From Static to Dynamic Regulation: Recent Developments in U.S. Telecommunications Policy. *Intereconomics: Review of European Economic Policy, 43*(1), 38-50.

Bauer, J. M., & Bohlin, E. (2018). *Roles and Effects of Access Regulation in 5G Markets*. Gothenburg, Sweden; East Lansing, Michigan.

Bauer, J. M., & Knieps, G. (2018). Complementary Innovation and Network Neutrality. *Telecommunications Policy, 42*(2), 172-183.

Bauer, J. M., & Obar, J. A. (2014). Reconciling Political and Economic Goals in the Net Neutrality Debate. *The Information Society, 30*(1), 1-19.

Benkler, Y. (2006). *The Wealth of Networks: How Social Production Transforms Markets and Freedom*. New Haven, CT: Yale University Press.

Benkler, Y. (2011). *The Penguin and the Leviathan: How Cooperation Triumphs over Self-Interest*. New York: Crown Business.

Benkler, Y. (2016). Peer Production and Cooperation. In J. M. Bauer & M. Latzer (Eds.), *Handbook on the Economics of the Internet* (pp. 91-119). Cheltenham, UK; Northampton, MA: Edward Elgar.

Bourreau, M., Cambini, C., & Doğan, P. (2012). Access Pricing, Competition, and Incentives to Migrate From "Old" to "New" Technology. *International Journal of Industrial Organization, 30*, 713-723.

Bourreau, M., Cambini, C., & Hoernig, S. (2012). Geographic Access Rules and Investments. CEPR Discussion Papers, 2012.

Breschi, S., Malerba, F., & Orsenigo, L. (2000). Technological Regimes and Schumpeterian Patterns of Innovation. *The Economic Journal, 110*(463), 388-410.

Bresnahan, T. F., & Trajtenberg, M. (1995). General Purpose Technologies: 'Engines of growth'? *Journal of econometrics, 65*(1), 83-108.

Brynjolfsson, E. (2011). Innovation and the E-economy. Unpublished paper. MIT, Sloan School of Management. October 1, 2011. In.

Cave, M. (2010). Snakes and Ladders: Unbundling in a Next Generation World. *Telecommunications Policy, 34*(1-2), 80-85.

Cave, M. (2014). The Ladder of Investment in Europe, in Retrospect and Prospect. *Telecommunications Policy, 38*(8-9), 674-683. doi:https://doi.org/10.1016/j.telpol.2014.04.012

Cave, M., Fournier, A., & Shutova, N. (2012). The Price of Copper and the Transition to Fibre. *Communications & Strategies, 85*(1st Quarter), 147-168.

claffy, k. c., & Clark, D. D. (2016). Adding Enhanced Services to the Internet: Lessons from History. *Journal of Information Policy, 6*, 206-251. doi:10.5325/jinfopoli.6.2016.0206

Cohen, W. M. (2010). Fifty Years of Empirical Studies of Innovative Activity and Performance. In B. H. Hall & N. Rosenberg (Eds.), *Handbook of the Economics of Innovation* (Vol. 1, pp. 129-213). Amsterdam: Elsevier.

DeNardis, L. (2009). *Protocol Politics: The Globalization of Internet Governance.* Cambridge, MA: MIT Press.

Ehrlich, E. M., Eisenach, J. A., & Leighton, W. A. (2010). The Impact of Regulation on Innovation and Choice in Wireless Communications. *Review of Network Economics, 9*(1).

Fransman, M. (1994). AT&T, BT, and NTT: The Role of R&D. *Telecommunications Policy, 18*(4), 295-305.

Fransman, M. (2010). *The New ICT Ecosystem: Implications for Policy and Regulation.* Cambridge, UK: Cambridge University Press.

Fransman, M. (2011). The Symbiotic Theory of Innovation: Knowledge Creation and the Evolution of the Capitalist System. In C. Antonelli (Ed.), *Handbook on the Economic Complexity of Technological Change* (pp. 120-137). Cheltenham, UK; Northampton, MA: Edward Elgar.

Garcia, D. L. (2016). The Evolution of the Internet: A Socioeconomic Account. In J. M. Bauer & M. Latzer (Eds.), *Handbook on the Economics of the Internet.* Cheltenham, UK; Northampton, MA: Edward Elgar.

Gertner, J. (2013). *The Idea Factory: Bell Labs and the Great Age of American Innovation.* New York: Penguin Books.

Hafner, K., & Lyon, M. (1996). *Where Wizards StayUup Late: The Origins of the Internet.* New York: Simon & Schuster.

Hashmi, A. R. (2013). Competition and Innovation: The Inverted-U relationship Revisited. *Review of Economics and Statistics, 95*(5), 1653-1668.

Hazlett, T. W. (2017). *The Political Spectrum: The Tumultuous Liberation of Wireless Technology, from Herbert Hoover to the Smartphone.* New Haven, CT: Yale University Press.

Henderson, R., & Clark, K. B. (1990). Architectural Innovation: The Reconfiguration of Existing Product Technologies and the Failure of Established Firms *Administrative Science Quarterly, 35*(1), 9-30.

Hodgson, G. M., & Knudsen, T. (2010). *Darwin's Conjecture: The Search for General Principles of Social and Economic Evolution.* Chicago, IL: University of Chicago Press.

Janeway, W. H. (2018). *Doing Capitalism in the Innovation Economy.* Cambridge, UK: Cambridge University Press.

Kamien, M. I., & Schwartz, N. L. (1982). *Market Structure and Innovation.* Cambridge, UK; New York: Cambridge University Press.

Kauffman, S. A. (1993). *The Origins of Order: Self Organization and Selection in Evolution.* New York: Oxford University Press.

Koppl, R., Kauffman, S. A., Felin, T., & Longo, G. (2015). Economics for a Creative World. *Journal of Institutional Economics, 11*(1), 1-31.

Krämer, J., Wiewiorra, L., & Weinhardt, C. (2013). Net Neutrality: A Progress Report. *Telecommunications Policy, 37*(9), 794-813. doi:http://dx.doi.org/10.1016/j.telpol.2012.08.005

Laland, K. N. (2017). *Darwin's Unfinished Symphony: How Culture Made the Human Mind.* Princeton, NJ: Princeton University Press.

Lee, R. S., & Wu, T. (2009). Subsidizing Creativity Through Network Design: Zero-pricing and Net Neutrality. *Journal of Economic Perspectives, 23*(3), 61-76.

Lerner, J., & Tirole, J. J. (2005). The Economics of Technology Sharing: Open Source and Beyond. *Journal of Economic Perspectives, 19*(2), 99-120.

Malerba, F., & Orsenigo, L. (1996). Schumpeterian Patterns of Innovation are Technology-specific. *Research Policy, 25*(3), 451-478.

Mazzucato, M. (2013). *The Entrepreneurial State: Debunking Public vs. Private Sector Myth.* London: Anthem Press.

Mueller, M. L. (2010). *Networks and States: The Global Politics of Internet Governance.* Cambridge, MA: MIT Press.

Nelson, R. R. (Ed.) (1993). *National Innovation Systems: A Comparative Analysis.* New York, Oxford: Oxford University Press.

Nelson, R. R., & Rosenberg, N. (1993). Technical Innovation and National Systems. In R. R. Nelson (Ed.), *National Innovation Systems: A Comparative Analysis* (pp. 3-21). New York, Oxford: Oxford University Press.

Nelson, R. R., & Sampat, B. N. (2001). Making Sense of Institutions as a Factor Shaping Economic Performance. *Journal of Economic Behavior and Organization, 44*(1), 31-54.

Nelson, R. R., & Winter, S. G. (1982). *An Evolutionary Theory of Economic Change.* Cambridge, MA: Belknap Press of Harvard University Press.

OECD. (2005). *The Measurement of Scientific and Technological Activities: Proposed Guidelines for Collecting and Interpreting Technological Innovation Data (Oslo Manual)* (3rd ed.). Paris: Organisation for Economic Co-operation and Development.

Parker, G. G., Van Alstyne, M. W., & Choudary, S. P. (2016). *Platform Revolution: How Networked Markets Are Transforming the Economy--And How to Make Them Work for You*. New York: W.W. Norton.

Perrow, C. (1984). *Normal Accidents: Living with High-risk Technologies*. New York: Basic Books.

Prieger, J. E. (2001). Telecommunications Regulation and New Services: A Case Study at the State Level. *Journal of Regulatory Economics, 20*(3), 285-305.

Prieger, J. E. (2002). Regulation, Innovation, and the Introduction of New Telecommunications Services. *Review of Economics and Statistics, 88*(4), 704-715.

Schumpeter, J. A. (1942). *Capitalism, Socialism, and Democracy*. New York: Harper.

Shapiro, C. (2012). Competition and Innovation: Did Arrow Hit the Bull's Eye? In J. Lerner & S. Stern (Eds.), *The Rate and Direction of Inventive Actitity Reconsidered* (pp. 361-404). Chicago, IL: University of Chicago Press.

Shapiro, C., & Varian, H. R. (1999). *Information Rules: A Strategic Guide to the Network Economy*. Boston, MA: Harvard Business School Press.

Stoneman, P. (Ed.) (1995). *Handbook of the Economics of Innovation and Technological Change*. Oxford, UK; Cambridge, MA: Blackwell.

Stoneman, P. (2010). *Soft Innovation: Economics, Product Aesthetics, and the Creative Industries*. Oxford, UK: Oxford University Press.

Teece, D. J. (2010). Technological Innovation and the Theory of the Firm: The Role of Enterprise-Level Knowledge, Complementarities, and (Dynamic) Capabilities. In B. H. Hall & N. Rosenberg (Eds.), *Handbook on the Economics of Innovation* (Vol. 1, pp. 679-730). Amsterdam: Elsevier.

Vogelsang, I. (2017a). Regulatory Inertia Versus ICT Dynamics: The Case of Product Innovations. *Telecommunications Policy, 41*(10), 978-990.

Vogelsang, I. (2017b). The Role of Competition and Regulation in Stimulating Innovation-Telecommunications. *Telecommunications Policy, 41*(9), 802-812. doi:http://dx.doi.org/10.1016/j.telpol.2016.11.009.

von Hippel, E. (2005). *Democratizing Innovation*. Cambridge, MA: MIT Press.

Yoo, C. S. (2016). Modularity Theory and Internet Regulation. *University of Illinois Law Review, 2016*(1), 1-62.

5G and the Future of Broadband

William Lehr[1]

Abstract

The future of broadband is 5G, which will provide the broadband infrastructure needed to realize the vision of pervasive computing, enabling ICTs to augment all aspects of economic and social life. The transition to 5G will lead to the convergence of fixed and mobile networks. For Mobile Network Operators (MNOs), 5G is the next generation of network technology that promises to deliver order-of-magnitude performance improvements over 4G, greatly expanding the capabilities and capacity of broadband platforms. Achieving these performance improvements will necessitate the widespread deployment of small cells. It will also drive network operators, including MNOs, to rely even more heavily on softwarization and virtualization in order to provide the capacity to handle the continued exponential growth in broadband traffic and to enable the dynamic scalability and customizability needed to meet the quality-of-service requirements of Smart-X, where the X represents any aspect of economic or social life that can be augmented with ICT support. That includes smart healthcare, energy grids, transport, and supply chains. Unlocking the potential of 5G has the potential to deliver trillions of dollars in economic growth and welfare improvements, but will require hundreds of billions in new investment across the broadband ecosystem. The drive to 5G will increase capital intensity and is likely to require further industry restructuring, but if successful, should unlock new avenues for competition from new kinds of facilities-based and MVNO broadband service providers.

Keywords: 5G, Broadband, Internet, Telecommunications Competition

---

1   Massachusetts Institute of Technology; wlehr@mit.edu. The author would like to acknowledge the support of T-Mobile in preparing an earlier version of this paper. All views expressed herein are the author's own.

109

1. Introduction

The vision of "Pervasive Computing" is one of everywhere/always available ICTs to support the transformation to the Smart-X digital economy. Smart-X refers to a vision of the future in which all sectors of the economy and our social lives are better able to make use of embedded ICTs to enhance economic efficiency. Smart-highways, smart-healthcare, smart-energy grids, and smart supply chains are some of the examples of how ICTs are envisioned helping enhance economic decision-making across the economy. Making this possible will require significant investments in all aspects of our ICT infrastructures, including greatly expanding the performance, capacity, and capabilities of our wireless networks.

The 5G vision describes the network infrastructure that is required to fully enable the Pervasive Computing vision of Smart-X. For MNOs, it represents the next generation of wireless networking technology and establishes ambitious targets for order-of-magnitude performance improvements relative to the 4G LTE networks that MNOs are currently in the process of maturing. Realizing these capabilities will require MNOs to invest hundreds of billions of dollars, much of which is needed in any case to keep up with the exponential growth in traffic (Morgan Stanley, 2017). Forecasts of the potential for Smart-X to contribute to economic growth and productivity are in excess of multiple trillions of dollars.[2] Already, it is estimated that the digital economy accounts for 6.5% of GDP ($1.2 trillion in 2016) and MNOs added over $282 billion to U.S. GDP (Barefoot et al., 2018; Entner, 2016). These are big numbers and staying on track to be at the forefront of the global digital economy transformation may determine how successful the U.S. is in sustaining economic growth and its competitive advantage in increasingly dynamic and competitive global markets. Ensuring that the U.S. has the wireless infrastructure it needs to stay on track is likely to depend on how successful we are in sustaining robust competition across the entire broadband ecosystem.

There is a lot of hype associated with 5G and a continuum of views regarding what 5G should mean, ranging from simply better mobile services than we have today (which might more appropriately be referred to as 4G+) to an order-of-magnitude improvement in the performance and capabilities of broadband networks along virtually every dimension. As with the vision of Pervasive Computing, realizing the most ambitious goals of

---

2   For example, McKinsey & Co. forecasted the potential global impact of IoT to be $3.9 to $11.1 trillion per year by 2025 (see McKinsey, 2015).

5G (and whatever may lay beyond) may best be understood as horizon goals,[3] but ones that are consistent with the trajectory of technical change and ICT-fueled economic growth that has been progressing in waves for decades. The focus here will be on those more ambitious goals since heading towards those goals offers the trajectory with the greatest promise of expanding market opportunities, innovation, and economic growth. The actual progress we realize toward achieving those goals will depend, in part, on how successful we are in promoting sustainable, robust competition on the road to 5G.

Realizing the 5G vision will have important implications for competition among MNOs and across the broadband ecosystem. For national MNOs, the challenge of scaling their network capacity and adding the network intelligence and capabilities to meet the 5G performance goals will compel each of the operators to invest tens of billions of dollars. Much of this investment will be directly associated with the need to transition to smaller, denser and hence more capital intensive network architectures. In addition to enabling the networks to support much faster data rates, lower latencies, and many more simultaneous connections, the investments will vastly expand the capacity of wireless networks. This capacity expansion is needed to meet the exponential growth in video traffic that is already happening, as well as to enable the new Smart-X services that are coming. In order for MNOs to manage this investment efficiently and to provide the flexibility and capabilities to offer customized, dynamic services to meet the needs of increasingly heterogeneous and demanding wireless applications and services, MNOs will be compelled to continue to implement softwarization and virtualization capabilities.

For the national MNOs, these complementary changes will increase their capital expenditure requirements and their potential to realize scale and scope economies required to operate a leading edge national-scale MNO. Although today there are four national MNOs, the scale of the top two gives them significant advantages in the effort to build national 5G networks. The best prospect for longer-term competition among the MNOs is for the third and fourth ranked MNOs to merge: the proposed merger of T-Mobile and Sprint would create a third national MNO with the scale to sustain the maximal extent of facilities-based competition

---

3   If and when we actually achieve the 5G performance targets identified in the ITU specifications (ITU, 2015), then we may choose to identify the next steps forward as "6G."

among MNOs that is likely to be economically feasible in the medium to longer-term.

This paper explores the following areas of 5G growth and its implications: (1) the broadband 5G future vision; (2) what MNOs require to transition to 5G and to compete as national-scale, full-service providers; and (3) what a 5G future will mean for competition in the evolving broadband ecosystem of increasingly converged networks and services.

2. *Broadband's 5G Future*

Pervasive computing is a vision of everything, always (24/7) and everywhere connect(able) to networked digital communication, computing, and storage resources wherever and whenever wanted. Networking digital communications, computing, and storage capabilities creates a powerful collection of resources that enhances the benefits of all three.[4] Everything means that individuals as well as "things" may be connected for any-to-any communications (i.e., the Internet of Things or IoT).[5] The IoT future promises to link the virtual and real worlds, opening up new frontiers for deploying ICTs productively throughout the economy and society.[6] In

---

4   Networking allows resources to be accessed, combined and shared. A networked computer is much more useful and powerful than a standalone computer. Moreover, networked computing, storage and communications (transport) resources can act as substitutes, expanding the productive potential when used together. For example, in telecommunication networks, transmission capacity needs (and hence, costs) and traffic loads may be reduced using computation (video compression) or storage (content caching). Such resource flexibility and substitutability expands options for load balancing and customizing service offerings.

5   The world of IoT includes individuals talking to appliances and machines talking to other machines ("m2m"). The appliances and machines may be big (*e.g.,* HVAC system in a building, factory machine tool, or mainframe computer) or small (*e.g.,* a sensor/actuator embedded in a pet or in the environment). In a 5G world of Pervasive Computing, the availability of networks and computing resources should not be limiting constraints on who or what is able be digitally networked.

6   The vision of Pervasive Computing expressed here is optimistic in so far as it describes how ICTs can expand the productive frontiers of the economy; however, this does not mean that we will succeed in operating at the productive frontier or that there will not also be problems or that everyone is or should be happy with the prospect of living in a world where computers and electronic communications are more ever present than already. Such normative considerations are beyond the scope of this paper.

such a world, much of the communications traffic may be between things (machine-to-machine or "m2m"). Always and everywhere connect(able) means that the networks will allow accessing the ICT capabilities wherever and whenever there is demand.[7] That implies that networked services are portable, mobile,[8] ubiquitously available,[9] and scalable.[10] The 5G vision is one of broadband networks capable of providing this sort of connectivity, one that requires significantly more wireless infrastructure, as well as many other complementary enhancements across the broadband ecosystem.

5G represents an important step toward achieving this vision, and relative to today's 4G LTE mobile technology, represents an order-of-magnitude improvement in performance along almost every dimension, including:[11]

- ***Faster data rates***: Ten-fold increase in user experienced data rates, including 20-fold increase in peak data rates. Faster data rates are needed to support richer, interactive multimedia applications (including streaming higher resolution video) and to support faster and more

---

7   Choice in connection modalities is important for many users and applications. For example, privacy and cybersecurity considerations call for nuanced control and support for multiple options over how end-users (whether individuals or devices) are digitally connected in the 5G future.

8   Mobility can mean a range of things: services should be sustained at both high speeds (*e.g.*, while flying in a plane or driving down the highway) and low speeds (*e.g.*, sitting at a café or walking through a mall). Indeed, fixed location services are just a special case of a mobile service. Portability is a form of mobility and implies the ability to move a service across platforms or to new locations or contexts (*e.g.*, accessing television services from multiple devices). Enabling seamless mobility allows end-users or their applications to connect via multiple devices and to have a predictable and satisfactory experience that is supported as they move through the environment where the movement can occur in any dimension (*e.g.* geo-space, time, or context). Ensuring seamless mobility presents a significant challenge since individual flows have to be protected from congestion and other network disruptions.

9   Ubiquitously available means everywhere in geospace (*e.g.* inside buildings, in the city and in the woods) and with sufficient capacity to meet demand over time whenever, wherever demand arises.

10   Since demands will naturally fluctuate as individuals and their devices change what they are doing, capacity and services will need to adapt in real-time, scaling as needed.

11   These performance targets are based on the ITU-2020 requirements. *See* IMT Vision.

robust content access.[12] Whereas 4G LTE offers user data rates that may be in the 10s of Mbps range today, the goal for 5G is to support data rates in the 100s of Mbps or more. Additionally, faster per-user data rates will drive the need for significant increases in area-traffic capacity to enable support for multiple users. Increasing the speed of mobile broadband services and the capacity of wireless access networks is necessary just to support the surging traffic associated with streaming mobile video.

- *Reduced latency*: Ten-fold reduction in latency from today's 10 ms norms to 1 ms latencies. Reduced latency is needed for near to real-time interactivity which is especially important when wireless networks are used for control (*e.g.*, managing autonomous vehicles on smart highways), as well as in highly interactive applications such as virtual or augmented reality, including gaming.

- *Enhanced mobility*: Seamless support for high-speed mobility across radio nodes which is important for sustaining continuous performance while a user may be moving at highway speeds. This level of support becomes more important and challenging when mobility requires more frequent hand-offs across radio nodes because of smaller cell sites (a key feature of the future, as will be discussed further below) that may be operating with different Radio Frequency ("RF") spectrum resources.

- *Massively increased connection density*: Increasingly, multiple devices per user are the norm, which in turn, drives the increase in the aggregate number of devices that need to be connected via the networks. With IoT, the connection density in any geolocation may increase substantially. Thousands of sensors may be embedded in the environment and built into our clothes and appliances to make them digitally enabled and allow them to participate in the online experience. Moreover, much of the communication in the 5G future will be m2m.

- *Improved spectral and energy efficiency*: Three-fold improvement in spectral efficiency and 100-fold improvement in energy efficiency.

---

12   Faster data rates provide additional head-room to accommodate fluctuations in performance. For example, faster-than-real-time delivery of content can feed buffers that can be used to smooth temporary congestion. This also contributes to lowering costs by enabling more efficient network management since increased tolerance for temporary congestion reduces the peak capacity provisioning requirements, allowing the network to be operated closer to full utilization.

Spectrum and power are two critical inputs that are necessary for wireless devices to operate. Improving the efficiency with which these inputs are used helps lower costs and enhances usability in terms of portability, longevity, and capacity.

The benefits of realizing this vision are several. First, 5G will dramatically improve the capacity and capabilities of using ICTs to enhance economic efficiency in all of its dimensions.[13] ICTs allow us to collect, analyze, share, and act upon information. 5G will enable better real-time intelligence (*e.g.*, situation awareness with the assistance of AI and big data analytics[14]) and increase control of complex production systems with the assistance of sensors and automation. ICT augmented reality can enhance adaptability, flexibility, and responsiveness on a more granular and dynamic basis, facilitating real-time responsiveness and customization.[15]

From the perspective of the end-user's experience, ICT improvements mean that existing mobile broadband applications and services like streaming video or mobile video conferencing will work better with higher resolution, more stable performance, and easier portability and mobility across devices and usage environments.[16] Faster and more capable networks make it feasible to take greater advantage of faster and more capa-

---

13　*Productive efficiency* means that goods and services are produced at the lowest resource cost; *allocative efficiency* means that scarce resources are devoted to their most valuable, welfare-maximizing uses; and *dynamic efficiency* means efficiency is preserved over time.

14　ICT-enhanced business intelligence can help improve forecasting, enable real-time monitoring for rapid response to changes, and empower operational management.

15　Network or application performance can be customized on a more granular and dynamic basis with respect to time, geo space, or context. This allows services to adjust as user needs change over time (*e.g.*, to accommodate fluctuating needs for faster data rate support based on what the user is actually doing), by location, or by context (*e.g.*, accommodating different traffic management or security requirements depending on the nature of the application). Finer granularity means customizations can occur over shorter time-scales (real-time), smaller geographic areas (personal-space wireless networks), and more complex (rich) contexts. Enhanced ability to customize services to supply-and-demand conditions unlock economic surplus (customer value and cost-saving opportunities). For example, the ability to respond automatically to faults (*e.g.*, re-route traffic, send alerts) can enhance the robustness and reliability of services, better managing risks and enabling more predictable services.

16　Users can control which device to answer a video call on and trust that the service will provide a good and predictable experience wherever they are (in town or in the country, indoors or outdoors, at home or at a concert, etc.).

ble complementary elements such as end-user devices and applications that offer users a richer experience. Of course, as devices and applications are enhanced they consume more network resources, driving growing demand for and increased investment in expanded capacity in the 5G ecosystem.

Providing the capacity and capabilities needed to serve the exponential growth in broadband traffic and enhancing the performance of legacy services provides a sufficient motivation for much of the investment in 5G. However, 5G's greatest promise is associated with its role in enabling the IoT future of Smart-X on which much of the hope for the digital economy rests. Examples include:

- **Smart highways and vehicles** (including autonomous vehicles) can contribute to safer roads, reduced congestion, and improved energy efficiency.
- **Smart energy grids** boost greener power generation and usage. Addressing global climate change will require shifting to more renewable energy sources and using energy more efficiently. ICT-enabled smarter power management systems and distribution grids will be needed, from generation to consumption, to control when renewable sources can feed into the grid and to help manage consumption through AI-assisted management of HVAC and lighting in homes and businesses.
- **Smart healthcare** can take advantage of networked, digitally-connected devices to allow continuous and remote health monitoring, earlier detection of health risks with crowd sourced data, and automated dispensing of drugs for real-time dosage management.
- **Smart supply chains** can enhance inventory management, production scheduling, and distribution control. This can enhance efficiency by enabling higher utilization rates of productive assets while supporting just-in-time, market-of-one demand customization. Costs can be lowered while customer satisfaction may be enhanced.
- **Smart agriculture and natural resource management** can fine-tune irrigation, fertilization, and harvesting decisions to take account of local environmental conditions, as well as market prices.
- **Smart finance and payments** ("FinTech") can provide better fraud detection, enable more flexible and secure e-payments, and lower transaction costs.

These are just some of the ways in which the transformation to Smart-X in the digital economy has the potential to open new opportunities for investment and economic growth across all sectors and layers of the economy. The world of 5G and Pervasive Computing expand options for embedding ICTs more deeply into the fabric of our economic and social lives—allowing virtually every aspect of economic production and markets to be ICT-empowered, from the distribution of final goods and services to the management of raw materials, from domestic commerce to international trade. ICTs enable just-in-time production, outsourcing, and market-of-one customization,[17] and in so doing help reorganize how markets and firms are structured and operate.

Although opportunities abound, some sectors are further along in upgrading their production methods and business processes to take advantage of ICTs. While it is uncertain precisely which Smart-X efforts will prove most successful, estimates of the potential benefits are huge. For example, a report from McKinsey & Co. forecasted the potential global impact of IoT to be $3.9 to $11.1 trillion per year by 2025, associated with smart cities, transportation, healthcare, retail, manufacturing, and other industrial sector applications.[18] Another report from Accenture forecasted that IoT could add $7.1 trillion to the U.S. economy by 2030 (Accenture, 2015). In yet another study, Accenture forecasted that 5G could help drive $275 billion in telecommunications investment in making cities smarter, and that the investment could contribute to creating 3 million jobs and add $500 billion to GDP (Accenture, 2017). Of course, realizing the benefits of 5G will require more than just the successful deployment of 5G infrastructure, although that is certainly necessary. The transition to the

---

17   *ICTs* allow richer, faster, and more flexible communications and decision-making by enabling electronic communication, information gathering, computation and control at a distance. This makes it feasible to reorganize economic activities to make them more responsive to changes in local conditions. *Just-in-time* production enables faster inventory turnover, higher factory utilization rates, and closer matching of market supply and demand, which helps businesses lower costs. Such capabilities have become increasingly necessary for firms to compete in the digital economy. *Market-of-one* customization refers to the ability of ICTs to allow economic decisions to be customized on a more granular basis, from real-time-control of factory production to on-demand manufacturing of custom-fit blue jeans.

18   See McKinsey (2015). Other analysts have produced similarly large estimates: Bain forecasts 2020 annual revenues for IoT could exceed $470B; General Electric predicts investment in industrial IoT to top $60 trillion over the next 15 years (Columbus, 2016). For additional estimates, see Thierer & O'Sullivan (2015).

digital "smart" economy will incur significant transition costs.[19] Workers, businesses, industry, and markets will confront disruptions and will need to experiment to determine how best to use ICT-smart processes in productive ways.

In the next section, I identify some of the important ways in which moving toward 5G will require MNOs to change the ways wireless networks are built and operate.

3. Economic Implications of 5G for MNOs

Each generation of mobile technology from the analog 1G mobile telephone networks of the 1980s to today's 4G LTE mobile broadband networks has propelled significant changes in how networks are designed and provisioned, with significant implications that resonated across the entire telecommunications and computer industries. The rise of mobile telephony, originally a luxury adjunct to fixed line telephony, eventually came to transform telephony into personalized "follow-me anywhere" service. The transition to digital with 2G and the addition of expanded data services with 3G expanded the modalities of mobile communications to include email, text messaging, chat, and other substitutes and complements to traditional voice telephony. With the advent of smartphones and the further expansion of wireless broadband platforms (including 3G, 4G, and Wi-Fi-enhanced fixed broadband services),[20] mobile wireless has been trans-

---

19   For example, the digital transformation will require workers with the appropriate digital skills and automation will reduce demand for labor in many traditional tasks. Acquiring the requisite skills is shifting education toward lifetime learning (something that eLearning solutions can help with). Within industries, some firms are more successful than others in adapting to the new digital economics, and the new digital capabilities are creating new markets and redefining market boundaries. The uneven growth can contribute to Digital Divides along many dimensions. A number of authors have pointed to the need for national strategies to help coordinate policies across all sectors of the economy in order to realize the benefits of investments in ICTs. See World Bank (2016) and Hanna (2016).

20   The fact that mobile users often access broadband data and other cellular services via Wi-Fi demonstrates how entwined the worlds of fixed and mobile broadband have become. Indeed, the ability to off-load cellular traffic to fixed broadband networks via Wi-Fi has enabled cellular traffic to scale faster than would have been possible if all of the traffic had to be carried with existing cellular capacity. For a discussion of the benefits of Wi-Fi off-loading (Thanki, 2012).

formed into a general-purpose platform for broadband access to the Internet, cloud computing, and other services.

Driven by the exponential growth in broadband traffic these cycles of innovation have enabled, businesses across the broadband ecosystem have had to invest in expanded capacity. The rise of the smartphone application ecosystem, the growth of streaming media services, the expanded reach and use of social media, and the rise of the sharing economy are all due, in part, to the expanded coverage, capacity, and quality of our mobile broadband infrastructure. Such changes herald the restructuring of the digital economy.

The transition to 5G will be similar and potentially even more significant in its impact. Meeting the performance targets for 5G will require enhancements in all elements of the networking ecosystem from chips to services, from radios to core networks, from hardware and software to content and applications. The focus of this paper, however, is on what is required to support the wireless elements of 5G and the implications of those for MNOs. As explained earlier, moving to 5G represents an order-of-magnitude improvement over 4G LTE. Meeting those performance targets will drive a number of important complementary changes in the design and operation of mobile networks that will have important economic implications. Among the many changes both large and small,[21] the transition to 5G is driving MNOs to embrace: (a) agile management of diverse spectrum assets; (b) small cells; and (c) softwarization and virtualization.[22]

---

21   Some of the advanced technologies that 5G will need to make use of include RF in millimeter wave bands (above 30 GHz), massive MIMO (using multiple antennas to allow disambiguation of digital signals that follow different paths from the transmitter to the receiver), beamforming (antenna technology to provide fine-grained focusing of radio signals), full duplex (enabling the same frequency for simultaneous reception and transmission which eliminates the need for paired frequencies for upstream and downstream channels), and small cells (to expand spectrum capacity, take advantage of smaller/portable base stations with lower power and smaller antennas, etc.). For a layman's description of these technologies, see Nordrum & Clark (2017).

22   *Softwarization* refers to the replacement of traditional "hardware" solutions with software solutions. Once business and technical functionality is moved into software it is easier to modify and relocate. *Virtualization* refers to the capability, enabled by softwarization, of creating a virtual machine platform that can simulate the operations of different hardware and software environments and isolate those simulations from the underlying hardware and software on which it is deployed and from other virtual machines that may share those resources. See Red Hat (2018a).

In the following sub-sections, I first explain at a high-level of abstraction what these changes mean for the design and provisioning of wireless networks, and then identify some of the important economic implications of those changes.

3.1 5G's Demands on Network Design

3.1.1. Agile management of diverse spectrum assets

Enabling 5G will require MNOs to implement the capabilities required to support *agile management of diverse spectrum assets*. The growth in wireless traffic, the need to support wireless applications with diverse requirements, and the need to enable the desired always on/everywhere connectable, seamlessly mobile end-user experience will require MNOs to manage their diverse RF spectrum assets efficiently. Traditionally, MNOs have relied principally on exclusively licensed spectrum and have built up their portfolios of spectrum in different bands as legacy inheritances through purchases at auctions or other business transactions, including M&A activity. The result is that MNOs have different patchworks of spectrum resources (that differ in terms of the frequency bands and locations for which they hold licenses). Those spectrum licenses are valuable assets and acquiring additional licensed spectrum is not always feasible, and when feasible, is expensive.

Simply meeting the capacity requirements of exponential traffic growth is posing a massive challenge for MNOs. Cisco has forecasted that mobile data traffic is expected to grow at an annual rate of 46% per year (Cisco, 2017a). Although each generation of mobile technology has enabled significant improvements in spectral efficiency, demand for spectrum resources has continued to outstrip the increase in supply. The growth of mobile video is currently the key driver for aggregate and per subscriber traffic growth.[23] Advertising supported and subscription media content providers are competing aggressively for consumer attention and the rapidly growing market of subscribers interested in accessing streaming media content over the Internet. To retain fickle consumers, content providers

---

[23] In 2016, video already accounted for 60 percent of traffic (Cisco, 2017b). By 2020, Cisco forecasts that Internet video traffic will be 82 percent of all consumer Internet traffic in 2020, up from 73 percent in 2016 (Cisco, 2017a).

are continuously enhancing the quality of the end-user experience[24] by expanding viewing options in terms of programming choices, the devices used to access the content (*e.g.*, new 4K and smart TVs, tablets, while still supporting legacy devices), and by providing better support for mobile access.

To meet the demand for additional spectrum resources, MNOs are expected to make use of shared spectrum that may be regulated as unlicensed (*e.g.*, in the 5 GHz band) or under a new framework such as the one recently established for the new Citizens Broadband Radio Service (3.5 GHz band). But even with these resources, spectrum is likely to remain scarce and MNOs will need to maintain diverse portfolios of spectrum assets. Furthermore, because the physics of RF propagation vary with frequencies and the challenges of supporting wireless communications varies with the local environment (*e.g.*, terrain, RF congestion and noise), spectrum assets are imperfect substitutes with complex implications for the costs of provisioning services using different spectrum.[25]

---

24   Audio and video offerings are being offered with differing degrees of resolution (but increasingly those options include higher-resolution options) and access to expanded libraries ("infinite" digital libraries). Providing access to ever-larger libraries of content imposes additional challenges on the underlying network infrastructure. For example, encoding content incurs a computation cost. For popular content that is to be viewed many times by multiple consumers on multiple devices (each requiring different resolution), it may be optimal for the content provider to incur the fixed encoding cost once and then incur the costs to cache multiple copies close to the consumers (to reduce access latency and transport costs). For rarely viewed content, the provider may elect to store the content at more remote servers, encode the content on the fly, and rely on faster (potentially real time) network delivery to get the content to the consumer so that the consumer has a responsive, high-quality experience regardless of what selection the consumer is making from the provider's digital archives. Meeting the more demanding requirements of content and application providers requires the MNOs to upgrade their networks. Failing to do so risks the largest content providers integrating forward to provision their own customized delivery networks, something that is also happening as I discuss further below.

25   Radio networks operating in different bands and local environments have quite different design and operating constraints. For example, lower frequency spectrum is less abundant (there is only 1 GHz below 1 GHz but lots more spectrum above that), more crowded, but has better non-line-of-site ("NLOS") propagation and requires fewer cell sites per area to provide coverage and is better at penetrating walls and other obstructions (*e.g.*, leaves). Higher frequency spectrum is more abundant (offering more bandwidth capacity), the antennas are smaller (good for multiple antennas and smaller radios), but it is less

Advances in wireless technology such as LTE have enabled MNOs to manage their spectrum assets on a more granular and dynamic basis. This allows MNOs more scope to mix-and-match spectrum resources (*e.g.*, paired and unpaired, licensed and unlicensed, contiguous and non-contiguous) to support seamless mobility. Access to more spectrum bands will result in lower cost and higher quality. The transition to 5G with its order-of-magnitude improvements in performance will require MNOs to become even more agile in their ability to manage diverse spectrum resources on a fine-grained dynamic basis.

As explained below, although adopting these capabilities is increasingly essential for national MNOs to meet traffic demands and reduce their spectrum costs, the availability of these capabilities also enables new potential sources of competition. For example, it facilitates new models for niche or specialized regional competitors or competitors that may target a narrow class of applications or customer segments. This is in contrast to the full-service, national-scale MNOs. The technologies enabling these new capabilities are also creating new options for end-user self-provisioning.[26] These and other aspects of how the technical and market environment for mobile broadband are contributing to intensifying competition in mobile broadband.

3.1.2. Small cells

The need to shift toward smaller cell network architectures is a complementary development associated with the need to manage spectrum more efficiently.[27] Key to this transition is spatial reuse of scarce spectrum resources—splitting an existing cell into multiple smaller cells allows the same licensed spectrum to be used multiple times.

---

capable of penetrating obstacles and supporting NLOS connectivity. However, advances in radio technologies from signal processing (*e.g.*, new modulation schemes and MIMO) to antenna design (*e.g.*, arrays) have allowed radio networks to better address the challenges posed by operating with different spectrum resources.

26 The same equipment and software solutions that the large national MNOs are using to more efficiently manage their large and diverse portfolios of spectrum assets are providing would-be competitors new options for overcoming asymmetric spectrum access costs.

27 For further discussion of what the transition to smaller cell architectures will mean Lehr & Oliver (2014).

The shift to smaller cells also has a number of other important implications. It means that lower power is needed for radios to communicate with the base station; there are likely to be fewer radios operating in the smaller coverage area and hence fewer potential sources of interfering radio transmissions; line of sight issues are therefore likely to be less important. With smaller cells, higher frequency spectrum may have an advantage over lower frequency spectrum. Another important difference is that while smaller cells are more expensive to provide area coverage, capacity can be added in smaller, more scalable increments.

In addition to addressing the spectrum capacity and performance issues, the transition to 5G will drive the move to smaller cells because of the need to push the edge of the MNO network (and its embedded capabilities and intelligent resources) closer to the end-user (Cisco, 2015; Tran et al., 2017). 5G base stations will include computing and storage (caching) resources that will be needed locally to support the performance requirements of 5G (*e.g.*, 1 ms latencies) and efficiently manage network costs (*e.g.*, edge-based caching of popular content to avoid excess retransmission costs). In the IoT future, many devices will be small and low power. Security and control considerations[28] may provide additional rationales for deploying small base stations closer to edge devices, to which the base stations provide communications and computing resources.

For a national-scale MNO whose business model depends on providing a full-menu of service options that includes national coverage and interoperability across customers with legacy and new devices and applications, building out small cells required by 5G is likely to necessitate a significant increase in capital costs. While no one knows for sure, some analysts have forecasted that the cost of upgrading to 5G will be up to $200 billion per year in the U.S. alone over the next five to ten years (Kharif & Moritz, 2017), while another study estimates that the cost will be $104 billion over

---

28 Not all 5G devices and networks will be connected to MNO networks or be globally accessible via the Internet. Privacy, cybersecurity, cost, market strategy or other concerns may provide a basis for end-users or 5G service providers to control how devices connect. For example, application developers for home, factory, or office automation may wish to deploy 5G sub-networks downstream of firewalls or even as isolated, standalone (sand-boxed) networks. Even if such networks never connect to MNO's networks, they will be part of the 5G wireless ecosystem and contribute to the aggregate demand for 5G technology.

the next ten years to upgrade networks (Goovaerts, 2015).[29] The costs will depend on the strategies operators choose to pursue, but SNL Kagan estimates that the transition to 5G will require building an additional 225,000 small cells by 2021.[30] A slow approach would involve only rolling out 5G radios in markets where a strong business case can be made. However, analysts at Bain argue that "5G has the potential to scramble the competitive game board for all three classes of operators—mobile-only, fixed-only and converged" and operators "that opt to wait and see how the technology will evolve risk exposing themselves to disruption from competitors that are more aggressive" (Blum et al., 2018).

In a portent of things to come, it is worth considering how per-subscriber traffic continues to grow with 4G LTE networks. For example, data traffic per smartphone has risen 50% per year from 0.3 GB/month in 2010 to 5.2 GB/month in 2017 (Evans, 2018). With the faster speeds and enhanced applications enabled by 5G, the traffic per subscriber will continue to grow. A forecast from Ericsson predicts that data usage per smartphone will grow to 26 GB per month by 2022 for a total of 9.8 Exabytes of data traffic![31] McKinsey has forecasted that the total cost of network ownership would need to grow by 60 percent if data grows by 25% per year, and significantly faster if the traffic growth unleashed by 5G-enhanced access connections grows still faster (Grijpink et al., 2018).

Meeting this challenge is one of the powerful market forces driving further industry restructuring among MNOs and elsewhere across the broadband provider ecosystem. At the same time, the technologies and architectures that small cells are enabling is opening up new models for niche facilities-based and other models for competition. To remain competitive in this environment, the national, full-service MNOs have to be even more aggressive in cutting costs and realizing scale and scope economies.

---

29   Another study by Deloitte Consulting estimates that an additional $130 to $150 billion in fiber investment will be required over the next five to seven years to support the transition to 5G (Deloitte, 2017).

30   SNL Kagan forecasts that there will be 138,000 small cells by the end of 2018 and 363,000 by the end of 2021 (Accenture, 2018).

31   An Exabyte is a billion Gigabytes ("GB") (Ericsson, 2017).

3.1.3. Softwarization and Virtualization

Moving network functionality out of hardware into software has significantly enhanced the flexibility, customizability, and performance of modern communication networks. This *softwarization* of network functions has been driven in part by an effort to lower costs. By shifting from specialized to commodity hardware in 4G LTE, for example, MNOs separate the radio and data network functionality and thereby allow MNOs to move toward all-IP data networks and benefit from the cost-economies associated with commodity IP hardware. In the radio domain, advances in developing software and cognitive radios (*i.e.*, moving radio functionality from specialized hardware into software and adding ICT-smart features to radios to make them capable of adapting their operations in response to changes in their local environment) are another example of softwarization that render individual radios better able to interoperate in diverse wireless environments by, for instance, becoming frequency agile.

In addition to lowering costs, softwarization expands flexibility and functionality. For example, in networks, the rise of Software Defined Networking ("SDN") and Network Function Virtualization ("NFV") have allowed better control and partitioning of network functionality (Tekkedath, 2016; Pretz, 2016; and Oguchi at al., 2017). One benefit of this is that it facilitates *delocalization* of functionality, allowing remote control from where the actual function or service may be delivered. This increases opportunities for MNOs to realize scale and scope economies.[32] For example, a single softswitch can implement the signaling and control functions for multiple (lower-cost) IP switches in a VoIP network, substituting for multiple legacy local switches based on dedicated hardware. The ability to centralize (or decentralize) where functionality is provided can also enhance security and privacy. The move to SDN and NFV takes these capabilities to the next level, enabling more control over how services are provided and managed to be shifted to end-users (or not, as desired).

These capabilities facilitate *virtualization*. Virtualization allows resources to be combined or shared by multiple higher-level applications and services. It is a key capability enabled by a layered architecture and is important in enabling resources to be sliced and combined to meet the heterogeneous requirements of different applications and users. A computer

---

[32] Oughton and Frias (2017) estimate that the transition to SDN and NFV can significantly reduce operating costs (63%) and capital costs (68%) relative to traditional cost models.

operating system provides a virtual layer that enables multiple applications to run on a shared CPU (Mathias, 2017; Red Hat, 2018b). In the 4G LTE architecture, separating the radio and IP network layers facilitates virtualization of the spectrum resources. Higher level applications do not need to know which frequency will be used to transmit the data over the wireless link and diverse combinations of spectrum can be used in different locations and at different times to support communications.

Cloud services from providers such as Amazon, IBM, Microsoft, and Google offer end-users the flexibility to scale there demand for computing and communication services. Analysts often describe cloud services as being organized into three market segments: Infrastructure-as-a-Service ("IaaS"), Platform-as-a-Service ("PaaS"), and Software-as-a-Service ("SaaS"). As one goes from IaaS to SaaS, more of the ICT functionality is off-loaded to the cloud service provider.

The benefits of adopting cloud services are several. First, cloud providers can realize scale and scope economies not available to individual enterprises. These arise from limiting data center costs for equipment, power, ensuring reliability, and the backbone networking services needed to tie the data centers together and make it accessible to end-users. Second, by outsourcing the ICT to cloud service providers, businesses can reduce their maintenance costs and turn what otherwise might be lumpy fixed cost investments into a variable cost that can scale more easily with their user needs. Moreover, as cloud services have evolved to become more user-friendly, the specialized ICT expertise required to make use of them is becoming less important and an ecosystem of intermediary service providers (market research firms, consultants, business process providers) exists to expand direct and indirect access to cloud services to businesses of all sizes. At this point, cloud services have evolved sufficiently that analysts are talking about "Everything-as-a-Service," or "XaaS," which highlights the rich portfolio of specialized and general-purpose cloud services available to allow businesses to outsource virtually all ICT functions to the cloud, turning them from CAPEX investments to service purchases (McLellan, 2017). According to the Gartner Group, the global market for public cloud services was $260 billion in 2017 and is expected to grow to over $400 billion by 2020 (Gartner, 2017).[33]

The evolution of cloud services would not be possible without the growth of the Internet and the telecommunications infrastructure that sup-

---

33 Public clouds are distinguished from private cloud services. Public clouds are accessible via the Internet and are shared infrastructure.

ports it. Increased demand for cloud services is helping drive demand for 5G networks since the two are complementary and progress in one helps drive progress in the other. By relying on virtualization to provide users slices to the shared resources, cloud services and the underlying 5G infrastructure enable the sort of shared access that makes on-demand XaaS possible.

All three of these developments are important and complementary changes in how broadband networks are being re-designed to address the 5G future. They are simultaneously being driven by the need to add cost-effective capacity and to support the order-of-magnitude enhanced performance requirements of 5G.

3.2. Network Changes Alter the Fundamental Economics of the Wireless Industry

The potential for 5G to unlock a wealth of opportunities for improved legacy and new mobile broadband services and to support the IoT future of Smart-X implies a need to support a growing range of heterogeneous wireless users and uses (from higher-resolution, interactive multi-media to IoT sensors). This will require expanded capacity for access and for core networks. It will also require the flexibility to customize services for diverse applications in varied usage environments. End-users will be using both fat and thin clients.[34] The 5G future will need to support both and having the flexibility to support both will expand opportunities for competition across the ecosystem, allowing device, application, content, and network

---

34 Fat clients are more substantial user applications running on more capable edge-devices like personal computers or higher-end tablets or smartphones that have on-board computing and storage capabilities to support a high-degree of functionality on the end-user device. Thin clients are less substantial and need to rely more heavily on network-hosted cloud resources and services for computing, storage and other communications functionality. Thin clients may run on high-end, capable devices (a question of application design) or on much less capable devices, such as digital appliances (sensors) that lack the on-board capacity to support fat client applications. Peer-to-peer computing (associated in the mass market with the rise of personal computing) is associated with fat clients, whereas client-server architectures are often associated with thin clients, and now with cloud architectures. The choice of fat or thin client involves a choice of where to put ICT smarts and has implications for power utilization, management control, security, reliability, and virtually every other aspect of computer system design.

service providers to tailor their solutions to best exploit their competitive advantages and appeal to the tastes of their target customers.

In addition to offering this functionality, the simple challenge of handling the continued explosive growth in mobile broadband traffic will compel MNOs to adopt more agile spectrum management, shift to small cells, and adopt softwarization and virtualization. These are responses to the rising shared, fixed, and sunk costs of provisioning smaller cell architectures associated with the move to 5G. These basic economics have characterized telecommunications networking from the start, but become more important with the move toward 5G.

A telecommunications network is a shared network. It needs to be provisioned to handle the expected peak loads that result from the aggregate behavior of all of the users who want to make use of the network at the same time. Because users do not perfectly coordinate their usage in time, location, or what they are trying to do,[35] the same resources can be shared by multiple users for mixed uses. Sharing reduces the total costs of providing capacity since the aggregate peak capacity can be shared and allows capacity to be used at higher utilization over time. However, because traffic needs are stochastic and uncertain, MNOs need to be able to scale and adjust capacity on a finer-grained, more dynamic basis.[36] Moreover, as we move toward further integration of the virtual and real worlds, the ICT systems are becoming more complex, involving more industry participants across multiple levels. The technical, market, and policy uncertainty is in-

---

35   The communications capacity of RF is limited by the ability of receivers to disambiguate the information in the signals they want to receive. The signals from other transmitters appear as noise to a receiver. Technology allows signals associated with different transmissions to be separated in many ways—in time, space (separate the transmitters and receivers in geo-space or by the direction in which the signals move through the air), in code (use digital codes to identify packets of information destined to particular receivers), or some other dimension in which RF waveforms may be modified. The limits of receiver technology and wireless network infrastructure limit the effective capacity of our spectrum resources.

36   With certain types of traffic (e.g., legacy voice telephony), well-known probability distributions (*e.g.*, Erlangs) can be used to model the stochastic behavior of traffic. However, in the rapidly evolving markets for wireless services, no one has a perfect crystal ball to forecast how the mix of traffic will evolve and the expanding matrix of players with control over traffic flows (from end-users to CDNs, from device manufacturers to ISPs) renders traffic planning inherently uncertain. This increases the need for the network flexibility and rapid scalability of 5G networks and cloud services that is supported by the fundamental trends discussed earlier.

creasing. In this environment, the benefits of flexibility, adaptability, and intelligence increase.

Virtualization and softwarization (enabling delocalization) accentuate the potential to realize scale and scope economies for MNOs, and are increasingly important for national-scale, full-service MNOs. For example, a single, larger network operations center ("NOC")[37] can be both more capable and lower cost than multiple smaller NOCs. A single customer account management center for bill processing, customer provisioning, and customer service can provide support for an MNO across multiple states, consolidating what may previously have been multiple facilities. This reduces the costs of operating an MNO and the opportunity to take advantage of these cost reductions increases with scale.

A byproduct of the movement from 3G to 4G was the convergence of the major MNOs on a common technology, LTE, which increasingly can be supported using commodity IP networking equipment. The adoption of a common technology platform has helped realize industry-wide scale and scope economies, reducing the per-MB costs of supporting mobile broadband network services. At the same time, common technology helps intensify competition among MNOs by making their network services closer substitutes. Meanwhile more capable end-user devices and more aggressive competition among content and application providers (to control the customer-relationship) are helping to reduce customer switching costs.[38]

The necessity to move to smaller cell architectures for 5G means that the capital costs of providing wide-area coverage *and* expanding aggregate capacity are increasing.[39] The increased fixed, shared and sunk costs in scale and scope economies combine to increase the scale required to sustain a national facilities-based, full-service network.

---

37   Typically, for network critical functionality for a large network, redundant "hot" facilities are needed, which means two network operations centers, each with the capability of assuming control of the functionality in the event that one of the NOCs goes down. The need to provision for highly reliable services further increases the costs of network provisioning (Lehr, 2012).

38   As will be discussed further below, these are forces helping to propel the drive toward more extensive MVNO and niche competition.

39   As noted earlier, with small cells it is easier to target capacity investments to local hot spots, enabling more fine-grained management of capacity expansions (rendering such investments less lumpy and more scalable); however, the significant growth in aggregate traffic volumes continues to require substantial investments in expanding capacity across the network.

Today, we have four national scale, facilities-based MNOs, each of which offers a portfolio of services: Verizon, AT&T, T-Mobile, and Sprint.[40] According to the FCC 20th CMRS, as of the end of 2016, these four were providing the underlying service (on a wholesale or retail basis) to 99% of the 417 million connections (which is more than the population because many subscribers have more than one device with a cellular subscription).[41] By way of comparison, in 2005, these same top four operators provided service to 80.7% of the 213 million subscribers, whereas in 1997, the top four operators were different (AT&T, SBC, Bell Atlantic, and BellSouth) and provided service to only 38.7% of the 55.3 million subscribers.[42]

These data points illustrate several important features. First, MNOs have experienced tremendous growth in subscribership as mobile services have approached saturation across the population. The number of subscribers has grown 816% from 1997 to 2016, and the volume of traffic has grown significantly more.[43] This growth was enabled first by the cellular operators building out national networks. The largest MNOs built their national coverage networks by sustained high levels of investment and through mergers and acquisitions to consolidate regional carriers, who in many cases had complementary coverage networks. In the early days (before 2000), there were numerous mobile telephony networks across the country and subscribers had to roam across multiple networks in order to use their cell phones nationwide, and many parts of the country lacked cell coverage because network infrastructure had not yet been deployed.

By 2005, the industry had substantially consolidated with the aforementioned top four mobile providers providing service to over 80% of combined retail and wholesale subscribers. The consolidation of the cellular industry is a natural outcome of the underlying economics confronting the industry. The market barriers to establishing a full-service, national cover-

---

40   It is worth noting that the enterprise offerings of T-Mobile and Sprint are much
      more limited than those available through AT&T and Verizon.
41   See Table II.B.1 (FCC, 2017). The FCC 20th CMRS only provides data on
      combined MNO retail and wholesale connections. The FCC does not provide
      data separately for retail and wholesale connections.
42   See Table 4 in FCC (1999) for 1997 data, Table 4 in FCC (2006) for 2005 data
      In 2005, AT&T had not yet acquired BellSouth (renamed Cingular Wireless),
      which occurred in 2006 (see *Cingular Merger Timeline*, AT&T,
      https://soc.att.com/2KyezYh, last visited Aug. 1, 2018).
43   Subscribership has grown from 46,375,849 (1997) to 378,554,642 (2016) (see
      Table III.A.ii in FCC, 2017). Wireless data use has increased from 388 billion
      MB (2010) to 13.7 trillion MB (2016) (see app. 1, Chart 1, FCC, 2017).

age mobile network are substantial and beyond the reach of all but very large enterprises, such as the major cable and internet companies. The annual investment requirements to operate a national MNO network run to the billions if not tens of billions of dollars per year and the scale and scope economies associated with larger size are substantial, as already noted. Building out coverage and then adding capacity and expanding capabilities to enhance legacy services and add new services, while keeping up with the rapid pace of technical change, induced the operators to invest approximately $205 billion from 2010 to 2016, which was when operators were completing their build-out of 3G and deploying 4G networks (Evans, 2018).

Although the top four MNOs are competing aggressively across the entire U.S., there are big differences between the top two MNOs. Based upon the data available from the FCC 20th CMRS, Verizon was #1, with a 37% share of all connections, and AT&T was #2, with a 33% share of all connections and the next two (#3 T-Mobile, with a 15% share of connections, and #4 Sprint, with a 13% share of connections).[44]

The size difference is also apparent in the different pace of investment the firms have been able to sustain. From 2010 through 2017, Verizon and AT&T have each averaged close to $10 billion per year in CAPEX, while Sprint and T-Mobile have each averaged closer to $4 billion. *See infra* Table 1.

Sprint and T-Mobile have also historically experienced substantially higher churn rates than either Verizon or AT&T.[45] Their smaller size means they are unable to realize the same level of scale and scope economies of the larger two firms.

---

44   See FCC (2017), Chart II.C.1 (2016 Revenue Shares). As discussed above, the FCC 20th CMRS does not provide data that would allow one to present shares separately on the basis of retail connections.

45   See FCC (2017), Chart II.B.6. Higher churn rates imply higher customer acquisition costs and other operating costs, adding to the challenges that T-Mobile and Sprint must confront.

Table 1: Capital Expenditures for Top Four MNOs ($ Millions)[46]

Year	Verizon	AT&T	Sprint	T-Mobile	Total
2002	$ 4,414	$ 5,302	$ 2,640	$ 1,700	$ 14,056
2003	$ 4,590	$ 2,774	$ 2,123	$ 1,734	$ 11,221
2004	$ 5,633	$ 3,449	$ 2,559	$ 2,138	$ 13,779
2005	$ 6,484	$ 7,475	$ 3,545	$ 5,045	$ 22,549
2006	$ 6,618	$ 7,039	$ 5,944	$ 3,444	$ 23,045
2007	$ 6,503	$ 3,745	$ 4,988	$ 2,667	$ 17,903
2008	$ 6,510	$ 6,021	$ 1,789	$ 3,603	$ 17,923
2009	$ 7,152	$ 5,924	$ 1,161	$ 3,687	$ 17,924
2010	$ 8,438	$ 8,593	$ 1,455	$ 2,819	$ 21,305
2011	$ 8,973	$ 9,764	$ 2,702	$ 2,729	$ 24,168
2012	$ 8,857	$ 10,795	$ 4,199	$ 2,901	$ 26,752
2013	$ 9,425	$ 11,191	$ 7,136	$ 4,025	$ 31,777
2014	$ 10,515	$ 11,383	$ 4,828	$ 4,317	$ 31,043
2015	$ 11,725	$ 8,697	$ 7,193	$ 4,724	$ 32,339
2016	$ 11,240	$ 8,384	$ 3,798	$ 4,702	$ 28,124
2017	$ 10,310	$ 7,870	$ 4,692	$ 5,237	$ 28,109
Cumulative	**$ 127,387**	**$ 118,406**	**$ 60,752**	**$ 55,472**	**$ 362,017**
Average 2010-2017	$ 9,935	$ 9,585	$ 4,500	$ 3,932	$ 27,952

In spite of these disadvantages and in part motivated by those disadvantages, T-Mobile has pursued an aggressive strategy of retail innovations to disrupt the market with novel pricing plans and new services. T-Mobile was the first to abandon subscriber termination fees and long-term contracts, making it easier for customers to switch carriers (which can result in higher churn rates). T-Mobile also innovated with new transparent pricing models, Wi-Fi calling, and programs to drive heavier mobile broadband data usage without risking exceeding data caps.

While this demonstrates the ability of smaller providers to impose significant competitive pressure on much larger rivals, this does not mean that it is likely that either Sprint or T-Mobile could significantly disrupt the dominant market position of the top two MNOs, which has remained remarkably stable for over a decade.

---

46   The data for this table is reproduced from Evans (2018), Exhibits 8-9.

In addition to lacking the scale of either Verizon or AT&T, both Sprint and T-Mobile suffer from additional important deficiencies that prevent them from competing as peers with the top two MNOs. First, Verizon and AT&T are both part of larger companies with wired networks and with significant investments in media content. The wired networks make it easier for Verizon and AT&T to offer their customers a converged, seamless broadband experience. Moreover, with their substantial wired core and access network infrastructure, both Verizon and AT&T have easier access to the back-haul transmission resources that are critical for connecting base stations into the backbone network. The costs of backhaul are a significant component of the costs of operating a mobile network.

In the move toward 5G, any MNOs that succeed in deploying 5G networks would have a significant advantage relative to other providers operating less advanced and less capable networks. Since most of the costs of building out the network will be shared, fixed or sunk, the 5G provider will have relatively low forward-looking incremental costs should it find it necessary to confront a rival. Consequently, if any national provider builds a 5G network, the other providers who want to compete on a level footing with that provider will also need to build 5G networks.

AT&T and Verizon have demonstrated in the past their capability to sustain the levels of investment that are required to keep pace with the leading edge of mobile technologies, and both have the scale to invest aggressively to deploy 5G networks. Hence, whether and how fast they choose to deploy 5G networks will be strategic choices. The same cannot be said for T-Mobile or Sprint as standalone MNOs.

In contrast, however, New T-Mobile would have both the resources and incentive to compete even more aggressively with AT&T and Verizon on quality-adjusted prices and would have stronger strategic incentives to more rapidly deploy its 5G network. First, New T-Mobile would be able to realize comparable scale and scope economies and would have the network, financial, and other business resources to compete head-to-head with Verizon and AT&T in a race to build out 5G networks.

Second, merging the networks (and operations) of Sprint and T-Mobile will require significant new investment and reconfigurations, costs which compare with upgrading to 5G, replacing radios, etc., and possibly may prove to be a major incentive for New T-Mobile to rapidly move forward with 5G upon merging. This cost-based justification would dovetail with the strategic benefits of being able to offer the enhanced services that having a 5G network portends. Moreover, the fact that Sprint and T-Mobile have quite complementary spectrum resources would help facilitate coverage and capacity for a joint network. T-Mobile has relatively lower frequency spectrum for expanding national coverage, whereas Sprint has relatively higher frequency band spectrum that is especially valuable for adding capacity and supporting faster data rate services. Pooling their spectrum will provide an easier transition path toward 5G while protecting the user experience of 4G LTE subscribers during the transition.[47]

Third, New T-Mobile also will have strong incentives to compete aggressively to add new customers to its new 5G network. Indeed, New T-Mobile will try to fill its network by capturing the high value customers who are served predominantly by AT&T and Verizon.

Rapid deployment by New T-Mobile of its 5G network would put added strategic pressure on AT&T and Verizon to accelerate their deployments of 5G. If either or both chose to sit on the sidelines, they would be taking significant risk that could jeopardize their current market positions. The pattern of follow-the-leader innovations in networks and service offerings has been an enduring characteristic of the history of competition among MNOs since 1G.

In short, the move to 5G will amplify the economic forces that have led to the increased size of MNOs. Those forces first drove the industry to combine to create national MNOs that have become dominant over time. Those forces resulted in an industry structure that is concentrated in traditional HHI terms with two leading firms of comparable size and two much smaller firms, also of comparable size. Although the industry has been concentrated for quite a while, there is ample evidence that the industry is highly competitive based on numerous performance metrics. Taking the next step to build nationwide 5G networks will require a level of investment that is feasible for the top two MNOs but unlikely for those ranked third and fourth. The merger of those providers to create a national, full-service MNO with the scale to compete on comparable terms with the dominant two MNOs is a pro-competitive response to the changing conditions in the market. Prospects for more rapid deployment of 5G networks *and* more aggressive quality-adjusted price competition among the national MNOs is likely if T-Mobile and Sprint are allowed to merge.

Likewise, European regulators have recently concluded that the substantial annual investments required to operate national scale MNOs

---

47   Sprint and T-Mobile are using their spectrum to support their 4G LTE customers and the need to continue providing service to those customers during the transition limits the spectrum and other resources available to build out their 5G networks.

supports consolidation, particularly in light of the growing investment needs in 5G networks. The French electronic communications regulatory authority, ARCEP, which formerly opposed several telecommunication mergers and even encouraged the introduction of a fourth operator in 2012, has now relaxed its opposition toward further consolidation in light of the benefits it has seen from the large investments by operators already (*e.g.*, €9.6 billion spent in 2017) and the need for substantial additional investment to deploy 5G networks across France.[48] Similarly, in an assessment of the future of telecom infrastructure, the British government concluded that "[a]s far as the Government is concerned, there is no magic number of mobile network operators. Each merger control case should be assessed on its own merits" (DCMS, 2018, ¶190). Indeed, "analysis suggests there is no significant difference in industry-level investment between four and three player markets" (DCMS, 2018, ¶191). There is concern in both circumstances that efforts to protect against hypothesized increases in retail prices in the short term will create substantial disincentives to allow for the large capital investments needed to promote robust and cost-efficient national wireless networks.

4.   5G Increases Competition in the Broadband Ecosystem

The preceding discussion has focused on the prospects for competition among MNOs, ignoring the implications of 5G for the larger broadband ecosystem. As I will explain further below, the transition to 5G is likely to intensify competition within the ecosystem. Additional competition from other vectors will alleviate remaining concerns over the shift from having four unbalanced national MNOs to three balanced MNOs. In the following subsections I describe three likely sources of intensified competition: (1) increased intermodal competition because mobile will be a more competitive substitute for fixed; (2) increased competitive pressure from a more robust market of MVNOs; and (3) new competition from local facilities-based providers that are expected to emerge with the transition to 5G.

---

48   The French government presented a roadmap for deploying 5G networks across France on July 16th (Cassini, 2018).

4.1. Intensified Intermodal Competition Between Fixed and Mobile
      Operators

If the services offered by mobile and fixed broadband were identical, then
they would be perfect substitutes and part of the same market from the
perspective of competitive analysis. Nevertheless, the merging of fixed
and mobile broadband services has been underway for some time and the
transition to 5G accelerates this convergence.

Historically, fixed and mobile broadband services were not close substitutes either in terms of the user experience (demand) or in terms of the
costs of providing the service (supply). Fixed broadband services tend to
be significantly faster, with more predictable performance, but lack the
mobility associated with cellular broadband services. Mobile broadband
services have tended to offer much more variable performance with average data rates that are typically below the speeds delivered by fixed
broadband services. Fixed broadband is typically shared by all of the users
in a household whereas mobile broadband services are more personalized.[49] In addition, mobile services have been more expensive on a per-
Mbps or per-MB basis and have been subject to monthly data caps or
thresholds for most subscribers. For these reasons, for most subscribers,
fixed and mobile broadband services have been viewed as complementary
services rather than as substitutes in the sense that most consumers want
both.[50] Furthermore, the opportunity to take advantage of Wi-Fi-
offloading to improve the price/quality of the user experience when using
cellular broadband services provides yet another reason for many subscribers (who can afford it) to want both fixed and mobile broadband services.

With continued improvements in the data rates, coverage, and capabilities of mobile broadband services, the performance of mobile services is

---

49 The personalization of mobile services has benefits and costs—it gives indi-
    viduals potentially better control over how their service is used but it may
    make it difficult to share resources with others. The ability to use cellular
    services as mobile hotspots (allowed under many subscriptions) or to pool data
    allowances can mitigate those differences.
50 For subscribers for whom the performance of mobile broadband is good
    enough or who are budget constrained, on a quality-adjusted price basis, mo-
    bile broadband may be a sufficiently good substitute to induce those subscrib-
    ers to cut the cord. In economic terms, however, mobile and fixed are likely to
    be substitutes in-so-far as an increase or decrease in the price of one is likely to
    result in an increase or decrease in the demand for the other (Lehr, 2009).

getting sufficiently better for a larger segment of the population (even in markets where fixed broadband speeds and pricing on a per MB basis may continue to be better). The question for many subscribers is how much speed and performance is enough and whether it will remain necessary to have both mobile and fixed broadband subscriptions. With telephony, we have seen a substantial number of customers choosing to cut the cord and switch to mobile-only telephony. As of 2016, the majority of households in the United States were wireless-telephone-only.[51] The cord cutting began when mobile telephone calling quality was not as good or reliable as fixed telephony, but today, mobile telephony or VoIP is often as good if not better than traditional wired telephony.[52] When it comes to comparing mobile and fixed broadband performance on a price/quality basis today, the services appear to be imperfect substitutes. Yet, we are seeing a growing trend toward mobile-only subscribers (Pressman, 2016).[53] The movement to 5G accentuates the capabilities of mobile broadband services, rendering mobile broadband (and fixed wireless broadband) an even stronger competitor for fixed broadband services.

Changes in the markets for upstream applications are also driving the convergence of broadband services. The shift toward delivering entertainment media (especially television and movies) via the Internet in order to take advantage of faster broadband services is inducing a growing number of households to consider cutting the cord to their traditional Multichannel Video Programming Distributor ("MVPD"). Historically, most customers of fixed broadband services purchased a bundle of services from their telephone or cable provider. That bundle included broadband, television services, and often, telephone services as well. Wired broad-

---

51   The data from the July-December 2016 survey found that 50.8% of the households in the U.S. were wireless-only (Blumberg & Luke, 2017).

52   Fixed line telephones have been declining for years. For quite a while, the need for dial-up Internet access, fax, and second lines for children drove many households to subscribe to multiple fixed telephone lines. With the rise of Voice over Internet Protocol (VoIP) telephone service, a growing number of subscribers started using their broadband access connections to support their telephone service. Today, providers like Comcast and Verizon provide their telephone service via VoIP, but do not route it via the broadband access service. Although increasingly, most who offer basic VoIP telephone service also offer an Internet application to allow their subscribers to use their fixed line telephone service as a mobile service wherever the subscribers have a broadband access connection.

53   Pew Research surveys found that 20% of adults do not use broadband at home, but have smartphones, which is up from 8% in 2013 (Pew, 2018).

band providers like to sell bundled services because it reduces their costs, enhances their subscriber revenues, and improves retention.

With more and more entertainment media becoming available via the Internet, customers are learning to appreciate the flexibility that over-the-top services provide (for instance, access to user content wherever the customer has a broadband Internet connection and on the device of the customer's choosing), and over-the-top may also be less expensive, depending on a subscriber's consumption habits. Traditional cable and telephone providers have been responding with their own services for accessing subscriber content via the Internet. As the range of Internet-available content and applications expands, and the broadband performance of mobile networks improves, more entertainment consumption can shift to mobile services. The expansion in viewing options and platforms is driving content and application providers to expand their distribution options to compete for viewer attention and to explore new ways to monetize their content assets. The shift from legacy MVPD models toward broadband-based models increases the potential for competition between mobile and fixed broadband access options.

At the same time that the mobile broadband user-experience is approaching the experience that previously was only available via fixed broadband services, fixed providers are adding mobile capabilities. Cable and DSL broadband providers recognized relatively early that allowing their subscribers to connect their broadband modems to Wi-Fi enhanced the usability and value of fixed broadband services within the home by allowing localized mobility. With the maturation of Wi-Fi and the proliferation of Wi-Fi services, Wi-Fi is increasingly seen as a substitute for mobile in many usage modalities that do not require support for high-speed movement. The wide-spread availability of Wi-Fi connectivity outside the home has prompted a number of new mobile offerings such as Google's Project Fi, Google's mobile telephone offering that uses Wi-Fi in place of cellular service when available (Martonik & Maring, 2018). Google purchases the cellular service as a MVNO wholesale from the MNOs. Comcast already offers its customers Xfinity Wi-Fi access via its installed base of Wi-Fi-enabled subscribers and is launching a new mobile service (Silbey, 2016; Finley, 2017).

In the small cell world of 5G, the capabilities of LTE and Wi-Fi are increasingly comparable, all else equal (Lehr & Oliver, 2014). Nomadic roaming (moving into the coverage area of a base station and then remaining stationary) is often well-suited for many attention-intensive broadband applications, which makes LTE and Wi-Fi better able to support comparable user experiences.[54] Additionally, in the small cell world, the economics of wired and wireless providers become increasingly similar since a greater share of the infrastructure is sunk in particular local locations (just as last-mile fiber has to be close to the end-users, so too do small cells). Providing the sort of local area-coverage required of 5G is analogous to the challenges of providing fiber to a town: the costs go up with the area covered, rather than with the number of subscribers. With earlier generations of mobile technology, it was easier to scale capacity with demand by starting with large cell sites and then adding sites as demand warranted.

Finally, the desire for a converged, seamless broadband experience is contributing to the convergence of wired and wireless services. Both providers are moving closer in terms of the capabilities they need to offer—wired and mobile providers are implementing SDN and NFV capabilities and connecting to cloud service providers and in so doing are becoming increasingly alike.

This assimilation is comparable to that which occurred with the first generation of broadband. Before broadband, telephone and cable television providers operated networks that were designed for distinct applications. Although both had wired infrastructure deployed to homes across the United States, the telephone-provider networks were designed for narrowband, two-way telephony while cable television networks were designed for one-way television distribution. With the move toward broadband platforms, the network architectures and the capabilities of the legacy telephone providers and cable television companies have coalesced. Today, Comcast and Verizon are more alike from a cost and product portfolio perspective than were the cable television and telephone companies of the 1980s. In an analogous process, the move to 5G will further drive convergence between wired and wireless network operators.

4.2. Stronger Competition Among MVNOs

The drive toward stronger MVNO competition will come from multiple sources. First, the increased capacity of the facilities-based networks will

---

54   For example, a user who wants to review a spreadsheet or watch a movie is unlikely to want to do that when driving a car (although the passengers may wish to). Moreover, seamless lower-speed service hand-offs are increasingly able to be supported in Wi-Fi networks (*e.g.*, keeping a telephone call connected while moving from one Wi-Fi access point to another at walking speeds).

make it more likely that the networks will be able to support new sorts of MVNOs models and provide assurance that robustly competitive whole-sale markets for capacity will be available to support the MVNOs.

Second, the intensifying competition among content (especially enter-tainment media providers noted earlier) and edge providers to offer more attractive offerings and to expand their control of the customer experience will create incentives for some to self-provision and manage more of the network functionality associated with the delivery of their products. The rise of CDNs, cloud services, and robust markets for the technologies that enable 5G will make self-provisioning a more viable option for the larger edge providers. This will create demand for MVNO strategies by larger content or application providers. In addition, increased retail market com-petition will provide increased opportunities for customer-segment-focused MVNOs (*e.g.*, focusing on a particular class of programming or customer segment, etc.). The entertainment and media industries are im-portant economic sectors and their intensifying competition will drive competition at the network and services level to support their growing demand for network capacity.[55]

Third, the potential to enable Smart-X opportunities will also contribute to expanded demand for MVNO business models. The greatest promise of 5G to contribute significantly to resurgent productivity and economic growth rests with these Smart-X opportunities, and because Smart-X ap-plications are likely to have quite a bit of domain-specificity to them, meeting the ICT needs of Smart-X is likely to expand opportunities for specialized MVNO providers. Thus, although there will obviously be sim-ilarities between the telecommunication services that Smart-healthcare and Smart-agriculture will require (*e.g.*, both will want users to make tele-phone calls), there are also likely to be important differences. For exam-ple, the cybersecurity requirements or the need to support particular types of IoT deployments may be quite different across application domains. When Smart-X takes hold, domain-specificity will be mission-critical for the businesses that are involved. In many contexts, that will make adopters

---

55 Although the changing dynamics of competition in the entertainment industries will drive additional economic growth, much of the economic impact will be associated with shifting revenues and profits among industry players rather than creating new economic opportunities. For example, the movement of vid-eo entertainment to Internet platforms accessed via broadband access results in revenues being displaced from traditional subscription cable and satellite TV services to new channels rather than the creation of wholly new revenue streams. For further discussion, see Lehr & Sicker (2017).

anxious to retain significant control, especially when the Smart-X applications are deeply embedded within their business processes. 5G networks are intended to enable the sort of functionality and flexibility to allow enterprise customers to assume more direct control over how their enterprise networks are provisioned and managed. The largest enterprises may elect to operate their own in-house MVNOs, while smaller enterprises may opt to purchase services from domain-specific MVNOs.

Additionally, it is reasonable to expect that there may be benefits of scale, scope, or learning economies associated with some business functions (*e.g.*, potentially some aspects of ePayments clearing or support for a cryptocurrency like Bitcoin) that may lead the providers of such services to operate purpose-built networks. In the world of Content Delivery Networks ("CDNs"), the largest content providers (Netflix, Google, Facebook) have opted to build their own customized CDNs rather than continue to rely exclusively on third-party CDN providers (Stocker et al., 2017).

These demand considerations suggest that the market for specialized MVNOs that are either directly integrated with the application providers (*e.g.* Facebook or Netflix becomes an MVNO for their customers, or a Smart-healthcare or Smart-agriculture MVNO emerges that caters to the customized needs of its focus sector) will increase. In many cases, the MNOs may choose to pursue such vertical market opportunities by integrating forward with their own specialized operations. However, such efforts are not without problems. They can lead to channel conflicts when the MNO finds its retail operations competing directly with its wholesale operations that are selling to competing retailers.

The history of long distance telephone competition provides a ready example of how this can work to the benefit of those in favor of robust retail competition. In the 1980s, there were three national facilities-based wired telephony providers of long-distance service: AT&T, MCI, and Sprint. In addition, there were a large number of resellers that varied from partial facilities-based providers (*e.g.*, ones that may have operated a few switches) to pure resellers (*i.e.*, those who fully outsourced their network operations to one of the facilities-based providers and only managed the customer-facing retail operations).

These long distance resellers were able to offer significant competitive discipline, including significant price competition, because there was an active and competitive market for wholesale long distance services. Each of the three large facilities-based providers had to have excess capacity in order to meet peak traffic needs, and because capacity in facilities-based telecommunication networks has to be added in lumpy increments. If there were only one facilities-based provider, it could have priced its wholesale services to extract the resellers' surplus, denying them the ability to offer competitive discipline.

With three facilities providers, there was excess capacity available and the incentives of selling this to resellers helped ensure that the national long-distance network operators could not collude to cartelize the wholesale market. The competitive market for wholesale long-distance telephone capacity contributed to ensuring a competitive market for resellers, which in turn, helped ensure aggressive competition in retail long distance services. Indeed, a reason the FCC concluded it was appropriate to deregulate markets for business telephone services in the 1990s (thereby helping advance the movement from legacy public utility regulation of telephone service toward market-based competition) was because of the widespread availability of bulk wholesale transport services in long-distance markets.[56]

In today's world of 3G/4G MNO competition, MVNOs are already playing an important role in sustaining robust retail service competition. These are especially relevant in the markets for discounted and pre-paid mobile services. With the transition to 5G, the scope of options for MVNO competition and their importance in the competitive landscape is expected to increase.

Moreover, the softwarization and virtualization capabilities noted earlier will make it easier for MNOs to offer MVNOs customized slices of their networks. These capabilities will make it feasible to support a robustly competitive wholesale market for the MNO services needed to support a robustly competitive ecosystem of MVNOs. Although the MNOs will be compelled to implement the softwarization and virtualization to lower their costs and to enable them to appeal to the increased demands for customized and enhanced services from ever-more-demanding end-users in order to compete against other MNOs, these same capabilities will make it harder for MNOs to collectively avoid the intensifying competition that will come from MVNOs.

---

56   In 1991, the FCC found the outbound business services market segment to be "substantially competitive" based principally on its finding "that the business services marketplace is characterized by substantial demand and supply elasticities" (FCC, 1991, ¶ 36). That finding was reaffirmed (FCC, 1995) and a similar finding was made with respect to inbound (i.e., 800) services in 1993, once 800 numbers were made portable (FCC, 1993).

4.3. Increased Competition From Specialized or Local Facilities-Based Entrants

A final vector for competition will come from local facilities-based entrants. In the 5G world of small cells and Smart-X environments the potential for small, localized providers are greater. To the extent that high frequency spectrum in the millimeter wave bands (above 20 GHz) becomes important for 5G, making use of this spectrum will require small cells. The siting of small cells requires a lot of complementary infrastructure (site access, power, management of interconnection to wider-area networks) that may make more sense to manage locally where the spectrum is actually being used.

For many of the Smart-X applications (such as Smart cities), the natural manager and deployer of much of the 5G infrastructure may be the city or municipality. The city may be able to justify the investment costs on the basis of specialized applications such as IoT for public safety (*e.g.*, using sensors to detect gunshots and enable faster responses), for traffic management (*e.g.*, to reduce congestion, improve public transportation, and manage parking), or for monitoring critical infrastructure (*e.g.*, repair statuses of roads and bridges). In stadiums, factories, malls or other venues, the owner of the venue may be well-suited for deploying the infrastructure.

In addition to the above business models, there is growing interest in so-called "neutral hosts" business models. The case for these is to take advantage of the natural monopoly elements of much of the local 5G infrastructure by enabling the infrastructure to be shared. Softwarization and virtualization techniques that are used at the core of the networks can also be used in edge components allowing those to be shared. A base station's resources could be reconfigured to support multiple MNOs or sliced to provide MNOs with on-demand access to local 5G capabilities. MNOs have demonstrated their willingness to outsource components of their networks and share those with other MNOs already in the case of large coverage area cell sites. Historically, MNOs built out their mobile telephone networks by building their own cell towers. Today, most of the macrocell towers are owned by third parties who lease space on the towers to multiple MNOs. The towers support multiple base station radios. In a world of software radios, the towers can be smaller and the radios themselves can be shared.

The increased incidence of end-user enabled Wi-Fi roaming (campuses and venues providing free Wi-Fi access, home-owners sharing Wi-Fi) is another example of how end-user provided local networking infrastructure can offer a new vector for competition that is only conceivable in the world of wireless. With the improvements in support for seamless mobility which 5G promises, additional technical barriers to end-users in venues and communities are falling, creating competitive alternatives to MNO services.

While 5G is likely to enable new models for wholesale and retail local or otherwise specialized wireless facilities-based providers, these business models will not displace the need for national-scale MNOs, nor will they be likely to provide a sufficient platform for a wholesale market for facilities that would allow national scale MVNOs to survive without relying on the wholesale offerings of the national MNOs.

5. Conclusion

The future of the global economy is digital. Remaining competitive and sustaining robust economic growth requires sustaining our critical ICT infrastructure's capacities for continued growth. Mobile broadband networks are key components of our national ICT infrastructure.

In the first four generations of their evolution, MNOs have been dominated by cellular networks. The fundamental economics of constructing and operating a national-scale telecommunications network implies that the industry structure will be oligopolistic, but can also contribute to conditions for intense competition with a small number of facilities-based providers. Today, we have four national cellular MNOs that are competing aggressively against one another. Collectively, for over a decade, these four MNOs have sustained a record of performance that includes expanding capacity and falling quality-adjusted prices. The MNOs have sustained exponential growth in traffic and contributed significantly to national economic growth and the increased vibrancy of the entire Internet ecosystem.

With the transition to 4G LTE, of which we are still in the midst, the MNOs have finally consolidated on a common technology platform that makes them better able to flexibly manage diverse spectrum assets on the radio side, while allowing them to make use of a unified IP-platform on the data network side. This sets the stage for closer convergence between fixed and mobile network providers and brings us one step closer to realizing the future of always and everywhere connectivity that is part of the vision of Pervasive Computing and the Smart-X future of converged real and virtual worlds. From an MNO network perspective, 5G represents the next round of order-of-magnitude improvements and investment that will be required to advance this vision and enable the potential for economic growth that Smart-X promises. However, even without Smart-X, MNOs need to continue to invest significantly in order to expand capacity and reduce the costs of carrying exponential growth in mobile broadband traffic. Most of this traffic growth in the near-term is associated with the explosion in entertainment video traffic as more content shifts from traditional delivery platforms to broadband-based platforms, including increasingly mobile broadband.

Addressing exponential traffic growth cost-effectively while enabling the enhanced service management capabilities that 5G requires (and are being demanded by today's more demanding 4G MNO enterprise and consumer customers), MNOs are being compelled to adopt more agile spectrum management capabilities, softwarization and virtualization network architectures, and small cells all at the same time. For the national MNOs that want to remain full-service providers, this is contributing to the potential and need to realize ever-larger scale and scope economies. The scale necessary for operating a national-scale MNO is increasing, rendering it less viable for smaller MNOs (like T-Mobile or Sprint) to sustain the pace of investment required to remain competitive with the largest two MNOs (Verizon and AT&T).

At the same time, market and technical trends are driving the convergence of fixed and mobile networking and the enhanced capabilities and localization of advanced wireless networking are creating new vectors for competition that further puts pressure on legacy national MNOs. The best prospect for sustaining robust competition among national MNOs is via the merger of T-Mobile and Sprint to form New T-Mobile. The merger represents a pro-competitive response by two providers with synergistic reasons for combining to better address the challenges of remaining a viable competitor in the 5G future.

The future of broadband and 5G is uncertain, but the success of robust competition and demand for 5G holds the promise of significant economic growth. Wireless networks of all kinds will be important if the 5G vision is to be realized. A merger of T-Mobile and Sprint offers important benefits in terms of helping to ensure sustainable and viable facilities-based competition among MNOs in the near to middle-term, and in promoting aggressive investment across the entire broadband ecosystem directed at enabling the 5G vision. Additionally, realizing the 5G vision will expand options for new vectors of competition from MVNOs, local providers, and more intense intermodal competition among fixed and mobile network operators.

References

Accenture (2018), *Impact of Federal Regulatory Reviews of Small Cell Deployment* 3, March 12, 2018, available at https://bit.ly/2JKXkRC.

Accenture (2017), *Smart Cities: How 5G Can Help Municipalities Become Vibrant Smart Cities*, 2017), available at https://bit.ly/2pMuM4y.

Accenture (2015), *Winning with the Industrial Internet of Things* 3, 2015, available at https://accntu.re/2mynldI.

Barefoot, Kevin, Dave Curtis, William Joliff, Jessica Nicholson, and Robert Omohundro (2018), "Defining and Measuring the Digital Economy," Working Paper, Bureau of Economic Analysis, U.S. Department of Commerce, Mar. 15, 2018, available at https://www.bea.gov/system/files/papers/WP2018-4.pdf.

Blum, Herbert, Darryn Lowe and Alex Dahlke (2018), *Why the 5G Pessimists are Wrong*, Bain & Co., June 28, 2018, available at https://www.bain.com/insights/why-the-5g-pessimists-are-wrong/.

Blumberg, Stephen and Julian Luke (2017), *Wireless Substitution: Early Release of Estimates from the National Health Interview Survey, July-December 2016*, National Center for Health Statistics, May 2017, available at https://bit.ly/2pC9LZ7.

Cassini, Sandrine (2018), *Sebastien Soriano: Sur la consolidation dans les télécoms, la porte de l'Arcep s'entrouve*, Le Monde, May 22, 2018, available at https://lemde.fr/2Lmcu5v.

Cisco (2017a), *Cisco Visual Networking Index: Forecast and Methodology, 2016-2021*, September 15, 2017, available at https://bit.ly/2mxglxY.

Cisco (2017b), *Cisco Visual Networking Index: Global Mobile Data Traffic Forecast Update, 2016–2021 White Paper*, March 28, 2017, available at https://bit.ly/2vu69MQ.

Cisco (2015), *Fog Computing and the Internet of Things: Extend the Cloud to Where the Things Are*, 2015, available at https://bit.ly/2eYXUxj.

Columbus, Louis (2016), *Roundup Of Internet Of Things Forecasts and Market Estimates,* Forbes, November 27, 2016, available at https://bit.ly/2Lw3ie0.

DCMS (2018), *Future Telecoms Infrastructure Review*, UK Department for Digital, Culture, Media and Sport, July 23 2018, available at https://www.gov.uk/government/uploads/system/uploads/attachment_data/file/732496/Future_Telecoms_Infrastructure_Review.pdf.

Deloitte (2017), *Communications Infrastructure Upgrades*, July 2017, available at https://bit.ly/2LJ9JY0.

Entner, Roger (2016), *The Wireless Industry: Revisiting Spectrum, The Essential Engine of US Economic Growth*, Recon Analytics LLC 8, April 2016, available at https://bit.ly/2mCOEE0.

Ericsson (2017), *Ericsson Mobility Report*, June 2017, available at https://bit.ly/2szKfGz.

Evans, David (2018), "Declaration of David Evans," In the matter of Sprint Corp. and T-Mobile US, Inc., Joint Application for Consent to Transfer Control of International and Domestic Authority Pursuant to Section 214 of the Communications Act of 1934, WT Docket No. 18-197, June 2018, available at https://bit.ly/2Lt25Ex.

FCC (2017), *Implementation of Section 6002(b) of the Omnibus Budget Reconciliation Act of 1993, Annual Report and Analysis of Competitive Market Conditions with Respect to Mobile Wireless, Including Commercial Mobile Services*, Twentieth Report, 32 FCC Rcd 8968.

FCC (2006), *Implementation of Section 6002(b) of the Omnibus Budget Reconciliation Act of 1993, Annual Report and Analysis of Competitive Market Conditions with Respect to Mobile Wireless, Including Commercial Mobile Services*, Eleventh Report, 21 FCC Rcd 10947.

FCC (1999), *Implementation of Section 6002(b) of the Omnibus Budget Reconciliation Act of 1993, Annual Report and Analysis of Competitive Market Conditions with Respect to Mobile Wireless, Including Commercial Mobile Services*, Fourth Report, 14 FCC 10145.

FCC (1995), *AT&T Corp.*, Order, 11 FCC Rcd 3271 ¶ 89 (1995)

FCC (1993) *Competition in the Interexchange Marketplace*, Second Report and Order, 8 FCC Rcd 3668 ¶ 10 (1993).

FCC (1991), *Competition in the Interstate Exchange Marketplace*, Report and Order, 6 FCC Rcd 5880 ¶ 36, 1991.

Finley, Klint (2017), *Comcast's New Mobile Service is a Good Deal, But Maybe Not Enough*, Wired, April 6, 2017, available at https://bit.ly/2o04jfA.

Gartner (2017), *Gartner Forecasts Worldwide Public Cloud Services Revenue to Reach $260 Billion in 2017*, Press Release, October 12, 2017, available at https://www.gartner.com/newsroom/id/3815165.

Goovaerts, Diana (2015), *iGR Study Forecasts $104B Cost to Upgrade LTE Networks, Build Out 5G Network*, Wireless Week, December 7, 2015, available at https://bit.ly/2mBjHjk.

Grijpink, Ferry, Alexandre Menard, Halldor Sigdsson, and Nemanja Vucevic (2018), *The road to 5G: The inevitable growth of infrastructure cost*, McKinsey & Co. Telecommunications, February 2018), available at https://www.mckinsey.com/industries/telecommunications/our-insights/the-road-to-5g-the-inevitable-growth-of-infrastructure-cost.

Hanna, Nagy (2016), *Mastering Digital Transformation: Towards a Smarter Society, Economy, City and Nation*, 2016.

ITU (2015), *Recommendation ITU-R M.2083-0: IMT Vision – Framework and Overall Objectives of the Future Development of IMT for 2020 and Beyond*, International Telecommunications Union (ITU), September 2015, available at https://bit.ly/2bl8QU2.

Kharif, Olga and Scott Moritz (2017), *Upgrade to 5G Costs $200 Billion a Year, May Not Be Worth It*, Bloomberg, December 18, 2017, available at https://bloom.bg/2Bb8nnK.

Lehr, William (2012), *Reliability and the Internet Cloud*, June 2012, available at https://bit.ly/2O9AruI.

Lehr, William (2009), *Mobile Broadband and Implications for Broadband Competition and Adoption*, Social Science Research Network 23-24, November 2009, available at https://bit.ly/2KFMo8p.

Lehr, William and Miquel Oliver (2014), *Small Cells and the Broadband Ecosystem*, 25th European Regional Conference of the International Telecommunications Society, June 2014, available at https://bit.ly/2OmczmL.

Lehr, William and Douglas Sicker (2017), *Would You Like Your Internet With or Without Video?*, Journal of Law, Technology & Policy, (2017), 73-140, available at https://bit.ly/2A0nNLl.

Martonik, Andrew and Joe Maring (2018), *What is Project Fi, how does it work, and why do I want it?*, Android Central, July 16, 2018, available at https://bit.ly/2OpZlWp.

Mathias, Craig (2017), *What is Virtualization?*, Network World, Oct. 26, 2017, available at https://bit.ly/2zRdAgr.

McLellan, Charles (2017), *XaaS: Why 'Everything' is Now a Service*, ZDNet, November 1, 2017, available at https://www.zdnet.com/article/xaas-why-everything-is-now-a-service/.

McKinsey (2015), *The Internet of Things: Mapping the Value Beyond the Hype* 3, McKinsey & Company, June 2015, available at https://mck.co/2gyPezB.

Morgan Stanley (2017), *Telecoms Send Mixed Signals on 5G Wireless*, Nov. 9, 2017, available at https://mgstn.ly/2vLY07U.

Nordrum, Amy and Kristen Clark (2017, *Everything You Need to Know About 5G*, IEEE Spectrum, January 27, 2017, available at https://bit.ly/2OV1Dhh.

Oguchi, Naoki et al. (2017), *Virtualization and Softwarization Technologies for End-to-end Networking*, 53 FUJITSU Science Technical Journal, 2017, available at https://bit.ly/2AT6H2v.

Oughton, Edward and Zoraida Frias (2017), *The Cost, Coverage and Rollout Implications of 5G Infrastructure in Britain*, Telecommunications Policy, 3, July 29, 2017, available at https://bit.ly/2M5Gymw.

Pew (2018), *Mobile Fact Sheet*, Pew Center Research, February 2018, available at https://pewrsr.ch/2inUJzB.

Pressman, Aaron (2016), *Why cord cutting is spreading to broadband Internet subscribers*, Fortune, October 5, 2016, available at https://for.tn/2OV3HWv.

Pretz, Kathy (2016), *The 'Softwarization' of Telecommunications*, IEEE, July 20, 2016, available at https://bit.ly/2bdCIpM.

Red Hat (2018a), *What is Virtualization?*, last visited Aug. 8, 2018, available at https://red.ht/2nlNDAn.

Red Hat (2018b), *Understanding Virtualization*, available at https://red.ht/2tZDa43 (last visited July 1, 2018).

Silbey, Mari (2016), *US Cable WiFi Hotspots Near 17 Million*, Light Reading, July 6, 2016, available at https://ubm.io/2LsBQOt

Stocker, Volker, Georgios Smaragdakis, William Lehr, and Stephen Bauer (2017), *The Growing Complexity of Content Delivery Networks: Challenges and Implications for the Internet Ecosystem*, 41 Telecommunications Policy 1003-1016 (2017), available at https://bit.ly/2Ol8AH8.

Tekkedath, Balamurali (2016), *Network Functions Virtualization for Dummies* (2016), available at https://bit.ly/2Ldi6iu.

Thanki, Richard (2012), *The Economic Significance of License-Exempt Spectrum to the Future of the Internet*, 36-40, June 2012, available at https://bit.ly/2LeGzEi.

Thierer, Adam and Andrea O'Sullivan (2015), *Projecting the Growth and Economic Impact of the Internet of Things*, Mercatus Center, George Mason Univ, June 15, 2015, available at https://bit.ly/2O7Reyd.

Tran, Tuyen, Abolfazl Hajisami, Parul Pandey and Dario Pompili (2017), *Collaborative Mobile Edge Computing in 5G Networks: New Paradigms, Scenarios, and Challenges*, IEEE Communications, Volume 55, Issue 4, April 2017, available at https://bit.ly/2nvF5Y1.

World Bank (2016), *World Development Report 2016: Digital Dividend*, May 2016, available at https://bit.ly/1IhG3Yo.

Telecommunication 4.0 – Investment in Very High Capacity Broadband and the Internet of Things

Iris Henseler-Unger[1]

Abstract

The Internet of Things (IoT) is part of Germany's (and Europe's) industrial and societal ambitions. It allows a variety of new combinations and interacting of different machines, the creation of dynamic new value chains by interlinking machines and people, the innovation in services and products. To make IoT a success story for users and industry the role of the telecommunications sector is a central one. It provides the basic infrastructure and the basic services for IoT applications. Thus, there will be two main challenges for them: to cope with a transformation of their business model and to finance investments in modern very high capacity broadband, often called gigabit networks.

Whereas we can expect privately financed deployment of very high capacity broadband in densely populated areas, we see major problems in rural areas. Disadvantages in terms of costs and population density cannot be overcome by the regulation/deregulation of players with significant market power. Our considerations have to go one step further: temporary monopolies (e. g. through concession models) could be part of the problem solution, in addition or alternative to subsidies.

Furthermore, telcos have to find their role in the IoT ecosystem. They have to supply new service classes with high quality standards, i.e. they have to innovate their offers. They have to streamline their processes. Telcos have the chance to define new business models. They have to develop their way to "Telecommunication 4.0".

Keywords: Broadband; Investment; Internet of Things; Very high capacity broadband

---

1   WIK GmbH, Bad Honnef; I.Henseler-Unger@WIK.ORG

1. Introduction

The Internet of Things (IoT) is a common vision of engineers, users, industry managers and politicians. The possibility of new combinations and interacting of different machines, the creation of dynamic new value chains by interlinking machines and people, the innovation in services and products is a fascinating perspective on the future years.

To make IoT a success story for users and industry the telecommunications sector will have to face new chances and new challenges. As the telecommunications sector provides the basic infrastructure and the basic services for IoT applications, telecommunications companies will have to cope with a transformation of their business model and will also have to finance investments in modern very high capacity broadband, often called gigabit networks, as a precondition for most of IoT applications. Without this transformation in Telecommunications 4.0 and without the investment in very high capacity networks IoT remains a vision.

2. Internet of Things

Digitisation, Internet protocol and packet-switched data traffic, the layered structure of the Internet, software-applications, virtualisation and smart networks are some of the keywords which pave the way to the Internet of Things. They are used to characterise what is often called the fourth industrial revolution. In fact, the paradigm shift in industry – and society – is significant. Value chains influenced by digitisation become complex ecosystems, in which, for example, subcontractors and manufacturers work together with new service providers, Internet platforms, social media and others. Some products such as cars will be transformed into a lifetime service for mobility. Today's production processes will be restructured by software engineers. Sharing platforms will challenge the way consumers use products today. Ownership, e. g. of a car, might no longer play a role. Industries have to manage their transformation, otherwise they face disruptive competition, as music labels and newspapers have already done.

The economic dynamics of the Internet of Things is expected to be significant. Cisco forecasts that machine-to-machine-communication as a central part of the IoT will reach 26,4% of global mobile data traffic in 2020 (2015: 7,7%)[2] and expects annual growth rates of 38%.[3]

---

2   Cisco (2016a).
3   Cisco (2016b), p. 15.

Figure 1:   Significant advantages over the next 5 years, as of April 2016

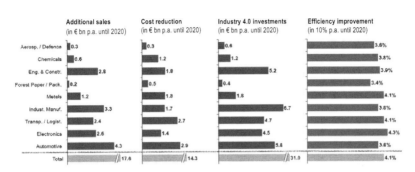

Source: in accordance with PwC (2016).

Drivers of this dynamic are economic factors, as competitive pressure and the opportunity to reduce costs. Figure 1 shows expected significant improvements in efficiency across all sectors that are on the verge of intensive use of IoT applications. Cost reductions are particularly prominent in the field of transportation/logistics and automotive. Especially in the automotive sector additional annual sales are expected. Another economic driver of IoT solutions is the prospect of developing future-proof business cases by innovation. Regulatory obligations (e. g. eCall) enforce the implementation of IoT solutions. The German "Energiewende" will rely on smart grids and smart networks. The regulatory obligation to use smart meters is only the beginning of the digitisation of the energy sector, as renewable energies enforce the decentralisation of energy generation and increase the need for intelligent coordination.

General economic implications might be significant. Roland Berger Strategy Consultants (2015) estimates additional annual value added of 250 bn. € in Europe until 2025. Cisco expects additional annual growth of 2 % in Germany over the next 10 years.[4] PwC (2016) is forecasting investment plans of annually 31 bn. € for the next 5 years.

---

4   Busse, C. (2014).

3. *Telecommunication 4.0: Telcos' two challenges to foster IoT*

3.1. 1st challenge: Managing the own transformation

The telecommunication industry will benefit from quite a few chances as a consequence of IoT. Their infrastructure, that is broadband communication networks, will become the basic infrastructure, which will be used for most of services and applications running in the IoT. Their strategic position in the electronic communications market will be confirmed and even strengthened, as they become an integral part of the new ecosystem, e.g. M2M applications or cloud computing need reliable connectivity. The demand for communication services will therefore grow beyond voice and today's Internet. If Cisco's forecast and other projections are correct, demand growth rates of the underlying infrastructure providers should also reach those expected for the whole industry, e.g. 2 % additional annual growth in Germany. That will help to fill the networks with traffic and thus to realise better economies of scale. New business cases are lying ahead as partners of IoT driven industries.

But where there is light, there is also shadow. IoT, especially M2M, might be a difficult market compared to today's mass consumer markets. It will force the telecommunications industry to reform its business model. Here are some aspects of the challenges lying ahead: There will be only a single customer with a huge amount of connections (e.g. all his manufactured cars). The customer will demand for data traffic and no voice, which is today's cash cow. Each of these single costumers will look for specialised solutions (e.g. car manufacturer) to differentiate themselves from competitors and to enforce innovation. Each individual user (e.g. car owner) will only realise a small business volume for telcos, IDATE expects 1-10 € instead of 40 € as ARPU of the mass consumer contract.[5]

The IoT market might in addition be highly attractive for newcomers, also using alternative technologies, e.g. in wireless solutions. So the battle between the new mobile generation 5G and Wifi has not yet been decided, as technical needs and the room for new business models is not foreseeable. We will observe the speeding up of innovation cycles, as they are reflecting now the innovation speed of applications. As they will be software driven, they speed up. Furthermore, costumers' innovation cycles are driven by international competition, which up to now reaches telecommu-

---

5   Godlovitch et al. (2016), p. 105 ff.

nications quite indirectly. Telcos will become only one part of new complex clusters of production and value added, quite differing from today's value chains which are comparable to ladders.

We expect fixed-mobile convergence, which co-occurs with the reallocation of value added from mobile operators to fixed network operators, as fibre networks are backbone, backhaul and fronthaul of the next mobile standard 5G.

Networks today dominated by best effort quality cannot cope with the high performance standards required by some IoT-applications. They require e.g. agreed qualities, real time transmission, high levels of security, high availability of nearly 100 %, symmetry of traffic between up- and download, qualities which cannot or can only partially be provided today. There have to be further investments in networks and in organisational issues.

Software-defined networks (SDN) can be part of the solution, as they enable the telecommunications industry to use the advantages of digitisation. They are more flexible, allow them to quickly participate in the software innovation process, and enable to define characteristics for each customer. But they might also lead to a loss of network control, as SDN-formed network slices could ultimately be managed by someone else as the infrastructure owner.

Differing quality of data transmission touches at the issue of net neutrality between Internet services and other services, a subject that is politically discussed. Can data packets and applications in the Internet be handled differently? Is it possible to define transparent and non-discriminating conditions? These questions will require a recalibration of net neutrality and specialised services.

We face future challenges for telecommunications markets, with changes for a whole ecosystem. Telcos have to cope with the challenges as starting point, but it is not only for realising their profit chances in the world of IoT. Their success will determine the future economical and societal welfare. The first challenge of IoT for telcos is to transform and adapt their business model to the expected demand of IoT applications. The second challenge is to manage investments in upgraded networks. As a consequence of the IoT, it follows that networks have to be capable to provide IoT services. Modern infrastructure is key for innovation and the new ecosystem. The first step must therefore be to invest in very high capacity broadband. They are a prerequisite for very high capacity broadband access, gigabit networks for a gigabit society. They contribute to future economic and societal competitiveness. But: How much risk does the commitment to CAPEX entail?

3.2. 2nd challenge: Investing in gigabit networks

3.2.1. Definition of gigabit networks

The common used buzzword "gigabit network" refers to broadband networks with very high capacity (VHC). The EU Commission[6] defines very high-capacity networks in its proposal for the recast of the legal framework for electronic communication as follows:

> "Very high-capacity network means an electronic communications network which either consists wholly of optical fibre elements at least up to the distribution point at the serving location or which is capable of delivering under usual peak-time conditions similar network performance in terms of available down- and uplink bandwidth, resilience, error-related parameters, and latency and its variation."

This definition tries to reflect the diversity of requirements following IoT applications. Probably, the variety of applications will not always require a high bandwidth (a "big pipe"), quite a few will need different quality standards, for example symmetry of traffic or real-time solutions. All these different requirements sum up to a gigabit network.

Table 1 shows some of the services with their expected needs. Only VHC networks should be able to cope with this demand.

---

6   EU Commission (2016), Article 2 (2).

Table 1:   Typical use cases and their demand for broadband quality

	Downstream (Mbit/s)	Upstream (Mbit/s)	Packet loss	Latency
Basic Internet	≈20	≈16	o	o
Homeoffice/VPN	≈250	≈250	+	+
Cloud Computing	≈250	≈250	+	++
Conventional TV (4K/Ultra-HD)	≈90	≈20	++	+
Progressive TV (8K/...)	≈300	≈60	++	+
Communication	≈8	≈8	++	+
Videocommunication (HD)	≈25	≈25	++	++
Gaming	≈300	≈150	++	++
E-Health	≈50	≈50	++	+
E-Home/E-Facility	≈50	≈50	o	o
Mobile-Offloading	≈15	≈12	o	o

O   = Low importance/significance
+   = High importance/significance
++   = Very high importance/significance

Source: WIK.

A closer look at fixed networks' technologies which are deployed or are near market maturity (see Table 2) leads to the conclusion that gigabit networks will be mainly relying on fibre networks.

Modern copper technologies will provide some of the required quality standards, but then they show strict length limitations for the very last copper meters. Copper technologies as G.fast and beyond are essential FTTB-technologies (Fibre to the Building). Cable being a shared medium will need fibre backhaul to provide the standards. The more traffic they handle, the more fibre has to be deployed till premises to reach the promised qualities. Only fibre technologies provide every requested demand of the IoT without limitations.

In the mobile world, 5G is considered to be the wireless solution that will be able to meet some/most of these requirements of IoT. It is for sure that this modern mobile standard will be based on a fibre network in fronthaul and backhaul as they need a high density of cells e.g. to meet the challenge of low latency.

Table 2: Characteristics of transmission technologies

Transmission technology	FTT...	Band-width [Gbit/s]	Length limitation [m]	Indiv./shared	Symm./asymm.	Stand-ard	Ma-turity	ODF unbund.	VULA (L2)
Copper pair									
ADSL2+	FTTC	0,01	2.600	i	a	y	y	y	y
VDSL2	FTTC	0,05	400	i	a	y	y	y	y
VDSL2 Vec-toring	FTTC	0,09	400	i	a	y	y	n	y
VDSL2 Su-pervect.	FTTC	0,25	300	i	a	y	y	n	y
G.fast	FTTS/dp	2 x 0,5	250	i	a	y	y	n	y
XG.fast	FTTB	2 x 5	50	i	a	n	+ 2 Y	n	y
Coax									
Docsis 3.0	fibre node	1,2	160.000	s	a	y	y	n	n
Docsis 3.1	fibre node	10	160.000	s	a	y	y	n	n
Docsis 3.1 FD/XG-Ca.ble	deep fibre	10	160.000	s	s	y	+ 4 Y	n	?
Fibre									
GPON (PMP)	FTTB/H	2,5	20.000	s	a	y	y	n	y
XG.PON	FTTB/H	10	40.000	s	a/s	y	y	n	y
XGS.PON	FTTB/H	10	40.000	s	s	y	y	n	y
TWDM GPON	FTTB/H	4 - 8 x 10	40.000	s	a/s	y	y	4 - 8 Ops	y
DWDM GPON	FTTB/H	1000 x 1	100.000	i	s	n	+ 4 Y	y	y
Ethernet P2P	FTTH	n x 100	80.000	i	s	y	y	y	y

Source: WIK

A future-proof scenario for VHC networks envisages that copper, cable and wireless are only used for short and very short distances to the customer. The goal of gigabit networks therefore leads to the demand for more fibre coverage nationwide.

But: in Germany fibre roll out is lacking far behind other European countries. Today, only 7.1 % of German households are passed by fibre, and take up rates are even worse. There is an urgent need for investment in fibre infrastructure. How can incentives be put in place?

3.2.2. Investment in gigabit networks

There is a comprehensive empirical literature that reflects the relationship among investment in broadband, competition and regulation in the telecommunication market - a true battlefield![7]
Two conflicting theses are discussed:

- Regulation prevents abuse of significant market power and thus fosters competition and efficient investment of all market players, incumbent as well as competitors.
- Regulation prevents the market dominant operator from generating sufficient revenue and thus prevents him from investing efficiently.

In their recent study Briglauer and Cambini (2017) see a majority of empirical work that supports the second thesis.

Of course, every empirical analysis is risky in regard to the underlying theses, the chosen methodology or data availability. It has to abstract from reality and to generalise. Theory and empirical work in the field of fibre network investment is an even more high-dangerous activity. Here are some of the obstacles:

Selected investment data is often the data for investment in NGA (Next Generation Access) networks. NGA networks cover all fixed network technologies that are capable to provide 30 Mbit/s or more, that is far away from gigabit networks and very high capacity networks. But even if one accepts this distortion in this context of 30 Mbit/s networks, analyses suffer from short time series. In the end these time series become extremely short for investment in very high capacity networks (gigabit networks), which are in our focus. This is especially true when looking for investment

---

7   E.g. Briglauer et al. (2015).

data comparable for a couple of countries since the deployment of fibre in most of the countries started only few years ago (frequently cited exceptions are South Korea, Japan).

Furthermore, researchers use take-up rates as a proxy for missing investment data. Take-up rates reflect market clearance volumes which rely on supply and demand. They reflect a wide range of market information, including preferences and price elasticities of consumers. Thus, their relation to investment in CAPEX is quite indirect. Neumann et al. (2016) chose the annual growth of fibre access lines as starting point for investment cost calculation to avoid this mixture of demand and supply elements.

Another challenge is to measure of the degree of competition and the level of regulation. It is not trivial. While indicators for competition seem to be relatively easy to achieve, e.g. the Herfindahl index, but there is no established and jointly shared regulatory index (yet). Modelling a regulatory index is a difficult task. The increasing complexity of regulation forces to address multiple communication markets with different wholesale levels and interdependent offers, such as traditional access via local loop unbundled or leased lines, but also virtual access via bitstream. An indicator measuring regulation should have to aggregate this information. Regulation varies and changes over time, markets are analysed every 2 or 3 years in the EU. Regulation also varies among countries, despite the European enthusiasm to harmonize policy. A comparison over time and across countries by an indicator and a stable scheme might not be easy. Impartial regulatory indicators are difficult to define (Has the German UMTS spectrum auction in 2000 been a disaster because of high spectrum prices? Is the result a consequence of regulation? Has it been a step forward in the direction of giving frequencies to the market at an early stage and in the liberalisation of their use?)

The analysis has to calibrate and to compare different impacts on different market players, i.e. incumbent and competitors, each with their specific business model. A comparable greenfield situation does not existing.

Empirical work in the field of regulation and investment in the telecommunications sector is a heroic task. A solid result would be urgently needed.

Against this background, which so far seems highly hypothetical about concrete conclusions, the transformation of results in concrete regulatory decisions becomes heroic. Briglauer and Cambini (2017) are very cautious in their wording: "(…) if full deregulation is not feasible due to monopolistic market structure (…)".[8]

In fact, the results of WIK's empirical work are mixed, e. g. for Ofcom[9] we don´t find solid results that support simple relations. Simple relations between competition and investment, as often cited in the political debate, are insignificant. Therefore, neither yes nor no can be concluded. Neumann et al. (2016) find a significant effect of the price for the last mile (local loop unbundled) on investment in fibre, but also warn to draw simplistic relationships as the relations appear mostly to be non-linear.

Many empirical studies show this result as a U-shaped curve between regulation and performance, so Briglauer and Cambini (2017), HSBC (2015) and also WIK with Elixmann et al. (2015). In a nutshell more effective regulation seems to foster investment (or an alternative performance indicator) up to a specific level (peak). Hereafter we find a negative impact (see Figure 2). The U-shaped curve is often explained by the interaction of Schumpeter-effect and escape competition effect [e.g. Bertschek et al. (2016) or WIK with Elixmann et al. (2015)].

Figure 2: Relationship between LLU-price and investment in FTTB/H connections

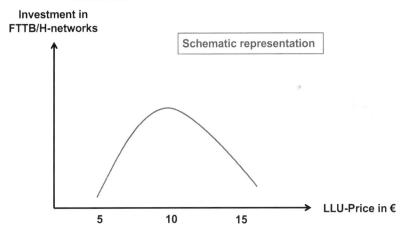

Source: WIK

---

8   Briglauer, Cambini (2017), page iii.
9   Elixmann et al. (2015).

This differentiated result questions the relevance for regulatory decisions. It does not make life easier for regulators in terms of concrete decisions. The regulator is especially interested in the peak point. Will his decision for a concrete parameter lie on the right or left side of the peak? How reliable is the deduction of the peak point? This information is essential for regulators seeking to calibrate competition and investment targets. Their regulatory decision is essential for all market players, incumbent and competitors. All market players rely on a fair regulatory decision to give them correct incentives to invest. A prominent example might be the regulatory price decision for access to the last mile. This price is essential for the incumbent, as it defines a large part of its profit at least in Germany. The competitors' business models are centrally influenced by this price, even if they demand other wholesale products, as their prices are based on the price for the last mile, LLU. At what price for the last mile will the peak be reached? What price fosters investment, which prevents investors? Neumann et al. (2016) conclude a peak price between 10.89 € and 11.43 €. The current regulated German price is 10.02 €, so can you expect it to be pro-invest? However, the calculation of the peak is based on an international sample. Can these results be transposed for the German regulator without any corrections, which one, in which respect?

The blur of empirical deduction, comparable to a fog, makes it quite courageous for regulators to found their decisions.

3.2.3. Pleading for a pragmatic approach: Rural regions are at the core of the problem

Econometric analyses might help us to understand the relation between regulation and investment a bit better than before. It might be a contribution to decrease the risk of the regulator to take a wrong decision. Even on the basis of a solid econometrical study the risk of a wrong decision will not vanish.

But my criticism goes deeper. From my perspective, econometric analysis gives an answer to a wrong question, at least if it focuses on the most important challenge. It addresses a minor part of the problem. In order to characterise the real problem it is worth to differentiate between different regional clusters and to take a closer look at them (see Figure 3).

Figure 3:   Households with gigabit-capable networks by clusters
(End-2016)

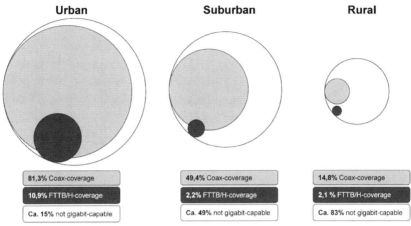

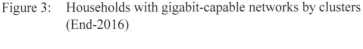

Source: WIK based on TÜV Rheinland (2017).

In Germany, three regional situations have to be clearly distinguished:

- In cities, competition at the end user level is highly developed. Coax coverage and FTTB/H coverage reach 85 % of households, corrected for overlapping. Here regulation is thus of minor importance today. Even the end of regulation seems to be achievable, as the situation itself benefits from infrastructure-based competition.
- In suburban areas, we face the above described dilemma between the level of regulation or competition and investment. More than 50 % of households are passed by gigabit networks. Indeed, optimising regulation in this area could provide an incentive for further investment. It could extend commercial deployment to areas that are now just at the margin, slightly unprofitable for investors.
- But the case is much more desperate in rural areas. Investors struggle with high burdens of cost and demand wide spread in the area. Today 83 % of rural households, the vast majority, are not gigabit-ready. Here we face the true problem on our way to gigabit economy and society that will be ubiquitous, so the vision. An optimisation of regulation to provide a better incentive for investment at the margin will be ineffective. The above described dilemma of regulation and invest-

ment is largely irrelevant at the country side. In rural areas we have to look for solutions beyond regulation. The above cited econometrical work does not and cannot address this problem.

Commercial deployment is difficult in rural areas, as their population density is low. For example, 80 % of the German population is living in one third of Germany, 15 % in the second third and 5 % in the last third of the area (see Figure 4).

Figure 4:   Area and participants per cluster

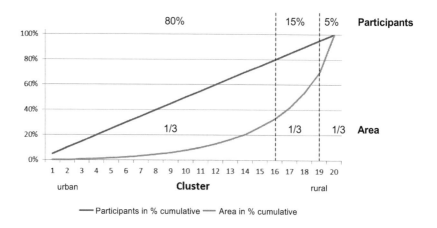

Source: WIK.

In order to reach the last 5 % of the population, an access network covering one third of the area is needed. As shown by the schematic representation of Figure 5, costs are extremely driven by low density. An average revenue per user (ARPU) of €40 per month and a take-up-rate of 40 % of the regional population could make an urban region profitable. The same ARPU requires a penetration near 70 % in suburban areas. In rural areas, a €40 monthly ARPU does not lead to any profitable business case. Only an average revenue per user and month of €70 and the same high penetration rate as in suburban areas can finance the deployment in a rural region. This difference in profitability between urban and rural areas is not marginal. It cannot simply be overcome by a better regulation.

Figure 5: Schematic representation of the cost of broadband deployment per customer depending on the penetration

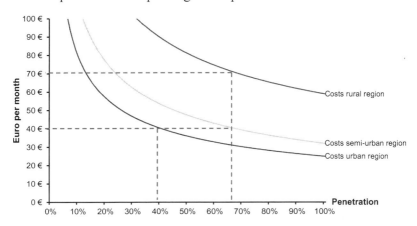

Source: WIK.

Therefore, one should search for other solutions to bridge the investment gap. Commercial deployment might be the first choice. In the case of market failure, we are looking for second-best solutions. Subsidies are paid by taxpayers' money, with all the risks of inefficient investment, crowding out of private initiatives and investors' attentism waiting for even better condition in public financing.

Other argumentations aim at other business models of other investors. Figure 6 gives a schematic example that illustrates the variance in investors' calculations. 0A is the investment a private investor would take. It covers all regions with positive profit and zero profit in the last deployed region. Public investment would increase coverage beyond to 0B by allowing cross-subsidisation of non-profitable regions through profits from profitable regions. If municipalities or other public investors take into consideration positive externalities caused by very high capacity broadband, the deployment of fibre could be even driven further without or with fewer subsidies.

Figure 6: Investment decision for broadband deployment

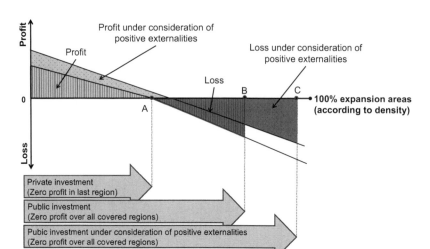

Source: WIK.

Other business models that would increase the footprint of gigabit networks in rural areas are wholesale-only and co-investment models. Wholesale-only business cases focus on the deployment of a structurally separated network that allows open access to each access seeker[10] and thus promotes penetration. Co-investment models allow to share investment costs and risks among investors. A combination of both, wholesale-only model based on a co-investment, would even lead to higher profitability in rural regions.

Although provoking some legal problems, concession models could be another solution. They guarantee investors conditions and obligations for a certain period of time that is longer than the standard regulatory period of 3 years. The duration could be e. g. 15 or 20 years, which is much closer to the expected depreciation period of fibre investment. Concessions could also include an exclusivity or a temporary monopoly for a certain period of time, which is also an incentive to invest. In doing so, they go beyond the questions about regulation discussed in Brussels about what price for

---

10   See Wernick et al. (2017).

the unbundled local loop is investment-friendly or do we need a five- or seven-year's period of regulatory holidays.

If the regulation of fibre optic networks in rural areas plays a minor or no role in creating incentives for further investment, is there a king's road to promote investment in rural areas? As international benchmarks show, the answer is no. Even countries that are well advanced in regard to fibre coverage compared to Germany struggle with deployment in rural areas, e.g. Switzerland and Sweden. In Australia, another example, there is widespread critique of the lack of rural coverage, although the Australian model is based on an ambitious national broadband plan.

Ultimately, commercial conditions (e.g. deployment costs, depreciation rates, time horizon) are key. Challenges as a consequence of economics have to be overcome. Here follows a further starting point for a cost-benefit analysis in practical situations than considerations at the theoretical level suggest. In theory and in empirical studies we discuss the optimal calibration of infrastructure investment versus regulatory intervention. In practical relevant situation we face another choice, the choice between inefficiencies as consequence of (temporary) regional monopoly and inefficiencies by spending tax payers money to subsidise infrastructure. That seems to be the choice between the devil and the deep blue sea.

4. Conclusion

The Internet of things, IoT, is part of Germany's (and Europe's) industrial and societal ambitions. To establish our region as a front runner in the IoT, it requires ubiquitous fibre networks. The IoT thus provokes enormous efforts to invest in broadband networks with very high capacity networks. Whereas we can expect their privately financed deployment in densely populated areas, we see major problems in rural areas.

Regulation might be an investment stimulus, but the fundamental business case cannot be changed in rural areas. Disadvantages in terms of costs and population density cannot be overcome by the regulation/deregulation of players with significant market power. Our considerations have to go one step further: temporary monopolies (e.g. through concession models) could be part of the problem solution, in addition or alternative to subsidies.

To overcome the obstacles on the way to IoT more is needed than just investment in infrastructure. Telcos are facing an additional challenge:

their transformation. They have to find their role in the IoT ecosystem at least as enabler. They have to supply new service classes with high quality standards, i.e. they have to innovate their offers. They have to streamline their processes. Telcos have the chance to define new business models. Since industries are facing a fourth industrial revolution and are on the brink of "Industry 4.0", telecommunications companies cannot step aside. They have to develop their way to "Telecommunication 4.0".

Both challenges are intertwined. VHC networks without the quality for IoT provided by telcos 4.0 will not be economically attractive, as they fail to realise all economies of scale. Telcos 4.0 will only deliver if their networks are upgraded. So if the telecommunications companies fail to deliver in regard to both challenges, investment in gigabit networks and transformation of the sector, IoT in Germany starts with a handicap.

In a nutshell: To make IoT a success, telecommunications companies have to deliver a modern fibre based infrastructure, provide adequate service quality and spur innovation in products and processes.

References

Bertschek, I.; Briglauer W.; Hüschelrath, K.; Krämer, J.; Frübing, S.; Kesler, R.; Saam, M. (2016): Metastudie zum Fachdialog Ordnungsrahmen für die Digitale Wirtschaft (Meta-study on the Dialogue Framework for the Digital Economy), commissioned by the Federal Ministry of Economics and Energy (BMWi), Zentrum für Europäische Wirtschaftsforschung GmbH (ZEW), University of Passau, March 2016, http://ftp.zew.de/pub/zew-docs/gutachten/Metastudie_DigitaleWirtschaft_2016.pdf

Briglauer, W.; Cambini, C. (2017): The Role of Regulation in Incentivizing Investment in New Communications Infrastructure, Study carried out on behalf of Deutsche Telekom AG, http://ftp.zew.de/pub/zew-docs/gutachten/Briglauer Cam-biniDeutscheTelekomApril2017.pdf

Briglauer, W.; Frübing, S.; Vogelsang, I. (2015): The Impact of Alternative Public Policies on the Deployment of New Communications Infratstructure – A Survey, http://ftp.zew.de/pub/zew-docs/dp/dp15003.pdf

Busse, C. (2014): „Deutschland kann weltweit führend werden" (Germany can become a world leader) – Interview with Cisco CEO John Chambers; in: Süddeutsche Zeitung, 01/01/2014

Cisco (2016a): 10th Annual Cisco Visual Networking Index (VNI) Mobile Forecast Projects 70 Percent of Global Population Will Be Mobile Users With 1.5 Connections per Capita by 2020, 02/03/2016, http://investor.cisco.com/investor-relations/news-and-events/news/news-de-tails/2016/10th-Annual-Cisco-Visual-Networking-Index-VNI-Mobile-Forecast-Pro-jects-70-Percent-of-Global-Population-Will-Be-Mobile-Users-With-15-Connec-tions-per-Capita-by-2020/default.aspx

Cisco (2016b): Cisco Virtual Networking Index: Global Mobile Data Traffic Forecast Update, 2015-2020 – White Paper, 02/07/2016, http://www.cisco.com/c/en/us/solutions/collateral/service-provider/visual-networking-index-vni/mobile-white-paper-c11-520862.html

Elixmann, D.; Godlovitch, I.; Henseler-Unger, I.; Schwab, R.; Stumpf, U. (2015): Competition & investment: An analysis of the drivers of investment and consumer welfare in mobile telecommunications, WIK-Consult, Bad Honnef, 3 July 2015, http://www.wik.org/fileadmin/Studien/2015/Competition_and_investment_mobile_telecommunications.pdf

EU Commission (2016): Proposal for a Directive of the European Parliament and of the Council establishing the European Electronic Communications Code (Recast), COM(2016) 590 final/2, Corrigendum of COM(2016) 590 final of 14.09.2016, Brussels, 12.10.2016, https://eur-lex.europa.eu/resource.html?uri=cellar:c5ee8d55-7a56-11e6-b076-01aa75ed71a1.0001.02/DOC_3&format=PDF

Godlovitch, I.; Lemstra, W.; Pennings, C.; Neumann, K.-H.; de Streel, A.; Stronzik, M.; Stumpf, U.; Kroon, P.; Lucidi, S.; Gantumur, T.; Plueckebaum, T.; Baldacchino, V.; Chaillou, V.; van den Peijl, S. (2016): Regulatory, in particular access, regimes for network investment models in Europe, WIK-Consult, Deloitte, IDATE, Studie für die Europäische Kommission, September 2016, http://bookshop.europa.eu/en/regulatory-in-particular-access-regimes-for-network-investment-models-in-europe-pbKK0216677/;pgid=GSPefJMEtXBSR0dT6jbGak ZD0000_d3RmiFd;sid=9do-O04fzX0-PhYN1-ignCw6VxlCa-zciYo=?CatalogCate goryID=CXoKABst5TsAAAEjepEY4e5L

HSBC (2015): Supersonic – European telecoms mergers will boost capex, driving prices lower and speeds higher, April 2015, https://www.orange.com/fr/content/download/33263/1086075/version/2/file/Supers onic+13.04.15.pdf

Neumann, K.-H.; Schmitt, S.; Schwab, R. with contribution of Stronzik, M. (2016): Die Bedeutung von TAL-Preisen für den Aufbau von NGA (The Importance of TAL Awards for the Establishment of NGA), WIK Discussion Paper No. 404, Bad Honnef, March 2016

PwC (2016): Industrie 4.0: Building the Digital Enterprise, Ergebnisse Deutschland (Results Germany), April 2016, https://www.pwc.de/de/digitale-transformation/assets/pwc-praesentation-industrie-4-0-deutsche-ergebnisse.pdf

Roland Berger Strategy Consultants (2015): Die digitale Transformation der Industrie (The digital transformation of the industry), Studie im Auftrag des BDI, 1.3.2015, http://bdi.eu/media/presse/publikationen/information-und-telekommunikation/Digitale_Transformation.pdf

TÜV Rheinland (2017): Bericht zum Breitbandatlas Ende 2016 im Auftrag des Bundesministeriums für Verkehr und digitale Infrastruktur (BMVI), Teil 1: Ergebnisse, Stand Ende 2016 (Report on the Broadband Atlas at the end of 2016 on behalf of the Federal Ministry of Transport and Digital Infrastructure, Part 1: Results, status at the end of 2016),
https://www.bmvi.de/SharedDocs/DE/Anlage/Digitales/bericht-zum-breitbandatlas-ende-2016-ergebnisse.pdf?__blob=publicationFile

Wernick, C.; Queder, F.; Strube Martins, S.; Gries, C.; with contribution of von Holznagel, B. (2017): Ansätze zur Glasfaser-Erschließung unterversorgter Gebiete (Approaches to the development of fiber optic access to underserved areas), WIK-Consult, Bad Honnef, August 2017, http://www.wik.org/index.php?id=907&L=1

Ecosystem Evolution and End-to-End QoS on the Internet: The (Remaining) Role of Interconnections

Volker Stocker[1]

Abstract

Tremendous evolutionary forces have produced a hugely diverse Internet ecosystem. Beyond disruptively shaping economies and societies, innovational activity has not only created a wealth of content and application services; it is also giving rise to unprecedented challenges. For example, the smartification of networks, the advent and increasing importance of the Internet of Things (IoT), and the emergence of Tactile Internet applications create pronounced demands for ultra-reliable and ultra-low latency communications, mobility, (local) big data capabilities, security, and privacy. In this chapter, we focus on performance-related challenges and describe how the different performance profiles can be met based on integrative (cross-layer) approaches that are based on the synergistic use of different mechanisms. We describe coordination problems and emphasize the interplay between QoS mechanisms and topological innovations that enable to modify the location where content is cached, applications are run, data is processed, and where traffic is exchanged strategically. Based on this, implications for the (remaining) role of interconnections are derived.

Keywords: interconnection, IXP, CDN, edge computing, Internet of Things

1   Chair of Network Economics, Competition Economics and Transport Science, Institute of Economics, University of Freiburg, Germany; Weizenbaum Institute for the Networked Society (German Internet Institute), Berlin, Germany; TU Berlin, Germany, vstocker@inet.tu-berlin.de. Volker Stocker gratefully acknowledges the support that he received during his time as a research assistant at the Max-Planck-Institute for Informatics in Saarbrücken, Germany.

171

1.   Introduction[2]

The economic and societal importance of Information and Communication Technologies (ICTs), particularly the Internet, have been continually increasing. The array of content and applications that are delivered via the Internet Protocol (IP) is rapidly evolving and highly diverse. For example, the smartification of networks (e.g., smart grids) and objects/things (e.g., smart TVs or connected cars) and the advent and anticipated importance of the Internet of Things (IoT), but also the emergence of Tactile Internet applications (like remote steering of haptic machines) are expected to benefit and transform economic activity in a disruptive fashion. Besides the tremendous potentials of these technologies, they create a wide range of differentiated demands for network services and traffic delivery. It is crucial to recognize the complexities that emerge with the delivery of a widening range of content and applications via multi- or general-purpose network infrastructures. In addition to growing numbers of connected users and things, the mix of content and applications is dynamically changing. While this implies that the ecosystem is in a 'state of constant flux', unprecedented challenges arise, for example, in terms of network investments and heterogeneous demands for (ultra-reliable and ultra-low latency) traffic delivery, (local) cloud capabilities (i.e., storage and processing), mobility, security, or privacy.

In this chapter, we focus on the evolving and highly differentiated demands for network services. More specifically, we examine how the way content and applications are delivered on the Internet has changed and discuss agile and flexible mechanisms and architectures that enable meeting the evolving and dynamically changing requirements for differentiated end-to-end QoS levels and (local) cloud capabilities. We provide some background on the role of integrative approaches, 'cross-layer' approaches synergistically combining different technologically complementary mechanisms and discuss the (remaining) role of interconnections. The remainder of this chapter is structured as follows. In Section 2, we will briefly describe evolution in the ecosystem. While this provides us with a basic understanding and appreciation of the growing diversity and complexity within the ecosystem, it helps us to describe the evolving demands that pose

---

2   This chapter is partially based on the author's doctoral thesis that will be published as: Stocker, V. (forthcoming). *Innovative Capacity Allocations for All-IP Networks: A Network Economic Analysis of Evolution and Competition in the Internet Ecosystem.* Freiburger Studien zur Netzökonomie, Baden-Baden: Nomos.

unprecedented challenges in terms of traffic delivery. In subsequent Section 3, we introduce and discuss different technologically complementary mechanisms that are available and can be used separately or in a synergistic fashion to address emerging challenges. In our discussion, we place a specific focus on explicating the role of innovative approaches enabling the strategic modification of the location where content is stored, applications are run, (big) data are processed, and traffic is exchanged. Against this background, and taking into account current trends in the Internet ecosystem, we examine the (remaining) role interconnections play on the Internet. Section 4 provides (tentative) conclusions and an outlook.

2. *Ecosystem Evolution: Growing Diversity and Evolving Complexity*

Since its commercialization in the mid-1990s, the Internet has evolved into a global platform for communications. It is facilitating the delivery of an evolving range of content and applications and has become a substantial driver of digital transformation processes that are fundamentally changing traditional business models, industry and market structures, and is also shaping how economic activity is organized. While the transition from a narrowband to a broadband Internet is closely linked to these transformation processes, it is instructive to take a look at the Internet's layered architecture and its modular structure provide in order to gain insights into the diverse evolution processes that have produced and shaped an increasingly complex ecosystem (e.g., Yoo, 2013; 2016). Innovational activity within the ecosystem can take place simultaneously at different layers. It is important to recognize that innovations can take place independently and separately. Still, (complementary or coupled) innovations might also interactively shape the ecosystem's evolution path. A formative force in shaping ecosystem evolution, broadband is widely recognized as an essential enabler of ICTs as General-Purpose Technologies (GPTs) (e.g., OECD, 2008; Bresnahan and Trajtenberg, 1995; Bresnahan, 2010; Briglauer et al., 2018). It provides the infrastructural basis for the delivery of an evolving range of content and applications and facilitates vertical (bidirectional) complementarities and associated innovation spillovers (e.g., Bauer and Knieps, 2018; see also the chapter by Johannes Bauer in this volume).

The integrated provision of a dynamically changing mix of content and applications with heterogeneous delivery requirements over the same physical (general-purpose) infrastructures gives rise to a series of challenges. In the absence of multiple parallel physical infrastructures that are designed for the delivery of a specific use case or a fixed set of applications, a variety of rivalry scenarios becomes relevant. The economically efficient sharing of network capacities between a range of applications with heterogeneous requirement profiles (e.g., regarding required data rates [upstream and downstream], tolerable levels of packet delays, jitter, or packet loss rates) gives rise to complex allocation problems. Heterogeneous requirement profiles, especially regarding the quality of end-to-end traffic delivery (i.e., Quality of Service, QoS), are not new. QoS-tolerant applications like e-mail or highly QoS-sensitive applications like Voice over IP (VoIP) have been around for more than two decades. What is new, however, is the anticipated essentiality of innovations that are expected to transform economic activity and merge the physical and virtual worlds. For example, innovations associated with the smartification of networks and objects/things, the projected success of 5G and the anticipated importance of the IoT,[3] the Tactile Internet, or virtual reality widen the range of applications and are often critically dependent on customized and reliable network services. Customized network services are considered essential enablers of new and innovative applications and associated business models. The digital transformation thus critically hinges on scalable and flexible network services that are capable of meeting the heterogeneous demands for end-to-end QoS and (local) storage and (big) data processing gain importance (e.g., Cisco, 2017b; Ofcom, 2018; DotEcon and Axon, 2018, pp. 105 ff.).[4] In this context, the synergistic and orchestrated use of multiple different and technologically complementary mechanisms gains importance.

Considering the evolving demands for network services, how has the Internet ecosystem evolved so far? Regardless of the considerable evolution and investments made in network infrastructures (see Section 3.1), the basic service model of the Internet has remained widely unchanged. While traffic service providers deliver data packets according to their 'best efforts', the

---

3   For example, Cisco (2017b) estimates that by 2021, more than 25 billion devices will be part of the global IP ecosystem – the majority of which (i.e., 51%) being used for Machine-to-Machine (M2M) communications.[3] While the share of PCs and non-smartphones is expected to decrease from 8% and 19% to 5% and 6% respectively (Cisco, 2017b, p. 6), the share of global IP traffic that originates from different devices presents a different picture. Smartphone traffic (33%) and TV traffic (30%) are expected to dominate global IP traffic by 2021. In contrast, M2M traffic is expected to contribute only 5% of global IP traffic (Cisco, 2017b, p. 7).

4   As is described in the chapter by Iris Henseler-Unger in this volume (especially in Table 1), requirements for upstream and downstream data rates, but also packet loss rates and latency vary significantly across different content and applications. See also Kurose and Ross (2013, Figure 2.4 at p. 93).

absence of network-based traffic differentiations implies that traffic services are not optimized or customized for the delivery of specific applications and do not provide specific performance guarantees. The growing mismatch between the capabilities of the Internet's basic service model and the evolving demands for differentiated traffic delivery has arguably contributed to the emergence of different complementary innovations we will describe in Sections 3.2 and 3.4. A common denominator of these innovations is that they can improve end-to-end QoS levels and (partially) address differentiated demands for traffic delivery while not requiring changes of the basic Internet service model. While this allows for the rapid deployment of innovations 'on top' of the basic Internet, the reliance on non-differentiated upstream traffic services implies a limitation on the customizability of service provision and the extent to which end-to-end QoS levels can be improved (e.g., Knieps and Stocker, 2016; Stocker et al., 2017). However, integrative approaches based on (vertical) collaborations and integration can be used to leverage and exploit the potentials between different technologically complementary upstream and downstream mechanisms.

Even in today's best effort-based Internet, a set of topological innovations have altered the way the Internet is interconnected and fundamentally changed the way content and applications are delivered. These innovations enable to modify the location where content is cached, applications are run, data is processed, and where traffic is exchanged strategically. The rise and growing importance of Content Delivery Networks (CDNs) and other (distributed) cloud computing approaches, but also innovations in the interconnection space have challenged conventional interconnection models and disrupted delivery chains (e.g., Stocker et al., 2017; Nygren et al., 2010). As we will describe in more detail in Section 3.4 below, remote peering allows providers to decouple the physical location of their network equipment from the geographical location where they exchange traffic (and thus interconnect) with other networks. Thus, a network's footprint no longer constrains the geographical locations where it can interconnect (e.g., Castro et al., 2014).

Similarly, Internet eXchange Points (IXPs) become increasingly important. They provide switching facilities acting as 'hubs' at which large numbers of networks can meet, physically interconnect, and exchange traffic (e.g., Chatzis et al., 2013; Giotsas et al., 2015). In recent years, IXPs have increased in numbers and become more geographically dispersed; large IXPs have even begun to build grids by connecting multiple geographically dispersed switching facilities via private Wide Area Networks (WANs). Thus, the location where traffic is exchanged can be decoupled from the geographical location where networks connect to the IXP grid (e.g., Reed et al., 2014; Nomikos et al., 2018). While related innovations are ongoing, they have caused a more densely interconnected and 'flattened' Internet. They disrupted traditional hierarchies and challenged conventional revenue-sharing approaches (e.g., Dhamdere and Dovrolis, 2010; Woodcock and Frigino, 2016; Bender et al., 2017; Stocker, 2015).

The innovations described so far have also changed industry structures. Beyond market entry by new players, other market players have tapped and ventured into new, typically complementary, markets based on various (horizontal and vertical) collaboration and integration strategies. Not only are legacy telco and cable ISPs venturing into content markets,[5] large content, cloud, or CDN providers are expanding the capacities and/or footprints of their clouds and also build their (proprietary) private backbone networks (e.g., Huston, 2017).[6] ISPs are collaborating with CDNs (e.g., Deutsche Telekom and Akamai) (Frank et al., 2013) and softwarize their networks (e.g., Telecom Italia or AT&T) (Stocker et al., 2017). Some large content, cloud, or CDN providers like Google, Facebook, or Netflix have grown into 'hypergiants', typically offering global services (at least partially) via their cloud infrastructures (e.g., Labovitz et al., 2010). Needless to mention, such developments have a profound effect on the ecosystem. Not only do they change network topologies and how content and applications are delivered; they have also contributed to changes in industry structures and disrupt the 'order' within the Internet ecosystem.

As a consequence, 'conventional wisdom' about traditional hierarchies and bargaining positions between market players, but also how revenues are shared on the Internet, are challenged fundamentally. From this arises a growing need to reassess the definition of relevant markets, competition, and the design of adequate Internet policies and regulations. In the following, however, we will focus on performance aspects related to the growing diversity and evolving complexity in the Internet ecosystem. More specifically, we examine mechanisms that can be used to meet the complex demands for QoS-differentiated packet delivery and local cloud capabilities and derive implications for the (remaining) role of interconnections.

---

5   Examples are the mergers of Comcast and NBC (Arango and Stelter, 2011) or AT&T and Time Warner (Gold, 2019).

6   For example, OTT provider Netflix operates its own (special-purpose) CDN to deliver content to their customers (Böttger et al., 2018; Netflix, 2018). CDN providers Akamai and Limelight Networks operate private backbone infrastructures to connect their distributed servers (Kaufmann, 2018; Limelight Networks, 2018). Similarly, Google operates its private network to connect its servers (Google, n.d.).

3.   *Meeting the Evolving Demands for Network Services*

In order to meet the differentiated requirements for network services by an evolving set of content and applications, a range of technologically complementary mechanisms is available. The relevant types of mechanisms are located in different (vertically complementary) layers and are illustrated in Figure 1. We distinguish between (i) network investments (see Section 3.1); (ii) network-based traffic management and traffic engineering (see Section 3.3); (iii) overlay-based traffic management and topological innovations (see Section 3.4); and (iv) (other) upper layer innovations (see Section 3.2). Before going into the details of the respective types of mechanisms, it must be recognized that both decision competencies and thus 'QoS control' might be dispersed among several different (and often competing) market players. As a consequence, end-to-end delivery chains, as well as associated value chains, are often complex (e.g., Stocker et al., 2017; Stocker and Whalley, 2018). For example, the provision of content or applications (or CDN services) typically relies on best effort-based traffic services as upstream inputs. In this case, ISPs (or traffic service providers) and content or CDN providers are involved in the provision of the service.[7] In Figure 1, the two bottom layers are typically controlled by an ISP, while other market players control the two upper layers. Exploiting synergies through the orchestrated use of complementary mechanisms is often contingent on the efficient coordination and cooperation between multiple market players. It can thus be assumed that much of the complexity associated with integrative (cross-layer) approaches are related to tussles between different market players. Issues may arise in the context of vertical coordination to orchestrate different instruments and horizontal coordination in the context of interconnections.

---

7   For example, decisions on network investments and capacity allocations based on active traffic management are typically made by traffic service providers (or ISPs). In contrast, overlay-based traffic management and various endpoint-based application layer innovations are located in downstream layers and are typically beyond the decision competence of the ISP. Instead, they are in the competence of other entities like content providers, OTT providers or CDN providers.

Figure 1: Mechanisms to Improve Traffic Delivery Performance: A Layered Perspective

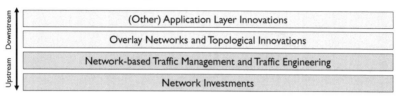

Source: Own representation

3.1 Expanding Network Capacities: The Role of Network Investments

We start by considering network investments. Expanding network capacities presents a fundamental and intuitive approach to lower network utilization and to increase end-to-end QoS levels. Network infrastructures are essential for ensuring (seamless) connectivity and provide the infrastructural basis for electronic communications between different endpoints. While one can distinguish between different types of network capacities like access, backhaul and backbone capacities, (broadband) access infrastructures have played a critical role in shaping ecosystem evolution. Network investments are necessary to ensure that networks are dimensioned in a way that available capacities enable high data rates (upstream and downstream) and high QoS levels. In local access loops, fiber optic elements increasingly replace metallic elements; thus, fiber reach is increasingly expanded towards end users. Perhaps less obvious, fiber is also becoming a common denominator — or 'unifying element' as it were — across different fixed and wireless access technologies. Fiberization and fiber densification processes not only yield substantial improvements in the service capabilities of many fixed (i.e., wireline) and mobile/wireless broadband access technologies; they also give rise to potentials for infrastructure sharing of fiber-based backhaul infrastructure components. For example, 5G deployments will in many cases be based on fiber-fed small cells (or 'microcells') and is expected to facilitate high capacity and low-latency mobile connectivity (e.g., Ofcom, 2018, pp. 23ff.; Adtran, 2018; Briglauer et al., 2018; Stocker and Whalley, 2017).

Several lessons can be learned from this. Most notably, perhaps, the insight that there is more to broadband than their maximum data rates. While the essentiality of network investments in general, and broadband access in particular, is beyond discussion, some caveats are attached. Network investments are necessary but not sufficient for ensuring high and stable levels of end-to-end QoS. Orchestrated investment and expansion efforts are required to prevent the creation of high-capacity network islands. Local and non-aligned investments in network infrastructures may not eliminate performance bottlenecks, but shift them to somewhere else in the network (e.g., Bauer et al., 2015; Stocker and Whalley, 2018). It is perhaps less obvious that the abundance of network capacities cannot eliminate all QoS-related problems. That is also why it does not constitute a perfect substitute for network-based traffic management. For example, jitter-related problems might occur and impair the performance of applications like VoIP or video conferencing even when network utilization levels are rather low (Ou, 2008, pp. 27ff.). Besides, achieving an abundance of network capacities requires excessive investments in infrastructure capacities (so-called 'over-provisioning'). These are economically inefficient and imply a wasteful use of resources (e.g., Berger-Kögler and Kruse, 2011, pp. 7f.; Knieps and Stocker, 2016; Ou, 2008, pp. 33 and 39). Additionally, even assuming very lightly loaded networks, best case end-to-end QoS levels vary across different access technologies. This is due to a host of factors. For example, access networks differ in terms of topology and configuration and imply different capacity sharing paradigms. Moreover, different transmission media vary in propagation speeds and how 'lossy' they are. This implies that while different broadband access technologies deliver comparable (maximum) data rates, they may differ across a number of other dimensions such as the symmetry of data rates, loss characteristics, or the performance in periods of peak demands (e.g., Stocker and Whalley, 2017; 2018; Peterson and Davie, 2012, pp. 504 and 513).

3.2   Endpoint-based Upper Layer Mechanisms

Endpoint-based upper layer mechanisms provide additional means to improve end-to-end QoS levels and to introduce traffic differentiations 'on top' of basic upstream traffic services. Generally speaking, endpoints can determine what, when, and how much traffic they inject into the network. While not requiring changes to the basic service model of the Internet, endpoints have a direct impact on network utilization and congestion. They can improve end-to-end QoS levels and enable some forms of traffic differentiations. The range of relevant mechanisms is wide, and so we only present a non-exhaustive overview to describe some of the major approaches commonly used in today's Internet. Innovations in transport layer protocols help to improve traditional flow or congestion control mechanisms. Additionally, compression and coding techniques can be used to significantly reduce data volumes, for example, of video or audio content (e.g., Kurose and Ross, 2013, pp. 587ff.).[8] Compression is typically performed at sending endpoints so that the actual amount of data traffic that needs to be transmitted between sender and receiver is reduced. As a result, utilization levels can be reduced, and end-to-end QoS levels can be increased. For example, the delivery of OTT services like YouTube or Netflix often use compression techniques and coding standards in the course of sophisticated mechanisms that facilitate rate adaptations in a congestion- or device-aware fashion. Endpoints can dynamically adapt sending rates on the basis of 'down-coding' or 'coding optimizations' to reduce video or audio resolutions to reflect either current network conditions or specific device characteristics (typically display resolutions) (e.g., Kua et al., 2017; Begen and Timmerer, 2017; Seufert et al., 2015). Two things are important to recognize here. First, endpoint-based rate adaptations can reflect current network states and improve QoS. Since this might require reductions in the 'quality' of the content that is delivered, the end-user experience might be impaired (e.g., Stocker and Whalley, 2018). Second, endpoint-based upper layer mechanisms impact on network utilization and thus shape the capacity allocation problems ISPs are confronted with (e.g., Seufert et al., 2015, pp. 484f.).

3.3 Enhancing Network Logistics: Active Traffic Management and QoS Differentiated Traffic Services

With the arrival of 5G, the IoT and the Tactile Internet, the array of content and application services that are delivered in an integrated fashion over shared physical traffic capacities is widening. Traffic that is highly QoS-sensitive (e.g., belonging to Tactile Internet applications) is delivered alongside traffic that is comparatively QoS-tolerant (e.g., email, or bulk data downloads). Since traffic compositions and thus QoS requirement profiles are dynamically changing and structurally evolving, diverse rivalry scenarios occur. This implies an obvious need for network management that is capable of flexibly adapting to the dynamically changing demands for network services. Generally, traffic engineering (i.e., based on routing differentiations) and active traffic management (based on the differentiated treatment of traffic at nodes along the path between sender and receiver)

---

8   A comprehensive overview of corresponding compression techniques and coding standards is provided in ZetaCast (2012, pp. 15ff.).

enable providers of traffic services (i.e., ISPs) to steer traffic, optimize network utilization, mitigate the adverse effects of network congestion, and improve cost-efficiency (e.g., Claffy and Clark, 2016; Knieps and Stocker, 2016).

Since QoS differentiation strategies that are capable of flexibly adapting to changing demands are becoming increasingly essential when considering anticipated demand structures and QoS requirement profiles as described above, enhanced network logistics based on flexible and versatile traffic architectures gain importance. The migration towards such logistics, however, implies a deviation from the basic Internet service model in which traffic service providers deliver data packets without guarantees and in a non-differentiated fashion according to their 'best efforts'. Traffic differentiations and the provision of performance guarantees imply innovations within the network. On the basis of active traffic management (e.g., based on packet prioritization or resource reservation and admission control), traffic service providers can implement innovative capacity allocations and provide differentiated traffic services that can be customized in terms of the QoS levels as well as the performance guarantees (i.e., stochastic or deterministic) they deliver. Active traffic management strategies are thus an essential component for solving capacity allocation problems that are characterized by heterogeneous and complex QoS requirements in an economically efficient fashion.[9] Another integral component is an adequate pricing

---

9   Knieps (2015) presents the Generalized DiffServ architecture, a flexible and versatile meta-architecture that facilitates a variety of active traffic management strategies based on several building blocks that are standardized by the Internet Engineering Task Force (IETF). Based on these building blocks, traffic differentiations and routing differentiations can be introduced by traffic service providers (or ISPs). Corresponding traffic architectures (e.g., the Integrated Services [IntServ] architecture combined with the Resource reSerVation Protocol [RSVP] or the Differentiated Services [DiffServ] architecture) facilitate a range of QoS differentiations based on prioritization or resource reservation (plus admission control) mechanisms. Elements of these architectures can further be combined with Multiprotocol Label Switching (MPLS). Thus, traffic differentiations and routing differentiations enable sophisticated traffic engineering (TE) capabilities (e.g., based on DiffServ-aware MPLS TE [DS-TE]). In the same context, the synergistic use of network softwarization and virtualization enables fine-grained and dynamic control over network resources and functions and facilitate the flexible and orchestrated provision of differentiated (application-specific) network services. Overviews are provided by Feamster et al. (2014), Kreutz et al. (2015), or Mijumbi et al. (2016). See also the analysis of virtual networks by Knieps (2017). In a similar context, related to 5G, Software Defined Networking (SDN) and Network Function Virtualization (NFV) constitute

scheme. In Knieps and Stocker (2016), we outlined a framework for the introduction of incentive compatible and non-discriminatory price and QoS differentiations that yield economically efficient and thus optimal capacity allocations for all-IP networks on the basis of entrepreneurial search processes (see also the chapter by Günter Knieps in this volume).

While we showed how (competitive) traffic service providers efficiently reflect the dynamic allocation problems that arise in all-IP networks, we did not focus on QoS differentiated interconnections between different traffic service providers. Extending the perspective to a scenario of multiple service providers adds significant complexities to the efficient solution of related allocation problems. While QoS control by a single entity is restricted to the boundaries of its own network, the Internet's very nature as a network of networks implies that QoS control is dispersed among a large number of entities. As a result, inter-provider traffic and the provision of inter-provider QoS gives rise to complex coordination problems in terms of service and business coordination. Not only may different providers be faced with different demand structures and thus pursue different QoS differentiation strategies, but problems might also arise when it comes to inter-provider compensations (e.g., Briscoe and Rudkin, 2005; Knieps, 2009; 2015; Stocker, 2015). In the following section, we want to turn our attention to approaches that can remedy or at least mitigate such coordination problems and further enable to improve end-to-end QoS levels by strategically modifying the geographical or virtual distance data packets need to travel between endpoints.

3.4 The Rise of IXPs and Clouds: Balancing Traffic Loads, Shortening Delivery Chains, and Defying the Laws of Physics

Other mechanisms can improve end-to-end QoS by enhancing the basic Internet's capabilities employing overlay functionality 'on top' of the basic Internet (e.g., Clark et al., 2006). Characteristic of these types of innovations is that they do not require changes or modifications of the basic service model of the Internet. While the basic Internet service model is increasingly unfit for meeting the differentiated delivery requirements of a widening range of content and applications, a set of innovations regarding network topologies can improve end-to-end QoS levels and at least partially address the demands for differentiated packet delivery (e.g., Nygren et al., 2010; Stocker et al., 2017). As we briefly described above, the impact of IXPs and

---

integral components of softwarized networks that enable network slicing (e.g., Nokia, 2016; Ofcom, 2018).

(local) clouds (e.g., those related to CDNs or edge computing approaches) changes the way content and applications are delivered on the Internet. Here, we want to describe how this affects the role of interconnections in delivering specific levels of end-to-end QoS.

In today's Internet, large shares of global IP traffic are delivered via CDNs (Cisco, 2017a; ARCEP, 2017; BEREC, 2017; Frank et al., 2013; Gerber and Doverspike, 2011). Broadly speaking, CDN providers operate networks of CDN servers that are strategically distributed across the Internet. Original content is typically copied and cached at multiple servers. Since the same content can thus be retrieved from different geographically dispersed servers, CDNs employ intelligent redirection mechanisms for matching incoming user requests for content with the 'closest' CDN server. In this way, content delivery performance can be optimized, and load balancing can be achieved (e.g., Dilley et al., 2002; Leighton, 2009; Nygren et al., 2010). The CDN ecosystem is continuously evolving and has produced a wide range of CDN approaches. The latter, in turn, reflect the business model CDN providers pursue, the scope of services they offer, and the subsequent performance requirements of the services that are to be delivered (for example, the delivery of highly cacheable and latency-tolerant software updates versus dynamic and interactive web applications). CDN providers may choose server deployment strategies that may vary across many dimensions. For example, (i) in the number of servers; (ii) their footprint (i.e., where they are deployed); (iii) whether they are clustered in large data centers or more distributed; (iv) whether the servers are connected via private networks or the public Internet, etc. Similar holds for decisions on where and for how long content is cached, etc. A fundamental difference can be observed in the service variety that is offered. Multi- or even general-purpose CDN (e.g., Akamai) approaches vary significantly from single-purpose CDN deployments (e.g., Netflix Open Connect platform) that are purpose-built for the delivery of a specific service. A comprehensive overview of the evolution of the CDN ecosystem and a typology of the different CDN strategies is provided in Stocker et al. (2017). Closely related is the edge computing paradigm which can be considered as a generalization of CDNs (Satyanarayanan, 2017). In addition to centralized cloud approaches, the geographically dispersed distribution of small-scale clouds facilitates to locally store and process (big) data in such a way that the growing demands for mobility, local storage/big data capabilities, and high and stable levels of end-to-end QoS can be met in a scalable fashion. While an overview of relevant approaches is provided by Ai et al. (2018), relocating cloud capabilities can be used to reduce the geographical and virtual distance data packets must travel, similar as in the case of CDNs.

Further innovations have been made in the field of interconnections (e.g., BITAG, 2014; Faratin et al., 2008). On the one hand, IXPs have become increasingly popular as communication hubs facilitating local and multilateral interconnections close to end users (e.g., Chatzis et al., 2013; Giotsas et al., 2015; Woodcock and Frigino, 2016; BEREC, 2017). On the other hand, remote peering approaches enable providers to interconnect with other providers at distant interconnection points directly — they facilitate to decouple the geographical location of a provider and the location of where it directly exchanges traffic with other networks. For example, providers might remotely access to a geographically distant IXP via direct connections — a physical presence at the IXP is no longer needed (e.g., Castro et al., 2014; Stocker et al., 2017). Similarly, IXP providers might operate and connect multiple interconnection facilities via private WANs. Gaining access to such an 'IXP grid' thus facilitates direct interconnections with all other networks connected to the same grid at all — even geographically distant locations — interconnection points of the grid (e.g., Reed et al., 2014; Nomikos et al., 2018). The growing possibilities to strategically modify the geographical and virtual locations at which servers are positioned, content and applications are cached, data is processed, and traffic is exchanged yield many benefits.

Distance in this respect can be considered to have two specific meanings. First, the *geographical distance*, i.e., the number of miles a data packets must travel through networks between sender and receiver. With increasing distance, throughput rates tend to decrease dramatically (e.g., Leighton, 2009, p. 47). While this might be associated with inefficiencies of Internet's most important transport layer protocol (i.e., the Transmission Control Protocol, TCP), the laws of physics critically determine the propagation speeds of signals (Smith, 2009). Thus, propagation delays (regardless of the transmission medium considered) can be reduced by reducing the distance data packets must travel. The relation between geographical distance and propagation delays is depicted in Figure 2 (see below). However, why is this so important? It clearly shows (i) how the laws of physics limit the problem-solving abilities of network-based active traffic management and traffic differentiations, (ii) how moving the endpoints closer together can be used as strategic means to defy the laws of physics and to improve end-to-end QoS levels, and (iii) that network-based active traffic management and topological innovations constitute (technologically) complementary mechanisms.

Figure 2:   How Far Can a Signal Travel in 1 ms (Round-Trip)?

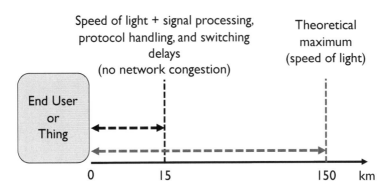

Source: Own representation based on numbers by Fettweis, 2014, p. 70
           and ITU-T, 2014, p. 16

Second, the *virtual distance*, i.e., the number of administrative hops (or in-terconnection points) a data packet must traverse between sender and re-ceiver. While a more comprehensive discussion is provided, for example in Stocker et al. (2017), this is important as it describes how many market players are involved in the traffic delivery process. It can be assumed that a reduction in the number of involved market players reduces bargaining complexity and improves QoS control. In the extreme case, content and ap-plications are hosted within the boundaries of the same network to which requesting customers are connected. Then, traffic delivery would constitute intra-provider communications — interconnections would not affect end-to-end QoS levels and performance bottlenecks at interconnection points can be avoided.

Figure 3:   The Role of Virtual Distance: A Schematic Illustration of Different CDN Approaches

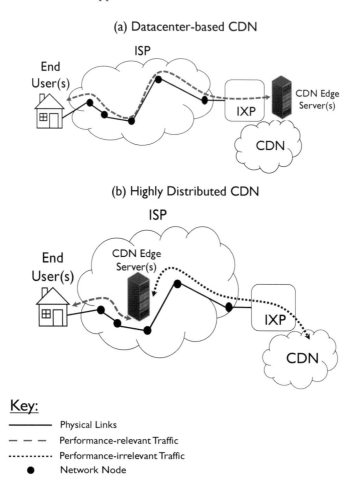

(a) Datacenter-based CDN

(b) Highly Distributed CDN

Key:
—————— Physical Links
— — — Performance-relevant Traffic
············ Performance-irrelevant Traffic
● Network Node

Source: Own representation

Figure 3 provides a schematic illustration of two different CDN approaches. In (a), we consider a datacenter-based CDN approach in which server farms are positioned at major hubs like an IXP. The delivery of content to end users involves that data packets traverse an interconnection point. Interconnections are thus considered performance-relevant. In (b), interconnections are used to deliver content to front-end CDN cache servers that are placed within ISP networks and are assigned an IP address that is administered by the ISP. Importantly, this CDN approach implies that interconnections are effectively decoupled from the delivery of content to end users. One can thus infer that the ISP gains end-to-end QoS control. Interconnections, in turn, have no impact on end-to-end QoS and are thus not performance-relevant.

4. (Tentative) Conclusions and Outlook

In this chapter, we described different mechanisms that, to some extent, act as substitutes in the provision of a specific range of non-deterministic end-to-end QoS levels and can also provide specific forms of traffic differentiations. We explained how, even in a best effort-dominated Internet ecosystem, end-to-end QoS levels can be improved, and differentiated demands for traffic delivery can be addressed through mechanisms that are technologically complementary to the traffic services provided by ISPs. The best effort service model of the Internet and its limited ability to accommodate the differentiated and evolving demands for traffic delivery have arguably spurred network investments but also the emergence of technologically complementary mechanisms that provide bypass solutions to mitigate the negative effects on non-differentiated best effort traffic services. However, as more recent developments in the ecosystem have shown, meeting more stringent delivery requirements, especially regarding deterministic performance guarantees, requires the synergistic use of (technologically) complementary mechanisms. QoS differentiated traffic services based on active traffic management become increasingly essential to meet the emerging demands for ultra-reliable and ultra-low latency communications and to ensure required performance guarantees. The benefits of the synergistic use of multiple mechanism has been recognized, for example, in the context of the 5G vision where network slicing approaches imply that ultra-reliable and ultra-low latency communications rely on QoS differentiated traffic services combined with local cloud capabilities (i.e., a mobile edge cloud) (e.g., DotEcon and Axon, 2018; Ofcom, 2018).[10]

---

10 See in this context also the discussion provided in the chapter by Günter Knieps in this volume.

Topological innovations enhance interconnection diversity and help to mitigate or even eliminate coordination problems between different and often competing market players. Reductions in the geographical and virtual distance data packets need to travel between sender end receiver are based on moving endpoints closer together. Improved QoS levels and enhanced QoS control can thus be achieved. Use cases of 5G that are related to the IoT emphasize requirements for ultra-reliable communications at ultra-low latencies and underscore the importance of integrative strategies based on enhanced logistics as well as the coordination and orchestration between complementary mechanisms. From a technological perspective, it needs to be recognized that the extent to which complementarities can be exploited crucially depends on the specific service under consideration. Trends towards a 'cloudification' imply that cloud infrastructures expand so that content, applications, and other cloud capabilities are be moved closer to end users and things (e.g., Huston, 2017; Pujol et al., 2014; Trevisan et al., 2018; Chiu et al., 2015). So, what can be learned from this for the (remaining) role of interconnections? Moving pairs of sources and destinations geographically and virtually closer together has a strong impact on the role of interconnections. Not only become traffic flows more regional and the ecosystem more fragmented, but changes in network topologies and the way content and applications are delivered challenge the conventional wisdom about hierarchies, bargaining power, and revenue-sharing on the Internet. As the order within the Internet ecosystem is changing, what can be described as the 'mental model' of the Internet ecosystem that has long served as a basis for analyses and policy-making is no longer valid. The role of interconnections has changed accordingly and requires reassessment.

References

Adtran (2018). *5G and Next Generation FTTH: A Symbiotic Relationship.* White Paper, available: https://www.telecompetitor.com/clients/adtran/5G_nextgen/5GandNext GenFTTH.pdf [accessed 20 November 2018].

Ai, Y., Peng, M. and Zhang, K. (2018). Edge Computing Technologies for Internet of Things: A Primer. *Digital Communications and Networks*, 4(2), 77-86.

Arango, T. and Stelter, B. (2011). Comcast Receives Approval for NBC Universal Merger. The New York Times, 19 January, available: https://www.nytimes.com/2011/01/19/business/media/19comcast.html [accessed 20 November 2018].

ARCEP (2017). L'état de l'internet en France. 30 May, available:

https://www.arcep.fr/uploads/tx_gspublication/rapport-etat-internet-france-2017-mai2017.pdf [accessed 20 November 2018].

Bauer, J.M. and Knieps, G. (2018). Complementary Innovation and Network Neutrality. *Telecommunications Policy* 42(2), 172-183.

Bauer, S., Lehr, W.H. and Hung, S. (2015). Gigabit Broadband, Interconnection Propositions, and the Challenge of Managing Expectations. Paper presented at the *43rd Research Conference on Communication, Information and Internet Policy (TPRC)*, 25-27 September, Arlington, VA, available: http://dx.doi.org/10.2139/ssrn.2586805 [accessed 20 November 2018].

Begen, A.C. and Timmerer, C. (2017). Adaptive Streaming of Traditional and Omnidirectional Media. *ACM SIGCOMM Tutorial*, 21-25 August, Los Angeles, CA.

Bender, B., Surdock, S. and Dhamdhere, A. (2017). The Internet is Flat: Revisited — A Small Transit Provider Case Study. Presentation at *NANOG 70*, 5-7 June, Bellevue, WA, available: https://www.nanog.org/sites/default/files/2_Bender_The_Internet_Is_Flat.pdf [accessed 20 November 2018].

BEREC (2017). BEREC Report on IP-Interconnection practices in the Context of Net Neutrality. BoR 17 (111), 1 June, Brussels, Belgium.

Berger-Kögler, U. and Kruse, J. (2011). Net Neutrality Regulation of the Internet?. *International Journal of Management and Network Economics*, 2(1), 3-23.

BITAG (2014). *Interconnection and Traffic Exchange on the Internet*. A Broadband Internet Technical Advisory Group Technical Working Group Report, A Uniform Agreement Report, November.

Böttger, T., Cuadrado, F., Tyson, G., Castro, I., and Uhlig, S. (2018). Open connect everywhere: A glimpse at the internet ecosystem through the lense of the Netflix CDN. *ACM SIGCOMM Computer Communication Review*, 48(1), 28-34.

Bresnahan, T. (2010). General Purpose Technologies. in: Hall, B.H. and Rosenberg, N. (eds.), *Handbook of the Economics of Innovation: Volume 2*, Amsterdam et al.: North-Holland, 761-791.

Bresnahan, T. and Trajtenberg, M. (1995). General Purpose Technologies 'Engines of growth'?. *Journal of Econometrics*, 65 (1), 83-108.

Briglauer, W., Stocker, V. and Whalley, J. (2018). Public Policy Targets in EU Broadband Markets: The Role of Technological Neutrality. Paper presented at the *29th European Regional Conference of the International Telecommunications Society (ITS)*, 1-4 August, Trento, Italy, available: http://hdl.handle.net/10419/184936 [accessed 20 November 2018].

Briscoe, B. and Rudkin, S. (2005). Commercial Models for IP Quality of Service Interconnect. *BT Technology Journal*, 23(2), 171-195.

Castro, I., Cardona, J.C., Gorinsky, S. and Francois, P. (2014). Remote Peering: More Peering without Internet Flattening. *Proceedings of the 10th ACM International on Conference on Emerging Networking Experiments and Technologies (CoNEXT '14)*, 2-5 December, Sydney, Australia, 185-198, available: https://doi.org/10.1145/2674005.2675013 [accessed 20 November 2018].

Chatzis, N., Smaragdakis, G., Feldmann, A. and Willinger, W. (2013). There is More to IXPs Than Meets the Eye. *ACM SIGCOMM Computer Communication Review*, 43(5), 19-28.

Chiu, Y.-C., Schlinker, B., Radhakrishnan, A.B., Katz-Bassett, E. and Govindan R. (2015). Are We One Hop Away from a Better Internet?. *Proceedings of the 2015 Internet Measurement Conference (IMC '15)*. 28-30 October, Tokyo, Japan, 523-529 available: https://doi.org/10.1145/2815675.2815719 [accessed 20 November 2018].

Cisco (2017a). Cisco Visual Networking Index: Forecast and Methodology: 2016–2021. 6 June.

Cisco (2017b). The Zettabyte Era: Trends and Analysis. 7 June.

Claffy, kc and Clark, D.D. (2016). Adding Enhanced Services to the Internet: Lessons from History. *Journal of Information Policy*, 6, 206-251.

Clark, D.D., Lehr, B., Bauer, S., Faratin, P., Sami, R. and Wroclawski, J. (2006). Overlay Networks and the Future of the Internet. *Communications & Strategies*, 63(3), 109-129.

Dhamdhere, A. and Dovrolis, C. (2010). The Internet is Flat: Modeling the Transition from a Transit Hierarchy to a Peering Mesh. *Proceedings of the 6th International Conference on emerging Networking EXperiments and Technologies (ACM CoNEXT 2010)*, 30 November-3 December, Philadelphia, PA, Article No 21, available: http://dx.doi.org/10.1145/1921168.1921196 [accessed 20 November 2018].

Dilley, J., Maggs, B.M., Parikh, J., Prokop, H., Sitaraman, R. and Weihl, B. (2002). Globally Distributed Content Delivery. *IEEE Internet Computing*, 6(5), 50-58.

DotEcon and Axon (2018). *Study on Implications of 5G Deployment on Future Business Models*. A Report by DotEcon Ltd and Axon Partners Group, No BE-REC/2017/02/NP3, BoR (18) 23, 14 March.

Faratin, P., Clark, D., Bauer, S., Lehr, W., Gilmore, P. and Berger, A. (2008). The Growing Complexity of Internet Interconnection. *Communications & Strategies*, 72(4), 51-71.

Feamster, N., Rexford, J. and Zegura, E. (2014). The Road to SDN: An Intellectual History of Programmable Networks. *ACM SIGCOMM Computer Communication Review*, 44(2), 87-98.

Fettweis, G.P. (2014). The Tactile Internet: Application and Challenges. *IEEE Vehicular Technology Magazine*, 9(1), 64-70.

Frank, B., Poese, I., Lin, Y., Smaragdakis, G., Feldmann, A., Maggs, B.M., Rake, J., Uhlig, S. and Weber, R. (2013). Pushing CDN-ISP Collaboration to the Limit. *ACM SIGCOMM Computer Communication Review*, 43(3), 35-44.

Gerber, A. and Doverspike, R. (2011). Traffic types and growth in backbone networks. *2011 Optical Fiber Communication Conference and Exposition and the National Fiber Optic Engineers Conference*, 6-10 March, Los Angeles, CA, 1-3, available: http://ieeexplore.ieee.org/stamp/stamp.jsp?tp=&arnumber=5875624&isnumber=5875055 [accessed 20 November 2018].

Giotsas, V., Smaragdakis, G., Huffaker, B., Luckie, M. and Claffy, kc (2015). Mapping Peering Interconnections to a Facility. *Proceedings of the 11th ACM Conference on*

Emerging Networking Experiments and Technologies (CoNEXT '15), 1-4 December, Heidelberg, Germany, Article No. 37, available: https://doi.org/10.1145/2716281.2836122 [accessed 20 November 2018].

Gold, H. (2019). Appeals court backs AT&T acquisition of Time Warner. CNN.com, 27 February, available at : https://edition.cnn.com/2019/02/26/media/att-time-warner-merger-ruling/index.html [accessed 30 March 2019].

Google (no date). Google: Our Infrastructure. Available: https://peering.google.com/#/infrastructure [accessed 20 November 2018].

Huston, G. (2017). The Rise and Rise of Content Distribution Networks. Presentation at the *8th Workshop on Internet Economics (WIE 2017)*, 13-14 December, La Jolla, CA, available: http://www.caida.org/workshops/wie/1712/slides/wie1712_ghuston.pdf [accessed 20 November 2018].

ITU-T (2014). The Tactile Internet. ITU-T Technology Watch Report, August.

Kaufmann, C. (2018). ICN – Akamai's Backbone. Presentation at *LINX Meeting 101*, 22 May, London, UK, available: https://www.linx.net/wp-content/uploads/LINX 101-Akamai-ICN-ChristianKaufmann.pdf [accessed 30 November 2018].

Knieps, G. (2009). Wettbewerb und Netzevolutorik. in: Vanberg, V.J. (ed.), *Evolution und Freiheitlicher Wettbewerb*, Tübingen: Mohr Siebeck, 193-210.

Knieps, G. (2015). Entrepreneurial traffic management and the Internet Engineering Task Force. *Journal of Competition Law & Economics*, 11(3), 727-745.

Knieps, G. (2017). Internet of Things, Future Networks, and the Economics of Virtual Networks. *Competition and Regulation in Network Industries*, 18(3-4), 240-255.

Knieps, G., and Stocker, V. (2016). Price and QoS differentiation in all-IP networks. *International Journal of Management and Network Economics*, 3(4), 317–335.

Kreutz, D., Ramos, F.M.V., Verissimo, P.E., Rothenberg, C.E., Azodolmolky, S. and Uhlig, S. (2015). Software-Defined Networking: A Comprehensive Survey. Proceedings of the IEEE, 103(1), 14-76.

Kua, J., Armitage, G. and Branch, P. (2017). A Survey of Rate Adaptation Techniques for Dynamic Adaptive Streaming Over HTTP. *IEEE Communications Surveys & Tutorials*, 19(3), 1842-1866.

Kurose, J.F. and Ross, K.W. (2013). *Computer Networking: A Top-Down Approach*. 6th ed., Boston et al.: Pearson.

Labovitz, C., Iekel-Johnson, S., McPherson, D., Oberheide, J. and Jahanian, F. (2010). Internet inter-domain traffic. *ACM SIGCOMM Computer Communication Review*, 40(4), 75-86.

Leighton, T. (2009). Improving Performance on the Internet. *Communications of the ACM*, 52(2), 44-51.

Limelight Networks (2018). Global Private Network. available: https://www.limelight.com/orchestrate-platform/global-infrastructure/ [accessed 20 November 2018].

Mijumbi, R., Serrat, J., Gorricho, J., Bouten, N., De Turck, F. and Boutaba, R. (2016). Network Function Virtualization: State-of-the-Art and Research Challenges. *IEEE Communications Surveys & Tutorials*, 18(1), 236-262.

Netflix (2018). Netflix Open Connect – Sample Architecture. Available: https://open-connect.netflix.com/en/sample-architectures/ [accessed 20 November 2018].

Nokia (2016). *Dynamic end-to-end network slicing for 5G - Addressing 5G requirements for diverse services, use cases, and business models.* Whitepaper.

Nomikos, G., Kotronis, V., Sermpezis, P., Gigis, P., Manassakis, L., Dietzel, C., Konstantaras, S., Dimitropoulos, X. and Giotsas, V. (2018). O Peer, Where Art Thou?: Uncovering Remote Peering Interconnections at IXPs. *Proceedings of the Internet Measurement Conference 2018 (IMC '18)*, 31 October-2 November, Boston, MA, 265-278.

Nygren, E., Sitaraman, R.K. and Sun, J. (2010). The Akamai Network: A Platform for High-Performance Internet Applications. *ACM SIGOPS Operating Systems Review*, 44(3), 2-19.

OECD (2008). *Broadband and the Economy.* Ministerial Background Report, DSTI/ICCP/IE(2007)3/FINAL, Paris: OECD, available: https://www.oecd.org/sti/40781696.pdf [accessed 20 November 2018].

Ofcom (2018). *Enabling 5G in the UK.* Discussion Document, 9 March, London, UK: Ofcom, available: https://www.ofcom.org.uk/__data/assets/pdf_file/0022/111883/enabling-5g-uk.pdf [accessed 20 November 2018].

Ou, G. (2008). *Managing Broadband Networks: A Policymaker's Guide.* The Information Technology and Innovation Foundation, December, available: http://www2.itif.org/2008-managing-broadband-policymakers-guide.pdf?_ga=2.198385327.1411444044.1542745432-1969726516.1542745432 [accessed 20 November 2018].

Peterson, L.L. and Davie, B.S. (2012). *Computer Networks: A Systems Approach.* 5th ed., Amsterdam et al.: Morgan Kaufman.

Pujol, E., Richter, P., Chandrasekaran, B., Smaragdakis, G., Feldmann, A., Maggs, B. and Ng, K.-C. (2014). Back-Office Web Traffic on The Internet. *Proceedings of the 2014 Conference on Internet Measurement Conference (IMC '14)*, 5-7 November, Vancouver, BC, 257-270, available: https://doi.org/10.1145/2663716.2663756 [accessed 20 November 2018].

Reed, D., Warbritton, D. and Sicker, D. (2014). Current Trends and Controversies in Internet Peering and Transit: Implications for the Future Evolution of the Internet. Paper presented at the *42nd Research Conference on Communication, Information and Internet Policy (TPRC)*, 12-14 September, Arlington, VA, available: http://ssrn.com/abstract=2418770 [accessed 20 November 2018].

Satyanarayanan, M. (2017). The Emergence of Edge Computing. *Computer*, 50(1), 30-39.

Seufert, M., Egger, S., Slanina, M., Zinner, T., Hoßfeld, T. and Tran-Gia, P. (2015). A Survey on Quality of Experience of HTTP Adaptive Streaming. *IEEE Communication Surveys & Tutorials*, 17(1), 469-492.

Smith, J.M. (2009). Fighting Physics: A Tough Battle. *ACM Queue*, 7(3), 20-26.

Stocker, V. (2015). Interconnection and Capacity Allocation for All-IP Networks: Walled Gardens or Full Integration?. Paper presented at the *43rd Research Conference on Communication, Information and Internet Policy (TPRC)*, 25-27 September,

Arlington, VA, available: http://dx.doi.org/10.2139/ssrn.2587833 [accessed 20 November 2018].

Stocker, V. and Whalley, J. (2017). Who Replies to Consultations, and What Do They Say? The Case of Broadband Universal Service in the UK. Paper presented at the *28th European Regional Conference of the International Telecommunications Society (ITS)*, 30 July-2 August, Passau, Germany, available: http://hdl.handle.net/10419/169499 [accessed 20 November 2018].

Stocker, V. and Whalley, J. (2018). Speed isn't everything: A multi-criteria analysis of the broadband consumer experience in the UK. *Telecommunications Policy*, 42 (1), 1-14.

Stocker, V., Smaragdakis, G., Lehr, W. H., and Bauer, S. (2017). The growing complexity of content delivery networks: Challenges and implications for the Internet ecosystem. *Telecommunications Policy*, 41 (10), 1003-1016.

Trevisan, M., Giordano, D., Drago, I., Mellia, M. and Munafo, M. (2018). Five Years at the Edge: Watching Internet from the ISP Network. *Proceedings of the 14th International Conference on emerging Networking EXperiments and Technologies (CoNEXT '18)*, 4-7 December, Heraklion, Greece, 1-12, available: https://doi.org/10.1145/3281411.3281433 [accessed 20 November 2018].

Woodcock, B., and Frigino, M. (2016). 2016 Survey of inter carrier Interconnection agreements. BoR, 16(237), 21 November, Brussels, Belgium.

Yoo, C.S. (2013). Protocol Layering and Internet Policy. *University of Pennsylvania Law Review*, 161(6), 1707-1771.

Yoo, C.S. (2016). Modularity Theory and Internet Regulation. *University of Illinois Law Review*, 2016(1), 1-62.

ZetaCast (2012). Technical Evolution of the DTT Platform. An independent report by ZetaCast, commissioned by Ofcom, Version 1.3, 28 January.

The evolution of interconnection in the Internet: New models of cooperation between Internet service providers and content

Falk von Bornstaedt[1]

Abstract

Today's Internet traffic is dominated by a small number of big content providers and content delivery networks (CDNs). How they interact with other Autonomous Systems largely shapes interdomain routing around the world.

Operator networks provide the infrastructure that enables these content providers to deliver their traffic to end users. These networks have to accommodate the diverse and volatile traffic of all the different popular content providers. This makes handling the traffic in the most efficient way on a capacity-constrained network a challenging task. Yet it is crucial to meet the individual best performance objectives for all types of traffic. Content providers have developed systems that aim to work intelligently around the limits resulting from constrained visibility into other network domains and aged protocols (e.g. BGP) to choose paths that meet their performance objectives.

BGP is not capacity aware and this leads to suboptimal results in case of congestion due to special events that boost traffic or in case of network or peering failures. Operator networks remain "dark" places for content providers regarding their actual network state thus adding risk to the optimal delivery.

Operator networks contain crucial state information that would aid content providers in making optimal delivery decisions. Given the high growth rates in traffic, network operators increasingly look for a closer partnership with content providers. This includes the use of measurement-based information about the network into the whole content delivery decision system.

Key words: IP-Interconnection, Peering, IP-Transit

---

1   Falk von Bornstaedt, Deutsche Telekom; bornstaedt@t-online.de

1. Introduction

The Internet consists of more than 60 000 networks. Interconnection is the glue that keeps the internet together. The interconnection market is the place, where different networks (=autonomous systems) exchange traffic via the Border Gateway Protocol (BGP). There are many networks with mixed functions; nevertheless it is helpful to classify networks in the internet as follows:

1. "Content Networks" specialize in hosting content, either their own like Google/YouTube, or offering this as a CDN service to third parties like Akamai,
2. "Transit Networks" act as intermediaries and neither carry traffic from their own consumers nor own content,
3. "Eyeball networks" specialize in serving internet access for end customers. Sub-categories are fixed networks with mostly broadband, and mobile providers,
4. Enterprise networks,
5. Others, such as research networks.

Content networks generally have an open peering policy; this means they do not impose a lot of restrictions to enter a peering relationship. Based on 2013 PeeringDB data, 76% of represented networks claimed to have an open peering policy, 21% selective, and 3% declared they are using a restrictive peering policy (Lodhi et al., 2014). PeeringDB does not cover all networks, it is a database which is not obligatory but gives some idea about the structure of the interconnection landscape: out of the 60000 networks 12203 have registered in PeeringDB, 627 public exchange points and 2740 private interconnection facilities are listed there (PeeringDB, 2018).

The bulk of traffic is exchanged between "Content" and "Eyeball networks". The role of "Transit networks" is getting smaller, but will not vanish completely, since there is always a need to serve the "long tail", the numerous medium and small size networks. Some networks cannot be classified in a single category. Century Link who took over Level 3 seems to serve all categories.

In the early days of the internet interconnection agreements were quite simple: There was peering to reach your customers and transit to reach the whole internet. This is still true for large parts of the internet. According to a study from Woodcock & Frigino (2016) over 99.9% of interconnection agreements were done by a handshake or a simple email exchange without written contracts. This is not true for the interconnection agreements between the top tier players. Peering is only given with a compensation which can be counter business or financial compensation. This is sometimes seen as a burden, but in other cases it is appreciated because a paid contract comes with a service level agreement (SLA).

A peering contract between one of the top content or transit network and a big eyeball provider may reach 20 pages or more, even a standard peering contract has 13 pages (Hall, 2007). The time for negotiation can last many months. Nevertheless, a peering contract can never foresee all possible conflict areas.

Figure 1: Value chain from content to eyeballs

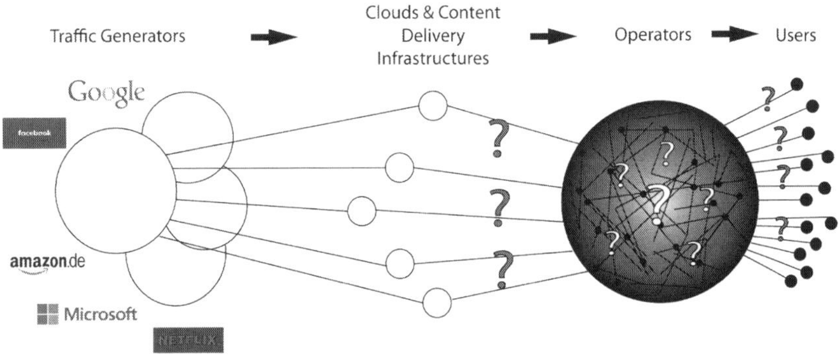

Source: BENOCS, 2018.

The eyeball networks own the last mile, the costliest element of the internet. Given the high growth of internet traffic, eyeball networks face a huge challenge. They need to invest into network infrastructure to enable a growth rate of about 30% per year. What is even more challenging is that peak hour traffic grows even faster. Networks must be dimensioned to carry the peak hour plus a reserve for even bigger peaks to come. From 2016 to 2021 CISCO expects peak hour Internet traffic to increase by a factor of 4.6, compared to average Internet traffic by a factor of 3.2 (CISCO, 2017a). Internet video is replacing traditional linear TV services and this is one of the driving factors. Traffic of mobile services makes up only a few percent of total traffic today but is on a strong rise. Eyeball ISPs have no control today where content traffic is handed over. The sending party controls where to hand over the traffic.

197

Content providers try to hand over the traffic to consumer ISPs in one of the following ways, in order of preference

1. private interconnection
2. interconnection via an Internet Exchange
3. distribution of content via a transit provider

The goal is always to have a short and reliable path to the end user.

At first glance, private interconnection between all networks seems to be the best solution since there is no need to rely on third party infrastructures. A full mesh of all 60000 networks would require n*(n-1) / 2 interconnects or 1,799,970,000 interconnections. 1.8 billion interconnects would be far too expensive to handle. The full mesh is only available between the so-called Tier 1 providers. By definition, Tier 1 ISPs do not buy transit to gain global connectivity. There may still be some settlements between Tier 1 ISPs, hidden behind non-disclosure agreements.

Medium and large eyeball networks and the top 10 to 20 content networks have reached traffic volumes that make a direct interconnection profitable. This is called PNI, private network interconnection, or private peering. There are only 2 port cards involved instead of 4, this reduces the single points of failure. As a rule of thumb, traffic flows above 2 to 3 Gbps are often handled via PNIs.

Interconnection via Internet Exchanges is especially efficient for small and medium sized ISPs. While in the USA commercially driven exchanges are prominent, most European Internet Exchanges are run by non-profit organizations. US Internet Exchanges are often restrictive in publishing traffic data, but it is generally acknowledged that DE-CIX is the biggest internet exchange globally when measured by traffic.

Figure 1 shows the Internet with different Over the Top providers (OTTs) sending traffic through a cloud and content delivery structure to eyeball operators and, finally delivered on the right side to the end users. As of today, there is no transparency about the traffic flows. Content providers have their own intelligence they know what they are sending, but they know little about what happens within the eyeball networks. ISPs have always considered this a business secret. Content providers like Google and Netflix have pushed for more transparency providing portals to publish end customer performance, e.g. the Netflix ISP speed index. This does not give any real time insight into networks.

ISPs do not like to admit that there might be congestion within their network, because "congestion free" is part of their selling proposition. That is true for most parts of their networks and most times of day, but there are also periods during the day, especially during busy hours like Sunday evenings, when networks reach their limits. Internet traffic during a day's most busy hour grew 51%, much more than the 32% growth in average during 2016 (CISCO, 2017a).

Internet Exchanges need to fight for their share of the total interconnection market since the big content networks place their caches directly into the eyeball networks. We might see disintermediation in this area, if internet exchanges do not succeed to deliver additional values to their customers. A first important step is already the offer of remote peering that added a lot of value for many smaller participants.

In the early days of the Internet, there were quite powerful so called "tier 1" providers. Traffic had to be hauled over big distances. For example, most of the European internet had to be hauled across the Atlantic. When the CDNs brought content closer to the eyeballs, and the large content providers built out their own networks, the situation changed dramatically. Content is now stored closer to the eyeballs. In many cases, the big content providers connect directly to the eyeball networks. There is no longer as much need for a Transit ISP to do the intermediation. With less partners involved it becomes easier to co-ordinate between the partners.

In the traditional setup there was a transit ISP involved:

Content Network → Transit ISP → Consumer ISP

The role of the transit ISP is shrinking more and more. OTT caches and stiff competition from CDNs with extreme price decreases have contributed to this situation. In the new setup we see disintermediation, the role of the "middle man" is made obsolete in many cases:

Content Network → Consumer ISP

Since the chain of involved parties in the delivery of content is now shorter, and since there are less parties involved, the cost of coordination is no longer prohibitive and real time coordination becomes possible. Now that the top content sources deliver directly to the consumer ISPs in many cases, only two parties have to coordinate, this is much more feasible, even in real-time.

Internet traffic levels increased heavily in 2015 due to increased video streaming. Eyeball operators needed to find ways of limiting the network invest to keep prices stable for their end customers without endangering customer experience. One way of reducing invest was to improve coordination with OTTs. This meant that ISPs had to change their mindset.

Deutsche Telekom, for example, decided to share internal load factors with OTTs to enable them to choose the best path for sending content to the end customer. They would no longer be forced to use trial and error to determine the best path.

The following scenario was a triggering factor for this new mindset. A typical OTT developed their traffic engineering for the United States market. There it is good practice to avoid foreign countries and prefer routes within the United States. These same routing policies were then applied to Europe. This is not always a good idea because in Europe, it may be better to serve traffic from a foreign country than to serve traffic within a country. For example, Duisburg end customers were served from Frankfurt 250 km away where the interconnection point was heavily congested rather than from Amsterdam which is only 200 km away and where interconnection capacity was still available.

Better coordination can save network costs. For a large network, 3% higher utilisation can yield several million Euro in cost savings. If the consumer ISP can run its core network at 33% average load after coordinating with the OTT, compared to 30% load at the same quality level as before, significant network cost savings can be realized.

With such a good case for cooperation, you may ask why it does not often happen: When a company is in an early stage in their life cycle, it will focus mainly on its core business. Only at a later stage, when the core business has stabilized, and the company is listed on the stock market, will controllers look at the positions on the cost balance sheet. At that time, companies will look for a deeper coordination with their internet peering partners.

In the current interconnection model there are manual provisioning procedures on both sides. If there are automated systems, there is no coordination between the different parties. There is no such thing as SAP for the interconnection business. Tracking of IP addresses is difficult. A first attempt to automate provisioning is done via peeringDB. Some ISPs require a peeringDB entry as a precondition for peering. A further limitation of traditional interconnection is the rigid business model. So far Internet Exchanges focus on exchange of packets, but this does not reflect the exchange of the associated values.

To sum it up, eyeball operators did not allow CDNs and OTTs to have insight into their own Network. Internal network statistics have always been a business secret, but maintaining this secrecy is more and more difficult since many different actors have started publishing network data. Traditionally, ISPs did not like to disclose internal load factors because they did not want to admit they have congestion from time to time. If the internet gets slow, it is quite difficult to find out which part of the chain is the limiting factor. Is it the Wi-Fi connection from the end customer, is it the access network, is it within the peering / IP Transit landscape, or is it within the area of the content provider?

2. A closer look on the content side

New forms of interconnections may show up first with the top players of the industry who have shown their power to innovate. On the other hand, these players do not want to do anything that endangers their free ride via settlement free peerings. We will now have a closer look at 7 of the top content providers of the western hemisphere.

Google / YouTube is one of the biggest sources of traffic. It is offering its own CDN, the Google Global Cache (GGC) to qualifying ISPs. The criteria to offer a GGC seems to have become stricter within the last few years; one reason could be that the cache hit ratio is smaller than initially expected. With YouTube Red a paid subscription model is being tested in a handful of countries. This will increase the willingness to work together with eyeball ISPs to guarantee quality of service.

Netflix started as a DVD distribution service in 1997. Ten Years later it began streaming content via the internet. Only 8 years later, in 2015, Netflix claimed to have reached 37% of the peak internet traffic in the USA (Hughes, 2016). Netflix offers a suite of purpose-built server appliances, called Open Connect Appliances (OCAs). Netflix can predict with high accuracy what their members will watch at what time of day. This enables Netflix to use non-peak bandwidth to update their servers, which is appreciated by the eyeball ISPs. Netflix does not operate its own backbone, so it is dependent on good connectivity from the internet through CDNs or Transit providers.

Akamai delivers peak traffic of around 60 Terabit per second (Tbps) from its massively distributed platform with over 200,000 servers across 130 countries (Akamai, 2017). In contrast to the other big content players, Akamai did not yet roll out their own network. So, Akamai depends even more on a close cooperation with other networks.

Amazon also runs their own server infrastructure, called Amazon CloudFront, part of Amazon Web Services, AWS. Netflix is using it for its services apart from the pure video streaming.

Facebook started renting CDN space from other providers. Facebook built up its own CDN for the simple tasks and leaves the complex ones to established CDNs as a first step. It is surprising to see how much internal traffic is necessary to deliver services to the consumer and advertising customers. Facebook admits that "BGP decisions can hurt performance" (Kim & Zeng, 2017). Facebook's BGP policy favours paths that are likely to optimize network traffic performance. Since BGP is not performance-aware, current Facebook policy relies on attributes such as path length. This is only an imperfect heuristic for proximity and performance and underlines the necessity of new cooperative ways of handling IP interconnection.

Microsoft Azure is the cloud computing platform of Microsoft. German customer data is stored within Germany in data centers managed under the control of a data trustee, T-Systems International, a subsidiary of Deutsche Telekom. Microsoft's cloud services in these data centers follow German data protection regulation. This model of cooperation between a Telco and a Cloud provider might be a blueprint for other content providers.

Apple initially relied on the CDNs of Akamai for iTunes and Level 3 for its radio. Since 2013 it invested around 100 million $ into its own CDN, and it seems to pay ISPs for direct network connections (Rayburn, 2014).

Backoffice traffic has a surprising large share of total traffic, the primary traffic within content networks is internal traffic to fill caches, provide advertisements, or exchange user data, not streaming the desired video towards the consumer (Leopold, 2017). The large content providers engage in their own networks to guarantee the desired quality of service. This is not only a short-term engagement to fill gaps, there is even massive invest into sea cables. As of March 2018, Amazon is active in 2, Facebook in 8, Google in 12, and Microsoft in 4 sea cables (Mauldin, 2017).

3. *Commercial relationships*

In many cases content players and OTTs offer their server infrastructure free of charge to the eyeball ISP. In countries with high IP transit prices like in Africa, content providers ask Internet exchanges for free access. In other areas, content providers sometimes pay for data center space and power, and in a few cases also for traffic (Brodkin, 2014). Since parties are bound by non-disclosure agreements, there is little transparency in this area. There is also a lot of emotion in this area, content players claim that some eyeball ISPs are "double charging" to their end customers and the content side.

Table 1: Interconnection overview

	Small content provider	**Medium size content provider**	**Large size content provider**
Small eyeball ISP	Settlement free peering at Internet Ex-changes	peering at Internet Exchange	Settlement free peering at Internet Exchange
Medium size eyeball ISP	Settlement free peering at Internet Ex-change	Settlement free peering	Settlement free peering
Large eyeball ISP	Content pays to eyeball ISP	Private peering some payments	Private peering some payments

Figure 2:   ARPU in the telecom industry by region

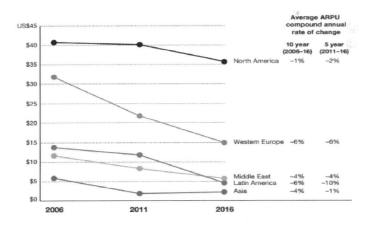

Average revenue per user in the telecom industry is falling in virtually every region

Source: El-Darwiche et al., 2017

The relationship also depends on the country. In 2016 European telecommunication companies had an average revenue per user (ARPU) of 15$ while in North America it was above $ 35 (El-Darwiche et al., 2017, p. 4). European Telcos have a much lower ARPU from end customers compared to US companies. As a result, they are very much more inclined to chase for revenues from content providers. Furthermore, it depends on the local market. In the United Kingdom for example settlement free interconnection is very common, while ISPs in France, Germany, Spain and Poland are more inclined to ask for money.

Figure 3: Schematic view of BENOCS Flow Director traffic steering as an example

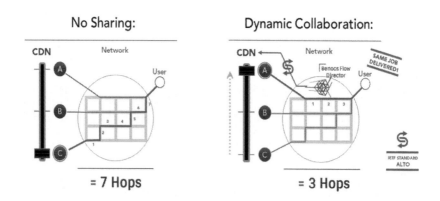

Source: BENOCS, 2018

Figure 3 illustrates how a cooperation model might look like. The eyeball network maintains a real-time map of its own network & capacities. Network state information is offered via Flow Director as Maps & Metrics to 3rd party CDNs & OTTs – on a real time request basis. CDNs and OTTs know beforehand on which paths to send traffic and on which not to go. Figure 3 shows a simplified version of the scenario. Without insight into the eyeball's network, the content CDN would hand over at point "C" and have 7 hops to reach the user. Using a real time mapping system, the CDN can switch their handover to point "A" (BENOCS, 2018). The result is a win/win/win situation for the content network, the eyeball ISP, and the consumer having a better quality of experience.

4. Summary

In the case of global OTTs there are enormous network effects. "Winner takes all" seems to be true for Facebook, in the search engine market Bing did not really succeed to challenge Google, Netflix may be a similar case, Amazon seems to be also very well entrenched. There are enormous economies of scale managing a customer base, rolling out a global CDN or even a global backbone. The same is true for the analysis of user data, big data needs big companies and big user data pools. Nevertheless, a much better product can make the existing service provider obsolete, like it happened to MySpace when Facebook offered a much better product.

On the other side, eyeball networks see enormous competition leading to a strong cost pressure. Video distribution and other real time services like Google Home and Amazon Echo require even better networks to reach the end customer.

For both sides, there is a strong argument to get into a deeper level of coordination and not just only "let BGP do the job". The traditional network protocols alone do not provide the most cost and quality efficient solution. The first pilots of such cooperation can already be seen.

Policy makers should have more focus on long term effects rather than short term consumer benefits. The market for internet traffic exchange does not need regulation, since it has proven to be highly competitive.

References

Akamai (2017): New Akamai Peak Traffic Record Demonstrates Increasing Importance Of Live Online Events. Press release, Sep. 15, 2017.
https://www.akamai.com/us/en/about/news/press/2017-press/new-akamai-peak-traffic-record-demonstrates-increased-importance-of-live-online-events.jsp
[Accessed 28 May 2018].

BENOCS (2018): BENOCS Flow Director. https://www.benocs.com/director/ [Accessed 28 May 2018].

Brodkin, J (2014): Apple reportedly will pay ISPs for direct network connections. https://arstechnica.com/information-technology/2014/05/apple-reportedly-will-pay-isps-for-direct-network-connections/ [Accessed 25 May 2018].

CISCO (2017a): The Zettabyte Era: Trends and Analysis. White Paper, June 2017. https://www.cisco.com/c/en/us/solutions/collateral/service-provider/visual-networking-index-vni/vni-hyperconnectivity-wp.html#_Toc484556816 [Accessed 28 May 2018].

CISCO (2017b): Cisco Visual Networking Index: Forecast and Methodology, 2016–2021. https://www.cisco.com/c/en/us/solutions/collateral/service-provider/visual-networking-index-vni/complete-white-paper-c11-481360.html. [Accessed 28 May 2018].

El-Darwiche, B./Péladeau, P./Rupp, C./Groene, F. (2017): 2017 Telecommunications Trends: Aspiring to digital simplicity and clarity in strategic identity. https://www.strategyand.pwc.com/media/file/2017-Telecommunications-Trends.pdf [Accessed 28 May 2018].

Faratin, P./Clark, D.D./Bauer, S./Lehr, W./Gilmore, P.W./Berger, A. (2008): The Growing Complexity of Internet Interconnection (December 31, 2008). Communications & Strategies, No. 72, 4th Quarter 2008. Available at SSRN: https://ssrn.com/abstract=1374285 [Accessed 28 May 2018].

Hall, Chris (2007): Bilateral Interconnect Agreement. http://www.highwayman.com/peering/peering_agreement.pdf [Accessed 28 May 2018].

Hughes, N. (2016): Netflix boasts 37% share of Internet traffic in North America, compared with 3% for Apple's iTunes. https://appleinsider.com/articles/16/01/20/netflix-boasts-37-share-of-internet-traffic-in-north-america-compared-with-3-for-apples-itunes [Accessed 28 May 2018].

Kim, H. & Zeng, J.H. (2017): Steering oceans of content to the world. Facebook code Blog. https://code.facebook.com/posts/565767133547005/steering-oceans-of-content-to-the-world/ [Accessed 28May 2018].

Leopold, G. (2017): Facebook Datacenters Get 'Express Backbone'. Enterprise Tech, May 1, 2017. https://www.enterprisetech.com/2017/05/01/facebook-datacenters-get-express-backbone/ . [Accessed 28 May 2018].

List of Internet exchange points by size. https://en.wikipedia.org/wiki/List_of_Internet_exchange_points_by_size#cite_note-ams-ixix-14. [Accessed 28 May 2018].

Lodhi, A./Larson, N./Dhamdhere, A./Dovrolis, C./Claffy, K. (2014): Using PeeringDB to Understand the Peering Ecosystem. CAIDA Center for Applied Internet Data Analysis. https://www.caida.org/publications/papers/2014/using_peeringdb_understand_peering/using_peeringdb_understand_peering.pdf [Accessed 28 May 2018].

Marcus, S.J./Elixmann, D./Carter, K.R. (2008): The future of IP interconnection: Technical, economic, and public policy aspects. Bad Honnef: WIK Consult. https://publications.europa.eu/en/publication-detail/-/publication/fb76a3c6-0b29-4ed3-809d-dd3557080c40/language-en.

Mauldin, A. (2017): A complete List of Content Provider's Submarine Cable Holdings. Telegeography. A Complete List of Content Providers' Submarine Cable Holdings. A Complete List of Content Providers' Submarine Cable Holdings. https://blog.telegeography.com/telegeographys-content-providers-submarine-cable-holdings-list [Accessed 28 May 2018].

PeeringDB (2018): www.peeringdb.com [Accessed 28 May 2018].

Rayburn, Dan (2014): Apple's $100M Investment Marks a Shift Away From Third-Party CDNs. In: Streaming Media Oct. 2014 Issue. http://www.streamingmedia. com/Articles/Editorial/Featured-Articles/Apples-%24100M-Investment-Marks-a-Shift-Away-From-Third-Party-CDNs-99832.aspx [Accessed 28 May 2018].

Woodcock, B. & Frigino, M. (2016): 2016 Survey of Internet Carrier Interconnection Agreements. Packet Clearing House. https://www.pch.net/resources/Papers/peering-survey/PCH-Peering-Survey-2016/PCH-Peering-Survey-2016.pdf [Accessed 28 May 2018].

Multi-objective technology selection for IoT solutions: A methodological approach

Marlies Van der Wee,[1] Frederic Vannieuwenborg and Sofie Verbrugge

Abstract

When deploying a new Internet of Things (IoT) service (e.g. smart water meter, air quality monitoring, smart parking application, etc.), a plethora of technologies are available. Examples of network layer technologies are WiFi, ZigBee, LoRa, Sigfox, LTE-4G, etc., while examples of application layer technologies are IP-based solutions like UPnP and CoAP or network-specific solutions such as the Zigbee Cluster Library. The technology choices for each specific service are however hard to make, especially from the point of view of non-technical providers like utility companies, local governments, public administration, etc.

This positioning paper presents a conceptual framework of parameters that need to be taken into account when selecting a technology for deploying an IoT service. Though the main focus of decision makers frequently aims at optimizing the technological performance, there are several functional (e.g., minimum number of messages to be sent each day), strategical (e.g., licensed versus unlicensed spectrum) and economic (e.g., investment and operational cost) parameters to take into account as well. By listing and prioritizing these parameters, the decision can be better supported, and the business case viability better assured.

Keywords: Internet of Things, techno-economics, technology selection

1. Introduction and motivation

The Internet of Things (IoT), a quickly emerging technological wave, is already finding its way in the market under the form of various applications such as pet trackers, smart thermostats, parking sensors and smart water meters. The result is about to flood our imagination. Various researchers report on market sizes of billions of devices within the next 5 years (Yeo et al., 2014).

---

1   Ghent University – imec; Marlies.VanderWee@UGent.be

IoT technology is embodied in a wide spectrum of networked products, services, systems, sensors and people that take advantage of advancements in computing power, miniaturization, electronics and network interconnections (Gubbi et al., 2013). However, given the strong diversity in platforms, applications, sensor types and stakeholders involved, the IoT environment is quickly becoming a stovepiped and very fragmented world where it becomes increasingly challenging to adequately connect all devices using a unified layer. When aiming to develop a new IoT application, difficult choices need to be made on which technology, platform or protocol to use for (1) gathering the information collected by sensors, (2) transmitting the information, (3) processing the data and offering value to the end user through the application, optionally controlling other IoT devices in the process.

Too often is this choice of architectural layers a consequence of technology-led thinking putting emphasis on the technical performance. In so doing, engineers tend to focus on technical parameters including time-behavior, resource utilization, capacity, operability, transmission rate and error protection (White et al., 2017).

Increasingly, however, the selection criterion tradition became criticized for being too technology-determined and for its lack of insights into more socio-economic factors that influence a technology's successful deployment. Given the overabundance of applications that are pushed into the market these days, strategic, economic and 'user experience' impact have become crucial differentiators in order to achieve market success. Functional, strategic and economic parameters include power consumption, vendor choice, investment versus operational cost considerations, etc. Actual user experience, represented by the Quality of Experience (QoE) concept, has become one of the ultimate business metrics (Palmer, 2010).

These particularities translate in pros and cons when considering a specific connectivity network for an IoT application. Since there is currently no 'one-size-fits-all' or best solution, making a balanced choice on each architecture layer that fits the needs of an IoT use case should be a careful trade-off between the ability of a technology to meet specific functional requirements, the related costs occurring during the lifetime of the application and the QoE of its intended users.

Furthermore, the technology choices for each specific application are hard to make, especially from the point of view of the IoT application provider (a public authority (government or city council for example), a factory, a health institute or hospital, etc.) which has to make long-term technology choices upfront, without having real technological expert knowledge.

This positioning paper presents a methodology that allows making the technology choice of IoT applications on different architectural layers in a smart and dynamic way. After having given a short overview of the Internet of Things in section 2, this methodology is presented in section 3. Section 4 gives a simple example of how the methodology could be applied, while section 5 summarizes this paper and provides some directions for future work.

2. The Internet of Things – an overview

Porter and Heppelmann (2014) describe three waves of IT-driven competition. First, there was digitalization: the automation of individual activities in the value chain. Second, internet connectivity made coordination and integration across individual activities possible. When IT becomes part of the product itself (third wave), new opportunities emerge because the nature of products changes and potentially disrupts the value chain. The Internet of Things (IoT) is one of the emerging trends on this third IT wave. Incorporating sensors, actuators, processing power and connectivity in physical devices presents the possibility of revolutionizing the way the economy works and society interacts. Some examples of smart services driven by IoT are:

- energy management systems in home and office environments to enable demand responses in the electricity grid,
- environmental monitoring (sound, air quality, etc.) in a city environment or large public buildings to support policy makers,
- smart city solutions for parking and mobility,
- car-to-car communication to solve or avoid traffic jams,
- health monitoring of patients to solve the problem of bed shortage in healthcare,
- monitoring of factory equipment to enable predictive maintenance to avoid disruptions in the manufacturing process.

In contrast to the first and second wave, the IoT impacts multiple sectors of the economy and hence leads to a high level of heterogeneity, on all three levels of required IoT functionality (Al-Fuqaha et al., 2015):

(1) The *perception layer* is responsible for generating and gathering the information, through the use of physical IoT hardware that has sensing

and/or actuating capabilities. The key building blocks of IoT devices include sensors to sense context parameters (e.g. acceleration, barometric pressure, location, light intensity, temperature and vibration), embedded intelligence in the form of a processor or micro controlling unit (MCU), a power circuit or power supply and a communication component.

(2) The *network layer* provides the wired or wireless network capacity that is required for transferring the data from sensor to central platform. Although in some application settings, IoT devices can rely on wired networks (IEEE 802.3) for communication purposes, most IoT devices require wireless connections for flexibility and operational simplicity. In wireless networks, the distinction can be made between cellular networks (3G, 4G-LTE, 5G), the newly emerging Low-Power Wide-Area Networks (LPWANs) such as LoRa, Sigfox and NB-IoT, Local Area Networks (LANs) such as Wi-Fi and Zigbee and Personal- or Body-Area Networks (PANs, BANs), that only require a wireless connectivity range of a couple of meters (e.g. Bluetooth Low Energy (BLE)) (Elkhodr et al., 2016). This plethora of available technologies has long resulted in a very fragmented environment.

(3) On the *application layer*, the information is processed and managed, transforming the raw data into valuable knowledge. This layer typically includes service management which abstracts away specific network and sensor details. Differences between technologies are not only present in the network layer. Depending on the underlying network technology and its limitations, a number of design decisions need to be taken with regard to the size and format of the data. The models used by the different technologies to give access to the services offered by the IoT device and the data it generates, are quite diverse. Examples are the Zigbee Cluster Library, GATT (Generic ATTributes), etc. When using IP, a whole range of other ways to model services and the accompanying data are possible, such as UPnP, CoAP and many others (Villaverde et al., 2012). Although many of these examples are closely tied to a particular underlying networking technology, these standards can in some cases also be used on top of other networking protocols (possibly encapsulated). Additionally, data management capabilities such as scalable processing tools and API provisioning are offered and finally a management layer which covers access including privacy and security measures is provided.

From the above, it is clear that there is a variety of choice on all layers of the IoT stack. When making a decision on what technology to use for an

IoT application, various authors compare a set of typical connectivity networks, based on technical parameters or hardware-related specifications (Akyildiz, 2002; Elkhodr et al, 2016). Often used parameters include bandwidth, latency, offered connectivity range, maximum number of nodes in the network, modulation techniques, authentication and encryption technologies, number of channels and orthogonal signals, etc. Choices on the application layer are typically driven by the functionality the IoT devices need to offer to the application, together with the accuracy, frequency, stability and maximum delay of the data needed by the application.

However, a much broader range of characteristics is needed in order to obtain a detailed basis for comparing these technologies on their applicability for a set of smart solutions.

3. The conceptual framework

This paper introduces a framework that allows to perform a more elaborate technology comparison based on an extensive parameter review, clearly going beyond a comparison on technical performance. The merit of this framework is its interdisciplinary approach focusing on the multidimensional character of an optimal user experience safeguarding techno-economic viability, instead of purely focusing on implementing the best possible technical architecture. The rationale for this project is that the success of IoT applications will not be driven so much by the technology itself, but rather by the ability to pursue economic feasibility and to provide a genuinely superior user experience, even if that would mean developers will not implement the best possible technological architecture.

The framework aims at linking the characteristics of IoT technologies and protocols to the requirements of smart services and applications, as can be seen from Figure 1 below. The followed methodology hence consists of three consecutive steps:
- Supply-side investigation,
- Demand-side investigation,
- Matching of supply and demand side.

Figure 1:   The conceptual framework

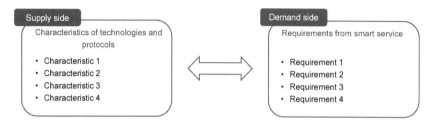

Matching characteristics with requirements
> Iterative approach
1. Technologies not matching **hard constraints** are removed from the search list
2. Multi-objective optimization approach on **soft constraints**
3. Identify trade-offs and calculate impact

3.1.   Supply-side investigation

On the supply-side (available technologies and protocols), the aim is to provide a detailed, categorized overview of the relevant parameters that should steer this technology choice. These parameters are not only technical, but also include functional, strategic and economic characteristics.

A non-exhaustive list of parameters that can be taken into account is given below:

- *Technical parameters* (as included in most traditional technology comparisons) include data rate and latency, frequency band, max payload size, max range, etc.
- *Functional parameters* of the communication network relate to public network accessibility, ability for private network deployments, etc. Functional parameters on the application layer relate to the amount of data that can be sent over the network, latency, power consumption, etc. Functional parameters on the perception layer indicate which services can be offered: what is the accuracy, frequency, stability, etc.
- *Strategic parameters* relate to dependence of a single network operator or single hardware manufacturer, impact of licensed versus unlicensed spectrum, etc.
- *Economic parameters* include cost versus lifetime considerations and availability of standards, operational aspects like required battery replacements, potential economies of scale in the network deployment, license cost where applicable etc.

214

3.2. Demand-side investigation

Whereas the previous step starts from the different technologies that define their performance in terms of different parameters, this step approaches the problem from the demand-side.

This step (although it can be executed in parallel to the previous one), aims at providing a set of tangible *quantitative as well as qualitative requirements for smart services*.

Examples of quantitative requirements are requested response time, or amount of data that should be sent from sensor to control platform. These requirements can often be "affiliated" to technology parameters (e.g. response time can be linked to a minimum latency requirement, or a minimum number of messages to be sent each day, while the amount of data to be sent can lead to a constraint on the minimum message size). An iterative process will be used to identify the various quantitative requirements, which will be based on input gathered from the different case studies linked to a feedback loop that involves the identified supply-side parameters.

Apart from these quantitative requirements, specific qualitative requirements should also be defined, including several experience-related parameters that cannot directly be quantified. Here, functional, strategic and economic requirements can be taken into account, but should be supplemented by Quality of Experience (QoE) parameters. QoE parameters are subject to a range of complex and interrelated 'influence factors' relating to the *human* (i.e. user characteristics including socio-demographics, attention level and affective state), *system* (i.e. properties of the application, network or device including bandwidth, delay, resolution, synchronization and design) and *context* (i.e. situational factors including physical, temporal, social and economic context). Hence, different users can have a different experience depending on the context in which IoT applications are used and the kind of technical architectures that are applied. By integrating objective parameters related to the technical aspects and subjective, user-related parameters, a comprehensive QoE approach allows for an optimal user experience and informs effective development of (IoT) technology.

Of course, these qualitative requirements should be quantified in order to be linked to the characteristics of the technologies. Different metrics are available in literature to do so, but the main metric is the Mean Opinion Score (MOS). MOS originates from measuring the perceived quality of audio and video fragments (Huynh-Thu et al., 2011), but is generally used as a measure of Quality of Experience (QoE) in telecommunications engineering. MOS ratings are often gathered in subjective quality evaluation tests but can also be estimated using algorithms. Using scales and ratings, these subjective results can then be translated into quantitative values, the latter used for evaluation. Only if the perceived quality/reliability of the service is good enough, the user of the smart application will experience a value in using the service. We can assume that the value of an application approaches zero as soon as the perceived quality drops below a certain threshold. Assume for example a farmer that uses a smart cow monitoring system, which gives him automatic notifications of urgent health issues with these animals. If this farmer receives too much false alarms at night, he might stop using the system, turning the system's value to zero.

3.3.   Matching supply and demand side

Finally, the technical, functional, strategic and economic IoT technology characteristics should be match to the smart service requirements in a *smart multi-criteria decision algorithm for IoT technology selection*. The idea is to go beyond transforming this technology choice from an "ad-hoc" decision based on own knowledge and experience to a multi-criteria optimization approach.

The identified parameters will lead to a large n-dimensional search space, which spans the different technical, functional, strategic and economic parameters offered by each technology choice. In order to map this large supply space with the user and application requirements, we will work in an iterative way to identify "best matches". For each identified match, the search result can be matched with the original requirements and the partial mismatches can be translated into user and application trade-offs.

The requirements will be categorized into hard and soft constraints. Hard constraints pose requests on the architecture layers, which some technologies might match, while others might not. Examples of hard constraints are minimum number of messages to be sent per day, minimum delay, etc. Similarly, functional parameters on the application layer can be used to limit the possible choices for the networking technology based on the availability of IoT devices. In the first iteration, the technologies not meeting the hard constraints, will be removed from the search space.

In a second step, existing algorithms are translated to the much more complex IoT environment, where the search space (in terms of technology options) is significantly bigger than for regular wireless networks.

Finally, multi-criterion optimization algorithms that allows incorporating the effect of technical, functional, strategic and economic parameters, will be proposed. A combination of weighted multi-criterion optimization and Pareto front visualization for the most important parameters can lead to optimal solutions. When no exact match is possible, the algorithms will allow to identify trade-offs, possibly leveraging combinations of technologies to further target optimal solutions across all parameters. Certain mobile sensor scenarios for example can perfectly rely on LPWAN technology during daytime, while at night the sensors are static (e.g. parked cars), thus enabling the use of cheap, high-bandwidth Wi-Fi connections.

Though we ideally target optimization methodologies (following operations research principles (Winston and Goldberg, 2004)), setting up and calculating these models might prove very time-consuming. We will hence learn from early results to deduct heuristics that can speed up the decision process for specific types of smart applications, while securing no loss of detail is incurred.

4. A small example

As this is a positioning paper describing the structure of a framework, no real use cases have been developed yet. However, to further clarify the framework, this section introduces a small example of how the framework could be applied.

The example focuses on deploying an IoT solution in an agricultural setting, more precisely a solution that allows tracking cows and monitoring their vital health signs. By monitoring the cows, the farmer is always up to date on their exact location (either in the meadows or in the stable) and furthermore knows if all his animals are healthy. The Flemish research project MoniCow (imec, 2017) reported that for every udder inflammation that is discovered too late, the costs can go up to about 150 Euros, and that a price tag of 250 Euros is attached to a missed malt or undetected crippled cow. In short: monitoring health indicators in real time allows to optimize the economic management of every growing dairy farm.

A system based on IoT sensors and communication technology can provide a solution for these problems. However, multiple technologies exist today, leading to a large search space.

If we apply the proposed framework on this – simplified – example, we first identify the available technologies (here limiting ourselves to the communication layer, although a similar exercise can be done on the other architecture layers), see Table 1.

Table 1: Overview of available technologies for cow monitoring example*

Technology	Bluetooth	LoraWAN	4G
Range	50 m	5 km	2000 m
Cost per collar	/	€2-3 yearly	€20-30 yearly

* Note that this is not an exhaustive list, but rather a shortlist to demonstrate the proposed framework)

On the other hand, different requirements are identified: the dairy farm has a grazing area of 1 km² and the farmer wants to have the lowest operational cost possible.

When comparing the technologies available to the requirements set above, we see that the range poses a hard constraint: the range of Bluetooth is simply not large enough to cover the entire grazing area, so Bluetooth should be eliminated from our search space. The second requirement – the operational cost – is a soft constraint, which makes us tend to choose for the LoraWAN solution. However, the coverage of Lora is not as good as the coverage of 4G today, so an own deployment might have to be considered. We hence identified a trade-off in the optimization problem that requires further details on the coverage or cost of deployment.

5. Summary and future work

The Internet of Things is a strongly emerging trend, and forecasts indicate that the number of connected objects will increase to rise exponentially. As IoT has applications across various sectors of the economy and society, there is no one standard technology to serve all emerging smart services. Choosing the right technology for the right application is hence not a straightforward task. This positioning paper presented a three-step methodology to identify the best solution for each type of application. In the first step, the supply-side investigation, a list of available technologies and their characteristics is made. Here, it is important that the focus not only lies on technical characteristics, but that functional, strategic and economic characteristics are included as well. The second step of the methodology investigates the demand side, by identifying the requirements (both quantitative and qualitative) set by the IoT service or application. Finally, in a third step, characteristics are matched to requirements in an iterative approach, using hard constraints to limit the search space and soft constraints to identify relevant trade-offs.

This paper gave a simplified example of how the framework could be applied. Future research is needed to further develop the methodology, to automate the decision process (e.g. identification of hard constraints and subsequent elimination of unfitting technologies) and to validate it on realistic use cases.

References

Al-Fuqaha, Ala, et al. "Internet of things: A survey on enabling technologies, protocols, and applications." *IEEE Communications Surveys & Tutorials* 17.4 (2015): 2347-2376.

Akyildiz, Ian F., et al. "Wireless sensor networks: a survey." *Computer networks* 38.4 (2002): 393-422.

Elkhodr, M., Shahrestani, S., Cheung, H. (2016) Emerging Wireless Technologies in the Internet of Things: a Comparative Study. ArXiv Prepr ArXiv161100861.

Gubbi, J.; Buyya, R.; Marusic, S. & Palaniswami, M. (2013). Internet of Things (IoT): A vision, architectural elements, and future directions. *Future Generation Computer Systems*, 29(7), 1645-1660.

Huynh-Thu, Q., Garcia, M. N., Speranza, F., Corriveau, P., & Raake, A. (2011). Study of rating scales for subjective quality assessment of high-definition video. *IEEE Transactions on Broadcasting*, 57(1), 1-14.

Imec (2017) MoniCow - More Efficient Cattle Monitoring Through an Advanced Data System. https://www.imec-int.com/en/what-we-offer/research-portfolio/monicow

Palmer. (2010). Customer experience management: a critical review of an emerging idea. *Journal of Services Marketing*, 24(3), 196-208.

Porter, M. E., & Heppelmann, J. E. (2014). How smart, connected products are transforming competition. *Harvard Business Review*, 92(11), 64-88.

Villaverde, B. C., Pesch, D., Alberola, R. D. P., Fedor, S., & Boubekeur, M. (2012, July). Constrained application protocol for low power embedded networks: A survey. In *Innovative Mobile and Internet Services in Ubiquitous Computing (IMIS), 2012 Sixth International Conference on* (pp. 702-707). IEEE.

Winston, W. L., & Goldberg, J. B. (2004). *Operations research: applications and algorithms* (Vol. 3). Boston: Duxbury press

White, G.; Nallur, V. & Clarke, S. (2017). Quality of service approaches in IoT: A systematic mapping. *Journal of Systems and Software*, 132, 186-203.

Yeo, K. S., Chian, M. C., & Ng, T. C. W. (2014, December). Internet of things: trends, challenges and applications. In *Integrated Circuits (ISIC), 2014 14th International Symposium on* (pp. 568-571). IEEE

5G and Net Neutrality

Christopher S. Yoo[1] and Jesse Lambert[2]

Abstract

Industry observers have raised the possibility that European network neutrality regulations may obstruct the deployment of 5G. To assess those claims, this Chapter describes the key technologies likely to be incorporated into 5G, including millimeter wave band radios, massive multiple input/multiple output (MIMO), ultra-densificaton, multiple radio access technologies (multi-RAT), and support for device-to-device (D2D) and machine-to-machine (M2M) connectivity. It then reviews the business models likely to be associated with 5G, including network management through biasing and blanking, an emphasis on business-to-business (B2B) communications, and network function virtualization/network slicing. It then lays out the network neutrality regulations created by the EU in 2015 as well as the nonbinding interpretive guidelines issued by the Body of Body of European Regulators for Electronic Communication (BEREC) in 2016 and assesses how they will be applied to 5G. Network neutrality's impact on 5G will likely be determined by the way that the exceptions for reasonable traffic management and specialised services are interpreted. A broad interpretation should accommodate network slicing and other new business models needed to support the deployment of 5G, while a narrow interpretation could restrict innovation and investment.

1 Introduction

One of the most striking changes in the Internet ecosystem in recent years is the growing importance of mobile broadband. Driven in large part by the advent of the smart phone in 2007, mobile has emerged as the primary

---

1   Center for Technology, Innovation and Competition, University of Pennsylvania; csyoo@law.upenn.edu
2   University of Pennsylvania Law School

source of Internet connectivity in most countries around the world. By the end of 2010, mobile broadband connections surpassed fixed-line broadband connections in the U.S. (Federal Communications Commission, 2012). Some estimates calculate that mobile IP traffic has grown by more than 100 times over the past ten years and is forecast to continue to grow at an annual rate of more than 45% per year through 2021 (Cisco, 2007, 2017).

Current discussions about mobile broadband are dominated by the impending deployment of the next generation of wireless technology, commonly known as 5G. The Korean government showcased 5G at the Winter Olympics in Pyeongchang in February 2018. Later that same month, 5G was the focus of seemingly every talk and every booth at the leading trade show for the wireless industry, known as the Mobile World Congress. In late 2018 and early 2019, U.S. and Korean companies raced to be the first to offer 5G to commercial subscribers.

Despite all of this hype, there is little understanding of what sets 5G apart as a technological matter and what the business case for its deployment will be. In addition, discussions of how the regulatory system might impact 5G and vice versa are only just beginning. For example, GSMA (2018) recently released a report on megacities underscoring the need to streamline the process for deploying 5G, a topic that is also the focus of the U.S. Federal Communications Commission's Broadband Deployment Advisory Committee (BDAC).

This Chapter focuses on another concern raised by the "5G Manifesto" released by a group of European telecommunications providers and equipment manufacturers in July 2016. This document warned that that strict implementation of network neutrality might hinder networks' ability to experiment with the kind of flexible, elastic configuration of resources and other innovative specialised services, which in turn could dampen investment in 5G (Patterson et al., 2016). A number of other industry observers have made similar questions about the compatibility of net neutrality and 5G (Lawson, 2015; Rysavy, 2017; Manion, 2017; Morris, 2018).

This Chapter seeks to examine the unresolved questions about how 5G will deploy and how network neutrality regulation will affect it. It begins by describing the technical underpinnings of 5G and identifying what sets it apart from previous generations of wireless technology, paying particular attention to new business model known as *network slicing*. It continues by looking at the potential impact of EU network neutrality regulations on 5G.

2   Defining 5G

Although some disagreement exists as to which 5G standard represents the definitive one, a broad consensus exists as to 5G's overall outlines and which technologies are the most characteristic of 5G. (For overviews appearing in the engineering literature, see, for example, Boccardi et al., 2014; Osseiran et al., 2014; Andrews et al., 2014; Gupta and Jha, 2015).

The operational goals for 5G are fairly well established: support for multiple gigabit speeds and millisecond latencies, the higher degree of reliability needed to support increasingly critical infrastructure, a greater diversity of devices, and reductions in energy consumption and cost. But a new generation of wireless connectivity requires more than just the ability to meet enhanced performance measures. It requires a sufficiently large technological step forward to be regarded as a paradigm shift. In addition to technological changes, the deployment of 5G appears to depend on the adoption of new business models. Finally, the potential use cases motivating 5G suggest that deployment is more likely to be driven by the Internet of Things (IoT) than the ability to expand network coverage or replace previous architectures.

2.1   New technologies

A consensus has emerged about the technologies most likely to prove essential to the deployment of 5G: use of millimeter wave bands of the spectrum, reliance on massive multiple input/multiple output (MIMO), and extreme densification through small cells. In addition, the 5G network needs to support multiple radio access technologies (multi-RAT) as well as direct device-to-device (D2D) and machine-to-machine (M2M) connectivity.

2.1.1 Millimeter wave bands

New services need spectrum. However, the spectrum bands traditionally used for wireless communication have already been fully allocated to other services. Improvements in semiconductor cost and power consumption have made available higher frequencies, such as millimeter wave (mmWave) spectrum in the 28, 38, 60, and 73 GHz ranges, that were previously regarded as unusable due to poor propagation characteristics. This increase in the range of usable frequencies allows the allocation of spectrum to 5G without having to displace any preexisting uses (Boccardi et al., 2014; Osseiran et al., 2014; Andrews et al., 2014; Agiwal et al., 2016) although interest has increased in deploying 5G in mid-band spectrum in the 1-6 GHz range.

2.1.2 Massive multiple input/multiple output (MIMO)

Wireless communications are plagued by a problem known as *multipath propagation*, which occurs when a signal from a source reaches the same point via multiple routes, such as when one signal arrives directly and one or more other signals arrive after reflecting off some nearby surface. A good example occurs when an echo in a room with bad acoustics causes listeners to hear the same message twice, with the signal travelling by the indirect path arriving slightly after the signal arriving by the direct path. Receivers that are unable to distinguish between these signals perceive the reflected signal as capacity-reducing interference or noise. The field of information theory, based on the seminal work of Shannon (1949), has long recognized that the usable capacity of a bandwidth-limited channel depends on its signal-to-interference-plus-noise ratio (SINR). Thus, multipath propagation has generally been regarded as reducing network performance (Yoo, 2016b).

A technique known as multiple input/multiple output (MIMO) can solve this problem. Deploying multiple antennas to both transmit and receive allows the systems to use the distance between the antennas to distinguish between signals that travel by direct paths from those that travel by various indirect paths. In addition, MIMO allows receivers to combine multiple signals that individually would be too weak to be a usable signal. Indeed, the latest generation WiFi standard (802.11n) and recent 3G and 4G technologies use MIMO employing two-to-four transmission and receiving antennas to improve throughput and deal with highly reflective environments. Massive MIMO uses a technique developed in 2007 to increase the number of antennas in use to more than one hundred (Boccardi et al., 2014; Osseiran et al., 2014; Andrews et al., 2014; Agiwal et al., 2016).

2.1.3   Ultra-densification through small cells

Another central technical commitment underlying 5G is the use of smaller, more densely packed cells. Increasing network capacity by making cells smaller is an approach that is hardly unique to 5G, as prior generations of wireless technology have long allowed more users to rely on the same spectrum by splitting cells and having the resulting base stations operate at lower power. That said, 5G takes densification to a new level, sometimes estimated to be as high as one base station for every twelve homes. In the limit, 5G base stations could be as small as a home router, with each one serving a single user. The use of smaller cells operating at lower power allows the same spectrum to be reused by a larger number of users (Andrews et al., 2014).

2.1.4   Multiple radio access technologies (multi-RAT)

Because microcells cover relatively small areas, they are not viable in areas where customer densities are too low to generate sufficient revenue to support the necessary investment. As a result, instead of being a replacement for 3G and 4G technologies, 5G will likely serve as a complement to legacy network deployments, relying on 3G and 4G macrocells to provide baseline connectivity and overlaying 5G microcells in those areas that require additional capacity (Osseiran et al., 2014; Andrews et al., 2014).

To deliver on its promise of reliable and ubiquitous high-speed service, 5G needs to be able to integrate multiple radio access technologies (multi-RAT). The standard must support the ability to connect to legacy 3G and 4G technologies as well as other technologies such as Wi-Fi and 5G. The 5G network must be able to manage handoffs seamlessly as users migrate from one radio technology to another. Finally, as discussed below in section 2.2.1, the need to optimize capacity in areas served by both microcells and macrocells requires extensive network management (Osseiran et al., 2014; Andrews et al., 2014).

2.1.5   Support for device-to-device (D2D) and machine-to-machine (M2M) connectivity

Lastly, 5G deviates from prior approaches by enabling the related, but distinct, concepts of device-to-device (D2D) and machine-to-machine

(M2M) communications. D2D is an approach to network management that deviates from the traditional centralized architecture by permitting nearby devices to communicate directly with each other without having to connect through a base station. Direct D2D communication can reduce the number of hops, transmission distances, power consumption, and path loss. As discussed below in Section 2.2.1, the elimination of a central infrastructure point to oversee individual connections poses complex management challenges (Boccardi et al., 2014; Osseiran et al., 2014; Andrews et al., 2014; Agiwal et al., 2016).

M2M differs from D2D in that it is not concerned with the mechanics of how end-nodes establish connections with one another. Instead, it focuses on the type of entity being connected, the type of data being exchanged, and the level of human involvement needed to initiate it. Prominent examples include connected cars, road and traffic management, health care, and smart cities. M2M differs from legacy architectures in that it envisions much larger numbers of connected devices, the need for very high link reliability and low latency, and the tendency to generate short blocks of highly sporadic data. M2M need not be D2D and can follow the traditional model of connecting through base stations. Unlike D2D, M2M communications need not involve devices that are located close to one another (Boccardi et al., 2014; Osseiran et al., 2014; Andrews et al., 2014; Agiwal et al., 2016).

2.1.6 Impact on spectral efficiency

These innovations both increase the amount of usable spectrum and the intensity with which the spectrum is used. Other technological improvements, such as slot aggregation, reductions in guard band size, elimination of the need of constant transmission of cell-specific reference signals (CRS), the use of code block groups to support more efficient transmission of large transport block sizes, and improved channel coding, promise to enhance efficiency still further (Khalid, 2018). Industry estimates that together these technological improvements can increase spectral efficiency by up to four times (Ghosh, 2017; Qualcomm, 2018).

2.2   New business models

In addition to employing new technologies, 5G systems are expected to incorporate new business models that have the potential to organize resources in a manner that is fundamentally different from the ways that prior networks were organized. It is also expected to place new functional demands on and require new functionality from the architecture.

2.2.1 Network management

5G deployments require more extensive and innovative forms of network management. As noted earlier, 5G applications are likely to place greater demands on the network, requiring the connection of many more devices as well as latency and reliability guarantees that are significantly more stringent than the current best-efforts architecture can support (Osseiran et al., 2014; Andrews et al., 2014).

Another challenge is posed by the fact that 5G service relies on a combination of microcells operating at relatively low power and macrocells operating at relatively high power. The overlapping operation of low-power and high-power transmissions raises difficult management problems. As noted above, SINR determines the amount of usable bandwidth. The low-power microcells perceive the signals of high-power macrocells as interference or noise. Moreover, because microcells operate at lower power, networks based on them are more vulnerable to interference than previous architectures (Andrews et al., 2014).

Innovative solutions exist to solve these problems. One technique known as *biasing* requires a user to connect through a microcell even when connecting to the macrocell would provide greater bandwidth. The reduction in macrocell usage benefits all other microcells, but disadvantages the user subject to biasing (although the microcell can compensate by allowing that user to access more of the microcell's resources). Another technique known as *blanking* shuts off macrocells and shunts all of the traffic to the microcells even when utilizing the macrocells might be more efficient for individual users (Andrews et al., 2014).

Proper application of these techniques requires knowing the load each user is placing on the network as well as the load, SINR, and resources available at every base station. In addition, because interference is the product of pairwise interactions between users, the network must integrate these data into a massive combinatorial optimization problem. Moreover, the standard governing the network must have the authority to implement the optimal result in a D2D architecture in which each node can act independently outside the central control of the infrastructure (Andrews et al., 2014). The issues presented by these control problems are demonstrated eloquently by the fact that Google is employing the centralized management features of 4G LTE to support both its since-abandoned, balloon-based connectively project known as Project Loon and its wireless replacement for the now defunct Google Fiber instead of ad hoc, unmanaged routing technologies, such as Wi-Fi.

2.2.2 Significant role for business-to-business (B2B)

The primary focus of 3G and 4G wireless networks was to support broadband access by consumers. It is possible that 5G's greater spectral efficiency may provide sufficient cost reductions to support the deployment of 5G. If supply-side considerations are not sufficient, the value added needed to support return on investment must come from the demand side.

The data on consumer willingness to pay for 5G services are mixed. On the one hand, a survey by Ericsson ConsumerLabs (2018) found that, contrary to the belief that consumers are uninterested in 5G, 44% of users are willing to pay for 5G. Another survey jointly conducted by Qualcomm and Nokia (2017) found that 50% of respondents indicated they were likely to be early 5G adapters and that over 60% would be willing to pay an average of USD 50 for a 5G-enabled device.

Other surveys suggest the contrary. A study by Deloitte (2017a) of German consumers found that 61% did not regard 5G as important. It also found that willingness to pay for 5G was quite limited, with 58% unwilling to pay anything more for 5G and another 22% only willing to pay 5 € or less. A related Deloitte study (2017b) of U.S. consumers found that they were unwilling to pay much for IoT and speculated that "consumers are beginning to view IoT services more as another utility, one for which they want to pay little or nothing at all." This is consistent with prior findings that consumers have shown little willingness to pay for higher download speeds (Lee and Whitacre, 2017; Liu, Prince and Wallsten, 2018).

Uncertainly about the consumer demand for 5G has led many providers to focus their efforts on business-to-business (B2B) connectivity as well. A brief perusal of the business cases typically cited as the potential drivers for 5G deployments underscores the likely importance of B2B. Implementations such as the Internet of things (IoT), connected cars, smart cities, other forms of connected transportation, and health care all are likely to require coordination with other business entities rather than with consumers (Agiwal et al., 2016).

The reasons for the emphasis on B2B follow directly from 5G's emphasis on microcells. The small geographic coverage of each cell means that the service area served by each base station will encompass relatively few customers. The smaller number of consumers served by each cell means that the economic viability of microcells depends on tapping into as many other sources of revenue as possible. To the extent that latencies are important, sharing becomes critical. In a two-dimensional space, halving the distance to the nearest node requires quadrupling the number of nodes (Weinman, 2015). In a small cell world, it is unlikely that a single application would have sufficient volume to support the investment necessary to build out 5G.

2.2.3   Network function virtualization/network slicing

Each of the different Internet-connected industries that 5G needs to serve (sometimes called *verticals*) requires different clusters of services from the network. The 5G architecture could create a unique package of services for each vertical offered on an integrated basis by a single provider. Another approach would be for network providers to offer building blocks of network components that end users or third-party integrators could assemble on a transactional basis to obtain the services that a particular vertical needs (Andrews et al., 2014).

This new business model is called *network function virtualization* or *network slicing*. These practices will enable the coexistence of independent virtual networks sitting side by side, much as cloud computing allows independent virtual machines to coexist on the same server. The comparison to cloud computing underscores the potential benefits of network slicing. In the traditional computing model, end users employ dedicated computing power and storage in the machines located on their desks and in their offices despite the fact that those resources were not in constant use and often lay fallow. The virtualization of computing and storage resources made possible by cloud computing allows multiple people to use the same servers. Instead of relying on dedicated machines, users instead obtain part-time access to virtual machines provided on demand on a set-up and take-down basis when they are needed (Weinman, 2015).

Network slicing applies the same rationale to networking. Rather than having network resources allocated to individual providers for extended lengths of time, network slicing allows network resources to be placed into new configurations on the fly in response to end users' immediate needs (Andrews et al., 2014). Network slicing thus results in multiple virtual networks sharing leased components in much the same way that cloud computing supports multiple virtual machines operating on the same server.

The resource sharing associated with network slicing yields a number of benefits, again illustrated by a comparison to cloud computing. Unless users' needs are perfectly correlated, computing power and storage can be shared in ways that allow the resources to be used more efficiently. Because users can expand their use of virtual machines to meet their demand means that they no longer need to maintain excess capacity to protect against potential surges in demand. These benefits can apply to networking resources to the same extent as to computer processing and storage. With the proper architecture, network slicing promises to allow users to access networking resources on a transactional basis to meet their immediate needs. This is done by decoupling the control and data planes and exposing the network capabilities to external applications through an application programming interface (API) (Andrews et al., 2014).

Network slicing is widely seen as critical to supporting the deployment of 5G. The small geographic areas served by microcells make it harder to maintain network components dedicated to any particular vertical. Creating configurable building blocks that can be assembled on a temporary basis maintains the flexibility of the network while allowing the network resources to be shared by all of the relevant verticals. So long as the usage of each different vertical is not perfectly correlated, network slicing should allow more intensive and efficient utilization of resources. Enabling multitenant usage of resources raises the possibility of parallel, independent virtual networks operating side by side (Andrews et al., 2014).

Different verticals require different types and levels of QoS. The configurability of these resources allows them to provide different levels of QoS as needed. In addition, the architecture must provide the primitives necessary to advertise, order, provision, meter, and bill resource usage. In addition, because slicing envisions short-term transactions that combine multiple components that are not part of a single, integrated system, the architecture must create interfaces to enable interconnection with other resources. Unless the information necessary to support such transactions are embedded in and conveyed by the network itself, such transactions will necessarily occur between firms in ways that reinforce the status quo, which would frustrate the vision of mix-and-match combinations of different elements among new providers on a dynamic basis (Yoo, 2015).

3. *Assessing the potential tension between network neutrality and 5G*

As noted in the 5G Manifesto, some commentators and industry observers have raised the concern that the EU approach to network neutrality may impede the business models needed to deploy 5G. EU network neutrality laws are embodied in Regulation (EU) 2015/2120 enacted on November 25, 2015, commonly known as the Telecoms Single Market (TSM) Regulation, which also included provisions addressing European roaming. The final language was the product of a protracted trilogue negotiation that resulted in a compromise that was less restrictive than the language initially adopted by the European Parliament. The Regulation calls upon the Body of European Regulators for Electronic Communication (BEREC) to issue nonbinding guidelines to help inform the National Regulatory Authorities' implementation of the regulation. BEREC issued these guidelines in August 2016.

The primary network neutrality obligations are laid out in Article 3 of the TSM Regulation. Article 3(1) recognizes end users'[3] "right to access and distribute information and content, use and provide applications and services, and use terminal equipment of their choice, irrespective of the end-user's or provider's location or the location, origin or destination of the information, content, application or service." Article 3(2) makes clear that these restrictions do not limit providers of internet access services and end-users from entering into agreements "on commercial and technical conditions and the characteristics of internet access services such as price, data volumes or speed" so long as these agreements do "not limit the exercise of the rights of end-users laid down in paragraph 1." The first subparagraph of Article 3(3) requires that providers of internet access services "treat all traffic equally . . . without discrimination, restriction or interference, and irrespective of the sender and receiver, the content accessed or

---

3   Unlike the repealed U.S. network neutrality regulations, which were limited in
     scope to consumer-facing Internet access services, consistent with the 2002
     Framework Directive, the scope of EU network neutrality regulation appears to
     cover both individuals and businesses (BEREC, 2016, at 4)

distributed, the applications or services used or provided, or the terminal equipment used."

The TSM Regulation recognizes exceptions for *reasonable network management* and for what are commonly known as *specialised services*. Regarding the first exception, the second subparagraph of Article 3(3) specifies that the rules "shall not prevent providers of internet access services from implementing reasonable traffic management measures." It further specifies that to be reasonable, "such measures shall be transparent, non-discriminatory and proportionate" and "shall not be based on commercial considerations but on objectively different technical quality of service requirements of specific categories of traffic."

Regarding the second exception, Article 3(5) recognizes that providers of electronic communications[4] to the public "shall be free to offer services other than internet access services which are optimised for specific content, applications or services, or a combination thereof," which the BEREC Guidelines note is simply a new name for specialised services. Specifically, this category includes services that "are optimised for specific content, applications or services, or a combination thereof, where the optimisation is necessary in order to meet requirements of the content, applications or services for a specific level of quality." Specialised services "shall not be usable or offered as a replacement for internet access services, and shall not be to the detriment of the availability of general quality internet access services for end-users."

Whether network slicing and the other practices associated with 5G will fall more naturally within the exception for reasonable network management or specialized services is not clear. On the one hand, the recitals of the TSM Regulation note that "[t]he objective of reasonable traffic management is to contribute to an efficient use of network resources and to an optimisation of overall transmission quality" (Recital 9). Specialised services, in contrast, are "optimised for specific content, applications or services, or a combination thereof" (Article 3(5)). Given that the network slicing and other business practices are designed to support the particular applications and services needed by particular verticals, it seems unlikely to fit within the ambit of reasonable traffic management measures, which are focused on the performance of the network as a whole. Instead, they

---

4   Article 3(5) specifies that providers of electronic communications to the public include both providers of internet access services and providers of content, applications and services.

seem more consistent with specialised services, which are focused on the performance of specific content, applications, or services.[5]

On the other hand, the distinction between the two categories may not be as sharp as the language would suggest. Traffic management measures that benefit the network as a whole do permit better operation of individual applications and services, whereas the benefits specialised services provide to specific applications and services also benefit the network as a whole. In many cases, the precise motivation may be difficult to discern.

On balance, practices such as network slicing appear to fall more naturally within the definition of specialised services than within the definition of reasonable network management. The idea of network slicing would appear to be more application oriented than network oriented. Moreover, footnote 26 to Paragraph 101 of the BEREC Guidelines acknowledges the link between specialised services and network slicing by noting, "Network-slicing in 5G networks may be used to deliver specialised services." But because of the ambiguity, this Chapter will analyze the application of both exceptions.

3.1 Reasonable traffic management

3.1.1 The EU Regulation

As noted earlier, subparagraph 2 of Article 3(3) of the TSM Regulation allows reasonable traffic management measures so long as they are "transparent, non-discriminatory and proportionate" and are not "based on commercial considerations but on objectively different technical quality of service requirements of specific categories of traffic." Subparagraph 3 of Article 3(3) specifies that traffic management measures "shall not block, slow down, alter, restrict, interfere with, degrade or discriminate between specific content, applications or services." The Regulation does specify three exceptions to this rule: (1) compliance with national legislation or a legal order; (2) preservation of the integrity and security of the network, the services provided through it, and the devices connected to it; and (3) prevention of impending congestion and the mitigation of exceptional or temporary congestion, "provided that equivalent categories of traffic are treated equally."

---

5   Paragraph 75 of the BEREC Guidelines appears to offer a similar suggestion, but is somewhat opaque.

In addition to repeating the operative regulatory language, the Recitals included in the TSM Regulation provide additional guidance as to what constitutes reasonable traffic management. Recital 9 provides, "The objective of reasonable traffic management is to contribute to an efficient use of network resources and to an optimisation of overall transmission quality responding to the objectively different technical quality of service requirements of specific categories of traffic, and thus of the content, applications and services transmitted." That said, "[t]he requirement for traffic management measures to be non-discriminatory does not preclude providers of internet access services from implementing, in order to optimise the overall transmission quality, traffic management measures which differentiate between objectively different categories of traffic." However, "[a]ny such differentiation should . . . be permitted only on the basis of objectively different technical quality of service requirements (for example, in terms of latency, jitter, packet loss, and bandwidth) of the specific categories of traffic, and not on the basis of commercial considerations." Also, "[s]uch differentiating measures should be proportionate in relation to the purpose of overall quality optimisation and should treat equivalent traffic equally. Such measures should not be maintained for longer than necessary."

Recital 11 makes clear that practices that go beyond the bounds of reasonable traffic management are prohibited unless they fall within the three exceptions specified above. In addition, "[t]hose exceptions should be subject to strict interpretation and to proportionality requirements." That said, prohibitions on altering content "do not ban non-discriminatory data compression techniques which reduce the size of a data file without any modification of the content," because "[s]uch compression enables a more efficient use of scarce resources and serves the end-users' interests by reducing data volumes, increasing speed and enhancing the experience of using the content, applications or services concerned."

Recital 12 makes clear that "[t]raffic management measures that go beyond such reasonable traffic management measures may only be applied as necessary and for as long as necessary to comply with the three justified exceptions laid down in this Regulation" specified above.

Recital 13 makes clear that compliance with law includes "requirements of the Charter of Fundamental Rights of the European Union . . . in relation to limitations on the exercise of fundamental rights and freedoms" and the procedural safeguards provided by the European Convention for the Protection of Human Rights and Fundamental Freedoms.

Recital 14 clarifies that protection of the integrity and security of the network includes "preventing cyber-attacks that occur through the spread of malicious software or identity theft of end-users that occurs as a result of spyware."

Recital 15 explains that congestion management is appropriate only "where such congestion occurs only temporarily or in exceptional circumstances" and includes both measures "necessary to prevent impending network congestion" as well as measures "to mitigate the effects of network congestion" after it has already occurred. The Recital defines temporary congestion as including "specific situations of short duration, where a sudden increase in the number of users in addition to the regular users, or a sudden increase in demand for specific content, applications or services, may overflow the transmission capacity of some elements of the network." Such congestion is likely to be more common "in mobile networks, which are subject to more variable conditions, such as physical obstructions, lower indoor coverage, or a variable number of active users with changing location." Even when such temporary congestion might be predictable, "it might not recur so often or for such extensive periods that a capacity expansion would be economically justified.

Recital 15 also characterizes exceptional congestion as "unpredictable and unavoidable situations of congestion" from causes such as "technical failure," "unexpected changes in routing of traffic," or "large increases in network traffic due to emergency or other situations beyond the control of providers of internet access services." "Such congestion problems are likely to be infrequent but may be severe, and are not necessarily of short duration." Measures to "prevent or mitigate the effects of temporary or exceptional network congestion should not give providers of internet access services the possibility to circumvent the general prohibition[s] contained in the TSM Regulation. Moreover, "[r]ecurrent and more long-lasting network congestion which is neither exceptional nor temporary should not benefit from that exception but should rather be tackled through expansion of network capacity."

3.1.2 The BEREC Guidelines

The BEREC Guidelines offer four pages and nineteen paragraphs of guidance on the implementation of the exception or reasonable traffic management. The provisions that are most important for 5G are those interpreting the regulatory requirement that reasonable traffic management measures "shall not be based on commercial considerations but on objectively different technical quality of service requirements of specific categories of traffic." Paragraph 62 reiterates the specific examples of what would constitute objectively different QoS requirements contained in the Regulation (latency, jitter, packet loss, and bandwidth). Paragraph 63 offers "real-time applications requiring a short time delay between sender and receiver" as an example of the type of application that is objectively sensitive to QoS requirements. Paragraph 66 offers that reasonable traffic management may be applied to "generic application types (such as file sharing VoIP or instant messaging)" only if it meets three requirements: (1) the generic application type "require[s] objectively different technical QoS," (2) "applications with equivalent QoS requirements are handled agnostically in the same traffic category," and (3) the justifications for the traffic management are specific to meeting those QoS requirements.

Most importantly for purposes of 5G, Paragraph 68 offers two examples of what the Guidelines believe constitutes a traffic management measure "based on commercial considerations" prohibited by the regulation. The first is "where an ISP charges for usage of different traffic categories." The second is "where the traffic management measure reflects the commercial interests of an ISP that offers certain applications or partners with a provider of certain applications."

Paragraph 75 distinguishes between what constitutes "categories of traffic" subject to reasonable traffic management on the one hand and specialised services on the other. Building on Recital 9 from the TSM Regulation, traffic management is intended to optimize overall transmission quality, presumably for the network as a whole, whereas specialised services are optimized "to meet requirements for a specific level of quality," presumably for specific content, applications, or services. Paragraph 21 specifies that traffic management practices do not require ex ante authorization.

3.1.3 Evaluation

Although the law is not completely clear, the best reading of the Regulation and the interpretive guidance put forth by BEREC suggests that the types of business models associated with 5G would not constitute reasonable traffic management. The recitals of the TSM Regulation note that "[t]he objective of reasonable traffic management is to contribute to an efficient use of network resources and to an optimisation of overall transmission quality" (Recital 9), as opposed to specialised services, which are "optimised for specific content, applications or services, or a combination thereof" (Article 3(5)). Given that network slicing and other business practices are designed to support the particular applications and services needed by particular verticals, it seems unlikely to fit within the ambit reasonable traffic management measures, because they are not primarily focused on the performance of the network as a whole. Instead, they seem more consistent with specialised services, which are focused on the performance of specific content, applications, or services.

Even if 5G business practices are regarded as traffic management measures, subparagraph 2 of Article 3(3) of the TSM regulation draws a sharp distinction between traffic management measures that are "based on commercial considerations" and those that are based "on objectively different technical quality of service requirements," with the latter being permissible and the former being forbidden. Charging for access to network slices would seem to constitute differential treatment based on commercial considerations rather than differential treatment based on objectively different QoS requirements.

That said, the examples cited in the BEREC Guidelines of prohibited commercial considerations (an ISP "charg[ing] for usage of different traffic categories" or "offer[ing] certain applications or partners with a provider of certain applications") would appear to take selling access to network slices outside the ambit of reasonable traffic management measures (Paragraph 68). The Guidelines do permit differential treatment based on "generic application types (such as file sharing, VoIP or instant messaging)." Any such differential treatment must be based on objectively different technical QoS and must handle "applications with equivalent QoS requirements . . . agnostically in the same traffic category" (Paragraph 66). Presumably, the illustrations contained in Paragraph 68 of the BEREC Guidelines would prevent providers from charging for network slices even if they were offered as generic information types.

3.2   Specialised services

3.2.1 The EU Regulation

As noted earlier, the types of business models expected to underlie 5G appear to fit more comfortably within the definition of "services other than internet access services which are optimised for specific content, applications or services, or a combination thereof" (more commonly known as specialised services).

Recital 16 of the TSM Regulation recognized the existence of demand for "electronic communication services other than internet access services, for which specific levels of quality, that are not assured by internet access services, are necessary." Specific examples include "services responding to a public interest" and "some new machine-to-machine communications services." National regulatory authorities overseeing specialised services should make sure that they are not "simply granting general priority over comparable content, applications or services available via the internet access service and thereby circumventing the provisions regarding traffic management measures applicable to the internet access services."

As noted above, specialised services are governed by Article 3(5) of the TSM Regulation. Per subparagraph 2, providers may offer specialised services "only if the network capacity is sufficient to provide them in addition to any internet access services provided." In addition, "[s]uch services shall not be usable or offered as a replacement for internet access services, and shall not be to the detriment of the availability or general quality of internet access services for end-users." Recital 17 emphasizes the same points. When determining whether specialised services are having a detrimental effect on internet access services, "national regulatory authorities should assess the impact on the availability and general quality of internet access services by analysing, inter alia, quality of service parameters (such as latency, jitter, packet loss), the levels and effects of congestion in the network, actual versus advertised speeds, the performance of internet access services as compared with services other than internet access services, and quality as perceived by end-users."

The Recital notes that anticipating traffic volumes can be more difficult in mobile networks, because variations in the number of users can cause unforeseeable variations in the quality of internet access services. As a result, in mobile networks, the fact that specialised services may have an unavoidable, minimal, and brief negative impact on internet access services should not be considered a sufficient detriment to bar the deployment of specialised services.

3.2.2 The BEREC Guidelines

The BEREC Guidelines offer six pages and twenty-nine paragraphs of guidance on specialised services. Focusing on the provisions most relevant to 5G, Paragraph 99 recognizes that "there can be demand for services that need to be carried at a specific level of quality that cannot be assured by the standard best effort delivery." Examples listed in Paragraph 113 include voice over LTE (VoLTE), linear broadcasting IPTV, real-time health services such as remote surgery, new machine-to-machine communications, and more generically "some services responding to a public interest." Paragraph 106 notes that certain applications have QoS requirements that are inherent in the nature of the application, while other applications may have QoS requirements that may vary. For example, real-time applications have an inherent requirement for low latency. The QoS requirements for video, in contrast, may vary depending on whether the resolution of the content is "standard definition with a low bitrate or ultra-high definition with high bitrate." Paragraph 114 observes that specialised services "might be especially important to corporate customers" and that such business services "have to be assessed on a case-by-case basis." As was the case for reasonable traffic management, Paragraph 21 specifies that specialised services do not require ex ante authorization.

The Guidelines provide language to help interpret the restrictions on specialised services contained in the Regulation. Paragraph 101 repeats the regulatory language that specialised services are "services other than [internet access services]," they are "optimised for specific content, application, or services, or a combination thereof," and "the optimisation is objectively necessary in order to meet requirements or a specific level of quality." Paragraph 102 repeats the Regulation's requirements that specialised services leave sufficient capacity for internet access services, are not usable or offered as a replacement for internet access services, and be to the detriment of the availability or quality of internet access services. Paragraph 123 echoed Recital 17's acknowledgement that QoS is harder to manage in mobile networks, where the number of uses and the amount of traffic are more difficult to anticipate, so that reductions in QoS that are "unavoidable, minimal and limited to a short duration" should not be considered detriments to internet access services sufficient to invalidate a specialised service.

Most importantly for 5G, Paragraph 110 indicates that specialised services "cannot be provided by simply granting general priority over comparable content." Instead, they can be offered, "for example, through a connection that is logically separated from the traffic of the IAS."

In addition, Paragraph 122 recognizes that end-user control can make a specialised service more justifiable. Specifically, enforcement officials should not consider competition for capacity between specialised services and internet access services to violate the regulations "[w]hen it is techni-cally impossible to provide the specialised service in parallel to IAS with-out detriment to the end-user's IAS quality," when end users are informed about the specialised service's impact on internet access services and de-termine for themselves whether to use it, and when the use of the special-ised service affects only the end users' own internet access services and not capacity that is shared by multiple end users.

3.2.3 Evaluation

The business models associated with 5G appear to fit more comfortably with the definition of specialised services. The BEREC Guidelines also acknowledge that specialised services will be characterized by M2M and B2B communications (Paragraphs 113, 114). Moreover, the examples of specialised services listed in the Guidelines (VoLTE, linear broadcasting IPTV, and real-time health services such as remote surgery) describe the types of verticals that 5G hopes to support (Paragraph 113). Furthermore, as noted above, the BEREC Guidelines specifically acknowledge that 5G may be delivered via network slicing (footnote 26 in Paragraph 101). This suggests that while network slicing does not itself represent a specialised service, it can provide the components from which a specialised service can be devised.

One potential ambiguity lies in the restriction that specialised services are those "optimised for specific content, applications or services, or a combination thereof." The vision for 5G is that the network can be recon-figured for the different demands placed by different types of content, ap-plications, and services. If so, the network at any particular moment may be configured to support a particular type of consumer demand. As a gen-eral matter, however, the overall network is designed to be flexible enough to support an arbitrary range of content, applications, and services rather than any one specific kind.

A further complicating factor is the catch-all phrase at the end of the list contained in Article 3(5) of the Regulation, which specifies that in addi-tion to supporting "specific content, applications or services," specialised services may also support "a combination thereof." If interpreted broadly, this catchall could encompass services offered by a 5G provider designed to support any arbitrary combination of content, applications, and services. However, an interpretation this broad encompasses everything and thus would effectively render this language meaningless. A narrower interpretation limited to specified, pre-envisioned capabilities may not be broad enough to encompass the type of flexible building block architecture associated with 5G networks.

Equally problematic is the language in Paragraph 110 of the BEREC Guidelines, which prohibits "simply granting general priority over comparable content" and suggests that specialised services should be offered "through a connection that is logically separated from the traffic of the IAS." The emphasis on logical separation arguably suggests that physical separation through the use of dedicated bandwidth is not required, as had been proposed and rejected in earlier stages of the debate. Instead, it suggests that both the internet access service and the specialised service may share the same resource so long as they are segregated by using distinct code, name spaces, or other digital means.

Paragraphs 101 and 110 rest in uneasy tension, as prioritization through the use of differential types of service or through virtual channels or circuits represent traditional ways to achieve logical separation. The criticism of relying on simple grants of priority raises questions about traditional prioritization techniques such as Differentiated Services (DiffServ) implemented through the *type of service* field that has always been part of IPv4 and has been maintained in IPv6 through the inclusion of the *traffic class* field. Determining what constitutes logical separation that is not simply granting general priority remains unclear. Indeed, many of the uses of these fields, which have been part of the internet architecture since the very beginning, would seem to contradict the prohibition on simply granting priority to certain types of content. Questions remain about how these restrictions permit increasingly mainstream techniques that assert even more control over the physical assets, such as Multi-Protocol Label Switching (MPLS), which are enabled still further in IPv6 by the addition of the *flow label* field into the IPv6 header (Yoo, 2016a).

The requirement that specialised services not starve internet access services of resources, not serve as a replacement for internet access services, and not evade the net neutrality rules also raises potential problems. Those skeptical of the motives of network providers may raise difficult questions about what constitutes sufficient bandwidth for internet access services, how people are using different network services, and the nature of the network provider's motivation behind different practices. Ironically, these conflicts are likely to become more acute to the extent that specialised services turn out to be popular with consumers.

Finally, to the extent that network slicing is requested by end users, the language on end-user control contained in Paragraph 122 of the BEREC

Guidelines offers some promise for enabling services supported by network slicing as a specialised service even when the specialised service does have some detrimental effects on internet access service. The logic underlying this provision is quite sensible: consumers are clearly in a position to ensure that the tradeoffs are made in a way that best suits their interests when they are the ones who dictate how those tradeoffs are made.

On closer inspection, the issue is not as simple as might be hoped. The language does not provide that end-user control automatically renders any completion between specialised services and internet access services unproblematic. Instead, end-user control provides a justification for the specialised service only "[w]hen it is technically impossible to provide the specialised service in parallel to IAS without detriment to the end-user's IAS quality." Read literally, this caveat has the potential to render end-user control irrelevant as a consideration. This is because, simply by deploying more bandwidth, it is almost always technically possible to provide specialised services in parallel with internet access services without degrading either. From this perspective, economic feasibility imposes the real limits, not technical impossibility. Thus, if read too broadly, the requirement of technical impossibility will never be met, and end-user control will never justify the deployment of specialised services despite the degradation

Even larger problems are raised by the requirement that the "use of the specialised service affect[] only the end users' own internet access services and not capacity that is shared by multiple end users." Networks have long moved past the day when each user connected to the Internet via dedicated twisted pair of coper wires that ran all the way to the telephone company's central office, the use of which was completely independent of and did not impose any detrimental impact on other people's usage. The increasing use of fiber nodes, in VDSL networks, hybrid fiber coaxial networks, and various fiber to the cabinet/node architectures means that bandwidth on the backside of the node is always shared. The advent of network slicing will accentuate the degree of resource sharing still further. Enabling users to access resources on a multitenant, transactional basis makes it almost inevitable that one person's usage will affect the use of others.

Lastly, it is far from clear whether end users will be able to exercise this discretion in an effective manner. Many end users may lack the expertise to make the necessary decisions. Moreover, end users care about services, not particular facilities, and the value of the services may depend on the behavior of other users both as competitors for limited resources and as potential partners whose demand can be aggregated to make resource usage more efficient. The issue is that end users can only see localized information and face collective action problems that place them in a poor position to make decisions based on what other network users are doing.

4.   *Conclusion*

This Chapter explores the extent to which the European network neutrality regime is consistent with the innovative technologies and business models expected to be a part of 5G. The task is complicated by the fact that the technologies and business models that will comprise 5G have yet to be definitively determined. It is likely, however, that 5G will connect a significantly larger number of devices and that those devices will place demands on the network that are increasingly diverse. The idea that the increasing diversity of demand will require increasingly differential treatment rests in uneasy tension with the principle of equal treatment of traffic underlying network neutrality.

The regulatory provisions most likely to make such practices permissible are the exceptions for reasonable traffic management and for specialised services. Unfortunately, the regulatory language and the nonbinding interpretive guidance provided by BEREC do not completely resolve which approaches to 5G will be permissible, if any. Ultimate resolution of these issues will have to await the deployment of 5G, enforcement decisions and actions by the national regulatory authorities, and any subsequent judicial challenges to the regulatory decisions. The hope is that enforcement authorities and courts will enforce these provisions with enough flexibility to give innovation the room to experiment that it needs in order to thrive.

References

Agiwal, M., Roy, A., and Saxena, N. (2016). Next Generation 5G Networks: A Comprehensive Survey. *IEEE Communications Surveys & Tutorials*, 18(3), 1617-55.

Andrews, J. G., Buzzi, S., Choi, W., Hanly, S. V., Lozano, A., Soong, A. C. K., & Zhang, J. C. (2014). What Will 5G Be? IEEE Journal on Selected Areas in Communications, 32(6), 1065-81.

Boccardi, F., Heath, R. W., Jr., Lozano, A., Marzetta, T. L., & Popovski, P. (2014). Five Disruptive Technology Directions for 5G, IEEE Communications, 52(2), 74-80.

Body of European Regulators for Electronic Communications (2016). BEREC Guidelines on the Implementation by National Regulators of European Net Neutrality Rules, BoR (16) 127.

Cisco (2007). Cisco Visual Networking Index: Forecast and Methodology, 2006–2011.

Cisco (2017). Cisco Visual Networking Index: Forecast and Methodology, 2016–2021.

Deloitte (2017a). Global Mobile Consumer Survey 2017 – Mobile Evolution: Ausgewählte Ergebnisse für den deutschen Mobilfunkmarkt. https://www2.deloitte.com/content/dam/Deloitte/de/Documents/technology-media-telecommunications/Global%20Mobile%20Consumer%20Survey%202017%20Study%20Deloitte1.pdf

Deloitte (2017b). 2017 Global Mobile Consumer Survey: US edition – The dawn of the next era in mobile. https://www2.deloitte.com/content/dam/Deloitte/us/Documents/technology-media-telecommunications/us-tmt-2017-global-mobile-consumer-survey-executive-summary.pdf

Ericsson ConsumerLabs (2018). Towards a Consumer 5G Future. https://www.ericsson.com/assets/local/networked-society/consumerlab/six-calls-to-action_report_screen_aw.pdf [Accessed 8 April 2018].

European Union (2015). Regulation (EU) 2015/2120 of the European Parliament and of the Council of November 25, 2015, laying down measures concerning open internet access and amending Directive 2002/22/EC on universal service and users' rights relating to electronic communications networks and services and Regulation (EU) No 531/2012 on roaming on public mobile communications networks within the Union. *Official Journal of the European Union* (L 310), 1-18. http://eur-lex.europa.eu/legal-content/EN/TXT/?uri=CELEX:32015R2120 [Accessed 8 April 2018].

Federal Communications Commission (2012). Internet Access Service: Status as of June 30, 2011. https://apps.fcc.gov/edocs_public/attachmatch/DOC-314630A1.pdf [Accessed 8 April 2018].

Ghosh, A. (2017). 5G New Radio – Technology and Performance. 2nd Workshop of the NSF Millimeter-Wave Research Coordination Network, University of Wisconsin-Madison. mmwrcn.ece.wisc.edu/wp-uploads/2017/05/5G-NR-Ghosh-Nokia-Keynote.pdf.

GSMA (2018). Delivering the Digital Revolution: Will Mobile Infrastructure Keep Up with Rising Demand. https://www.gsma.com/publicpolicy/wp-content/uploads/2018/02/GSMA_DigitalTransformation_Delivering-the-Digital-Revolution.pdf [Accessed 8 April 2018].

Gupta, A. & Jha, R. K. (2015). A Survey of 5G Network: Architecture and Emerging Technologies. IEEE Access, 3, 1206-32.

Khalid, A. (2018). How 5G Wins the Spectral Efficiency Race. Our Technology Planet. https://ourtechplanet.com/how-5g-wins-the-spectral-efficiency-race/ [Accessed 8 April 2018].

Lawson, S. (2015). Suddenly, net neutrality doesn't look so great for 5G. *PC World.* https://www.pcworld.com/article/2893032/5g-net-neutrality-may-be-headed-for-a-showdown.html [Accessed 8 April 2018].

Lee, H. J., and Whitacre, B. (2017). Estimating willingness-to-pay for broadband attributes among low-income consumers: Results from two FCC lifeline pilot projects. *Telecommunications Policy*, 41(9), 769-80.

Liu, Y.-H., Prince, J., and Wallsten, S. (2018). Distinguishing Bandwidth and Latency in Households' Willingness-to-Pay for Broadband Internet Speed. *Information Economics and Policy*, forthcoming. https://www.sciencedirect.com/science/article/pii/S0167624517301609

Manion, P. (2017). Net Neutrality's fall is 5G's gain. *Electronic Products*. https://www.electronicproducts.com/Digital_ICs/Communications_Interface/Net_n eutrality_s_fall_is_5G_s_gain.aspx [Accessed 8 April 2018].

Morris, I. (2018). Ericsson CEO: Net Neutrality Threatens 5G. *LightReading*. https://www.lightreading.com/net-neutrality/ericsson-ceo-net-neutrality-threatens-5g/d/d-id/740854 [Accessed 8 April 2018].

Osseiran, A., Boccard, F., Braun, V., Kusume, K., Marsch, P., Maternia, M., Queseth, O., Schellmann, M., Schotten, H., Taoka, H., Tullberg, H., Uusitalo, M. A., Timus, B., & Fallgren, M. (2014). Scenarios for 5G Mobile and Wireless Communications: The Vision of the METIS Project. *IEEE Communications*, 52(5), 26-35.

Patterson, G., et al. (2016). 5G Manifesto for timely deployment of 5G in Europe. http://telecoms.com/wp-content/blogs.dir/1/files/2016/07/5GManifestofortimely deploymentof5GinEurope.pdf [Accessed 8 April 2018].

Qualcomm (2018). Predicting real-world performance of 5G NR mobile networks and devices. *OnQ Blog*. https://www.qualcomm.com/news/onq/2018/03/07/predicting-real-world-5g-performance

Qualcomm and Nokia. (2017). Making 5G a reality: Addressing the strong mobile broadband demand in 2019 and beyond. https://www.qualcomm.com/system/files/document/files/whitepaper_-_making_5g_a_reality_-_addressing_the_strong_mobile_broadban.pdf [Accessed 8 April 2018].

Rysavy, P. (2017). Analyst Angle: How "Title II" net neutrality undermines 5G. https://www.rcrwireless.com/20170503/opinion/net-neutrality-5G-tag9 [Accessed 8 April 2018].

Shannon, C. E. (1949). Communications in the Presence of Noise. *Proceedings of the I.R.E.*, 37(1), 10-21.

Weinman, J. (2015). Cloud Strategy and Economics. In C. S. Yoo & J.-F. Blanchette (Eds.). *Regulating the Cloud: Policy for Computing Infrastructure* (pp.21-60), Cambridge, Massachusetts: MIT.

Yoo, C. S. (2015). Cloud Computing, Contractibility, and Network Architecture. In C. S. Yoo & J.-F. Blanchette (Eds.). *Regulating the Cloud: Policy for Computing Infrastructure* (pp.115-33), Cambridge, Massachusetts: MIT.

Yoo, C. S. (2016a). Modularity Theory and Internet Policy. *University of Illinois Law Review*, 2016(1), 1-62.

Yoo, C. S. (2016b). Wireless Network Neutrality: Technological Challenges and Policy Implications. *Berkeley Technology Law Journal*, 31(2), 1410-59.